The Crisis of Soviet Industrialization

The Crisis of Soviet Industrialization

SELECTED ESSAYS

E.A. Preobrazhensky

Edited and with an Introduction by Donald A. Filtzer

Routledge
Taylor & Francis Group
LONDON AND NEW YORK

First published 1979 by M.E. Sharpe

Reissued 2018 by Routledge
2 Park Square, Milton Park, Abingdon, Oxon OX14 4RN
711 Third Avenue, New York, NY 10017, USA

Routledge is an imprint of the Taylor & Francis Group, an informa business

A Library of Congress record exists under LC control number: 78073225

ISBN 13: 978-1-138-89676-5 (hbk)
ISBN 13: 978-1-315-17904-9 (ebk)

Dedicated to the memory of Isaac Deutscher.
More than any other thinker of the postwar years,
he helped make clear to my generation that
despite the turmoils of the last half-century,
socialism and Marxism are still relevant to human needs.

Contents

Acknowledgments

Thanks must go, first and foremost, to Michel Vale, a colleague and friend of many years, who helped me to initially organize this project and gave me intellectual encouragement to learn Russian and to make a proper study of the Soviet Union, and Preobrazhensky in particular. Without his further practical assistance in editing some of the translations when my time was short, I do not think this book would ever have been finished. Thanks also to Hillel Ticktin, editor of the journal *Critique*, who, in addition to providing important theoretical guidance in the course of supervising my Ph.D. thesis at the University of Glasgow, also helped iron out some of the thornier terminological problems in the texts. Despite the intellectual debt I owe to both these people, it goes without saying that they bear none of the responsibility for whatever shortcomings remain in this volume.

Finally, acknowledgement is due to Alec Nove and Alexander Erlich for helpful criticisms and comments on the Introduction and notes to this collection, or on my Ph.D. thesis, that directly or indirectly found their way into the present volume.

Introduction
by Donald A. Filtzer

With the revival of interest in Marxist ideas over the past ten or so years, Evgeny Preobrazhensky, one of the leading political and intellectual figures to emerge from the Bolshevik Revolution, has become known to a far wider circle than just the occasional specialist in Soviet history.[1] In part this is due to the monumental work of Isaac Deutscher, whose biography of Trotsky did a great deal to keep alive the vitality of Marxist thought during a period when the continuity and traditions of the socialist movement had not yet emerged from the shock of postwar reaction.[2] For the English reader, direct familiarity with Preobrazhensky's writings became possible only in 1965, with the publication of a translation of his most famous theoretical work, *The New Economics*.[3] For the first time, English-speaking scholars who did not know Russian were able to assess firsthand Preobrazhensky's contribution to the early years of Soviet economic theory and the relevance of his discussions of Soviet industrialization to problems facing the contemporary neocolonial world. Unfortunately, since then we have had only one other translation of an important Preobrazhensky work, *From NEP To Socialism*. A glance at the bibliography of Preobrazhensky's major writings at the end of this book will show a significant body of valuable material that remains accessible only to those who read Russian. We hope, of course, that the present book will go some way toward filling this gap, but we by no means consider our effort sufficient.

As we have had cause to note in a previous essay,[4] this lack of attention to the vast body of Preobrazhensky's writings is surprising, since the scope of his theoretical interests was enormous and encompassed such problems as the development of working-class culture in postrevolutionary society, the history of socialist thought, the theory of money and questions of finance and inflation under the capitalist and Soviet systems, the theory of capitalist crises, and, of course, the theory of economic development in the USSR.

The volume and theoretical sophistication of his writings appear all the more impressive when it is remembered that he was truly a self-made scholar, having had only a high-school education and having been a full-time (and leading) Bolshevik militant from his mid-teens onward. Nor can anyone doubt his political courage and skill, for it was precisely the years of intense political struggle inside the Bolshevik Party—a struggle in which Preobrazhensky played one of the two or three leading roles within the Trotskyist Opposition—that saw his most abundant and fruitful intellectual output. This is not to gloss over Preobrazhensky's sudden political collapse, when after years of fighting against Stalin's growing incursions on Party democracy and against the catastrophic policies of Party leadership, he was one of the first Oppositionists to break under the strains of exile and isolation and make his peace with the man Trotsky had so aptly called the "gravedigger of the revolution." Such acts are to be explained, perhaps, but never justified.

Preobrazhensky's Political Career

Preobrazhensky was born in 1886 in the town of Bolkhov in Orel Province. His father was a priest, and Preobrazhensky was to attribute much of his early radicalism to his reaction against what he termed "all the religious quackery" he could see going on around him. Although he attended the gymnasium, he did not continue his studies on leaving school. He had already become a political militant by the age of 15, and with a friend had founded his own political school journal. Soon, however, Preobrazhensky graduated to more sophisticated political activity. At 17 he joined the Russian Social Democrats, and by 1905 had already led a general strike of educational institutions in Orel. It is worth reflecting on this early history, because it indicates that Preobrazhensky was a completely self-taught scholar and theoretician. The types of clandestine literature he read during these early days in politics were to greatly influence his later theoretical preoccupations: the history of culture, general and revolutionary history, and basic works in political economy. It is equally notable that unlike many other great Bolshevik leaders of erudition, Preobrazhensky did not spend time abroad, nor even in the "cultured" metropolises of Petersburg and Moscow, but had his political activity confined to organizing work in the Russian provinces.

In the years following, and through the time of the Civil War, Preobrazhensky was assigned by the Bolsheviks to the Urals, where he was to do most of his political work—by and large in positions of responsibility. He spent these years constantly on the run from the tsarist police, and was apprehended, jailed, or exiled, on more than one occasion. When the February revolution broke out in 1917, Preobrazhensky was part of a Bolshevik minority that did not support Prince Lvov's provisional government, and was one of the early supporters of Lenin's April Theses.[5] From this early date Preobrazhensky was to find himself on the left of intra-Party disputes.

It was in the years after 1920 that Preobrazhensky came into his own as a major political thinker and Bolshevik leader. At the Sixth Congress of the Bolshevik Party (1917) he was elected an alternate to the Central Committee, and a full member at the Ninth Congress in 1920. At the same time Preobrazhensky was elected one of the Party's three secretaries, together with A. Krestinsky and L. Serebriakov, all three of them later members of the Left Opposition. It is ironic that Preobrazhensky and his two other comrades of the Left were early holders of the post that was later given over to Stalin, who was to use his position as General Secretary to stamp out Party democracy and build up his own base of power.

It is equally ironic that one of Preobrazhensky's early comrades in opposition was the young Nikolai Bukharin, later to be Preobrazhensky's opponent in the debate over industrialization, a faithful defender of "socialism in one country," and one of the more able executioners of intra-Party democracy. Both were members of the "Left Communist Group" which in 1918 opposed the treaty of Brest-Litovsk.[6] Although at first reading the Left Communists' theses appear hopelessly out of step with the dire realities then confronting the Bolsheviks—who had to consolidate power in a decimated, war-torn country—a closer look at their platform shows an uncanny insight into the painful options that both Party and country were to face in ensuing years. The "annexationist peace" with Germany, argued the Left Communists, would dull the internationalism of the world proletariat, thus throwing the prospects of world revolution dangerously into the future. At the same time, the proletarian populations of Russia's two major centers, Petersburg and Moscow, were becoming declassed and lost in the petit bourgeois sea that dominated Russian society. This and the need to reestablish economic order within the country would lead, the Left Communists predicted, to dependence on foreign capital (this did not prove true, and Preobrazhensky would later note the importance of maintaining access to the world division labor as long as there was no question of foreign capital gaining domination over any arena of the domestic economy) and to a bureaucratic centralization of industry that would divorce the proletariat from control over economic and political life. Capitalist methods of labor organization would be introduced, with a concomitant reliance on bourgeois specialists. In the end, the Left Communists concluded, "the Russian workers' revolution cannot 'save itself' by leaving the path of international revolution, constantly avoiding battle and retreating before the onslaught of international capital, by making concessions to 'native capital.' "

The theoretical legacy of Left Communism in Preobrazhensky's later political development is often overlooked. However, the problems that the Left Communists had pointed to were real, and found their place in Preobrazhensky's (and other Bolsheviks') thinking. On the one hand, the Civil War and War Communism compelled the Bolsheviks to implement certain parts of the Left Communist platform (e.g., the call for extension of nationalizations) simply as a matter of survival. On the other hand, the critical state of the Soviet economy made their worst fears come true, as well. Industry did have to be organized in a centralized and bureaucratic manner (one-man management, profit and loss accounting) and capitalist forms of labor incentives did have to be applied (especially piece wages). The physical annihilation during the Civil War of leading elements of the urban proletariat—the Bolsheviks' main political support in the early years of the Revolution—had brought about a drastic change in the social composition of the work force, thus raising the problem of building modern industry with a work force with a rural psychology. Finally, the problem of the regime's continued isolation placed the economy—and social peace within the country—under terrible strain. All of these difficulties, so aptly foreseen by the Left Communists (though not necessarily rectifiable in the manner they had proposed), read like a catalogue of Preobrazhensky's writings of the 1920s. The fact that

Bukharin later abandoned the Left Communist standpoint is no reason to doubt that many of the ideas of that movement continued to influence its other adherents.

The War Communism experience taught Preobrazhensky a great deal. Politically he was one of its great supporters, but he was quick to absorb the real import of these events for Soviet Russia's later development. In terms of economic theory, the problems of finance and inflation would be central preoccupations of his writings for the rest of his career. It is testimony to his mastery of financial matters that, although he had been one of the most over-enthusiastic advocates of the use of inflation as an "indirect tax" to help finance the socialist sector of the economy, he was appointed by the Central Committee and the Council of People's Commissars (Sovnarkom) to direct its work on adapting the monetary system and financial mechanisms to the market conditions of NEP.[7] His interest in financial policy brought him into almost constant conflict with G. Sokol'nikov (Commissar for Finance until 1926) over what Preobrazhensky saw as the finance commissariat's financial conservatism in the issue of credits for industrial development.

Preobrazhensky was one of the first Bolshevik economists to grasp the impact that the economic devastation brought by the Civil War (and reflected in War Communism) would have on the Soviet Union's industrialization. This, too, was a constant theme of his writings, and the reader will come across it on a number of occasions in the present book (see in particular the first part of Preobrazhensky's article "Economic Equilibrium in the System of the USSR," and references to this theme in later sections of this Introduction).

The years 1923 to 1927 were Preobrazhensky's most active both politically and intellectually. He was one of the founding signatories of the "Platform of the 46" in 1923, which marked the first Left Opposition.[8] Here Preobrazhensky, Serebriakov, G. Piatakov, and the other leaders of the Left, though political confidents of Trotsky (whom many of the signatories had supported in the trade union dispute of 1920–21), acted independently of Trotsky—and probably more resolutely—in opposing what they saw as the twin evils of internal bureaucratization and the leadership's blindness to the country's economic crisis. The Platform was a critical document in that it expressly linked the country's economic difficulties to the political bureaucratization of Party life.[9] This theme was repeated in the debate at the Thirteenth Party Conference in January 1924, where the Opposition (whose main spokespersons were Piatakov and Preobrazhensky) unsuccessfully called for greater emphasis on industrialization and democratization within the Party.

Preobrazhensky thereafter retained a place alongside Trotsky as one of the two or three main Opposition leaders. These were also the years of his most productive theoretical work, including the publication of *The New Economics* and all but the first two of the articles collected in the present volume. We will discuss the main ideas of these writings in subsequent sections of this Introduction.

In 1929, after the Opposition had been finally crushed (late 1927) and its leaders exiled (1928), Preobrazhensky was one of the first Oppositionists (together with I. Smilga and K. Radek) to break with Trotsky and reconcile with Stalin. The political pretext was, of course, the Party leadership's sudden turn toward rapid industrialization, a turn that appeared to echo the main economic demands of the Left. But we must exercise caution here, for it is doubtful that any of the recanting Oppositionists was ever intellectually "convinced" of the correctness of Stalin's policy. Rather, the strains of exile and isolation from what the old Bolsheviks must have seen as the main battlefield of a great historical struggle no doubt took their toll on people's judgment. This is not to exonerate Preobrazhensky, Radek, or others; other Oppositionists did hold out and were only forced to capitulate much later.

Preobrazhensky was again expelled from the Party in 1931, after the publication of his book *The Decline of Capitalism* (*Zakat kapitalizma*) and the submission of an article attacking the five-year plans.[10] He was again readmitted in 1932, thereafter (to judge from the evidence) a crushed figure. In 1934 he made a pathetic recantation at the Seventeenth Party Congress (the so-called "Congress of Victors") in which he renounced his former views and attacked Trotsky. His recantation, as Alec Nove notes, was not, however, without its ironical twist.[11] After being arrested and jailed in 1935, he served as a prosecution witness against Zinoviev at the infamous Moscow trials of 1936. Somehow, however, Preobrazhensky seems to have gathered the moral strength and courage to make one last act of defiance. Arrested once more in late 1936, and scheduled to be a defendant at the second series of trials, he did not appear. He had refused to confess, and so could not be allowed to appear publicly for the world to hear. He was shot, presumably in 1937, the date for his death listed in official Soviet sources.

Preobrazhensky's Plan for The New Economics

The New Economics was to have been part of a larger work of the same title, of which five other chapters were published as articles (the portion that appeared as a book was to be the first, abstract-theoretical section of the work). Two of these five chapters, the twin articles "Socialist and Communist Conceptions of Socialism,"[12] were intended to make up most of part 2 of vol. I, which was to be devoted to a history of socialist theory. The remainder of that volume, which was to have covered Lenin and the Bolsheviks, was never written. The three other chapters are the articles on "Economic Equilibrium Under Concrete Capitalism and in the Soviet System," which form the major part of the present collection. These were intended for part 1 of vol. II, which was to be "devoted to a *concrete* analysis of the Soviet economy, that is, Soviet industry, Soviet agriculture, the system of exchange and credit, and the economic policy of the Soviet state, together with an examination of the first rudiments of socialist culture."[13] The three published chapters were to have been the theoretical portion of vol. II, presenting an analysis of the regularities of expanded reproduction under modern capitalism and in the economy of the Soviet Union. The remainder of vol. II was to be taken up with "filling in the algebraic scheme of reproduction in the USSR" (already outlined by Preobrazhensky in the article "Economic Equilibrium in the System of the USSR") "with concrete data provided by Soviet statistics and, above all, by the Control Figures of Gosplan." It would equally "touch upon certain theoretical questions that, in the interests of shortening the purely methodological section of the study," Preobrazhensky preferred "to illustrate with figures from the present-day living Soviet economy."[14]

Preobrazhensky was never to carry out this ambitious theoretical plan. Political events—the intensification of the intra-Party struggle, the defeat of the Opposition, and the eventual suppression and liquidation of ex-Oppositionists—made this virtually impossible. Even the three articles on "Economic Equilibrium," ostensibly able to stand on their own, are marked by the time of their writing: Their hasty preparation meant that numerical examples are rife with errors (though this often appears the result of misprints), the arguments are often sketchy, and the political implications of the theoretical conclusions are drawn without the boldness of even one or two years before. By 1927, certainly, Preobrazhensky no longer felt free to state openly what seemed perfectly obvious to him and others on the Left.

If these articles seem incomplete, however, it is also due to the larger theoretical context in which they must be placed. Preobrazhensky did not so much abandon his plan for the completion of *The New Economics* as rework it and adapt it to the constraints of the deteriorating political situation. After rejoining the Party fold in 1929, he shifted his attention from direct concern with the Soviet economy (save for an occasional article on money) to the problem of capitalist crises. This was certainly not a topic that he had ignored in the 1920s, and the second of the three articles on "Economic Equilibrium" is devoted to an analysis of the process of declining reproduction in capitalist Europe after World War I.[15] Yet it remains true that the theoretical problems that had increasingly preoccupied his thinking in these years—such as the temporal discontinuities in the process of expanded reproduction, the peculiar difficulties attached to the restoration and accumulation of fixed capital, especially in a poor, war-devastated country, and the role of money and the effects of monetary depreciation upon conditions of production and exchange—were fully worked out by him only in the early 1930s, and then only under the guise of their application to the economies of the capitalist world. We must stress that it is not speculation on our part when we say that the books and articles written after his recantation and capitulation were a direct continuation of his theoretical work of the 1920s. Preobrazhensky was sufficiently honest politically and intellectually to acknowledge this fact, and in so doing left his critics little need to guess his intention of extending his theoretical work on the nature of crises within the Soviet economy.[16]

The Historical Background to the "Law of Primitive Socialist Accumulation"

It is difficult for those of us who have grown up in advanced industrial societies to grasp the extent of the problems that confronted the Bolsheviks when they came to power in 1917. The working class had successfully led a revolution in a backward, peasant country. Its industry, though modern and extremely large-scale by the standards of pre–World War I Europe, was weak in comparison to the economy as a whole. What is more, this industry, now the possession of the proletarian state, had been devastated by the years of world war and civil war: aside from outright destruction, normal replacement of plant and equipment had not been made; the country's fixed capital was worn out, badly in need of replacement, and ill-suited to the tasks of building a modern, socialist economy. How, under these circumstances, was the state to proceed?

The years of the NEP were a constant succession of crises, all of which had their roots in the backwardness of the economy and the weakness of its heavy industry. It is worth pointing out that virtually all the participants in the so-called "debates" over industrialization shared certain premises and objectives. They were all, for instance, opposed to using coercion against the peasantry, even against its more prosperous layers, the so-called kulaks. Instead, it was accepted that the only way industrialization could take place would be for industry to develop strong market relations with the private economy, from which it needed vital supplies of foodstuffs and raw materials, and agricultural surpluses that could be marketed abroad for foreign currency (which was to be used for the purchase of foreign-made commodities). For these market relations to be successful, state industry had to satisfy the private economy's demand for consumer goods and agricultural means of production. No one disagreed on these points. Where they did disagree was on the implications of these problems for the country's short-term development.

The first crisis came in 1921–22. With the transition to a market economy agricultural prices went up considerably—a healthy phenomenon in that it augured well for an agricultural recovery. Industry, however, found itself hard put. Cut off from state credits and required to meet normal operating costs, all under the constraints of profit and loss accounting, the individual enterprise had no other recourse but to liquidate its stocks of finished products at any obtainable price. The more industrial prices fell, the more difficult it became to make even normal replacements of fixed and circulating capital. This was the so-called *razbazarovanie*, or "squandering" crisis of 1921.

The response of state enterprises was to combine into "trusts," which were successful in pushing industrial prices back up until 1923, when the famous "scissors" crisis reached full force. The terms of trade between agriculture and industry had become counterproductively detrimental to agriculture. The responses of the Party leadership and the Trotskyist Opposition (and Preobrazhensky in particular in his pamphlet *Economic Crises Under NEP*) were indicative. The official leadership acted by curtailing industrial credits and forcing industrial prices down. The Opposition agreed that agricultural prices were too low (so low, in fact, that the peasantry could not meet its tax obligations) and that enterprises were pushing industrial prices up way beyond rational considerations of proportionality between these two economic sectors. However, they also claimed that agricultural prices could only be raised if there was a corresponding increase in agricultural exports; otherwise, higher agricultural prices would simply produce a drain on industry. Parallel with this analysis went a call for an emphasis on heavy industry as the only long-term method for reducing industrial costs and boosting supplies for the peasant consumer.

Equally germane to the Opposition's argument (and a point made by Preobrazhensky in "The Outlook For the New Economic Policy," the first article in this collection) was the warning that any increase in the prosperity of the countryside, if left to develop spontaneously, would lead to a "differentiation" favoring the kulak strata at the expense of the medium-sized and poorer peasantry. It was therefore logical to insist that industrialization should in large part be financed by taxing (either directly or through the judicious setting of industrial prices) these prosperous elements, a move that would also keep rural inequality within limits.

The scissors crisis was really only a symptom of the more fundamental crisis that plagued the economy throughout these years and finally brought the country to the brink of social collapse: the so-called "goods famine." Here the two competing strategies for industrial development offered by the Opposition and the ruling group of Stalin, Bukharin (and until 1925, G. Zinoviev and L. Kamenev) simply had no point of contact, either in terms of policies or objectives. The ruling majority had committed itself to a short-term strategy of encouraging maximum, marketable agricultural surpluses. This in turn meant a commitment to favor that section of agricultural producers who in fact could supply that surplus, the kulaks. Official policy in the years 1924–25 went openly in that direction: kulaks were allowed to lease additional land and hire wage laborers, and their tax burden was eased.

The Opposition, with Preobrazhensky as a major spokesperson, countered by pointing out that, even accepting the logic of the majority case, the supply of industrial consumer goods could not expand while industry remained poor in fixed capital. The longer the country waited to carry out long-overdue replacements of plant and equipment, the worse the shortage of industrial products would be. In the end it was a question of making a commitment to heavy industry in the present for the sake of adequate supplies in the future.

Preobrazhensky's analysis of the goods famine (see the first of his "Economic Notes") pointed to the fact that peasant purchasing power was swelling, partly due to the agricultural recovery under NEP and partly because the peasantry was no longer subject to the kinds of heavy exactions that had been imposed under the tsarist regime. Unless industrial production could be boosted, there would be no economic reason for the peasantry to sell its output to the state. Further, the time when industry could improve its performance simply by bringing unused plant and equipment back into operation (the so-called recovery period) was rapidly drawing to a close. Henceforth, all major increases in industrial output would require the prior construction of new plant and equipment; the "restoration" period was about to begin. Events were to prove the power of the Opposition's case. The peasantry refused to market all of its surplus following the harvest of 1925: it did not need to, especially with no industrial goods forthcoming.

Although these events greatly shook the Party leadership (they compelled Zinoviev and Kamenev to break with Stalin and Bukharin and to move toward their bloc with Trotsky) there was a good harvest in 1926, which dulled the impact of the Opposition's argument. A year later, however, they were vindicated with a vengeance. There was another good harvest, but kulaks and even middle peasants hoarded their grain; they would not sell. The entire official policy was in danger. The train of events leading to collectivization and the industrialization drive of the late twenties was set in motion. The grain was collected, but only at the expense of increasing resort to "administrative" methods. But the problems of industry still had not been broached in any concerted fashion.

It was in this context that Preobrazhensky presented his famous theory of primitive (in the sense of primary, *pervonachal'nyi*) socialist accumulation. As long as industry was unable to expand on the basis of its own, internally generated surplus, it would have to draw this surplus from elsewhere—specifically, from the private economy. He was not unaware that this policy had its economic and social contradictions, a point to which we will later return. The thrust of his argument was that "equilibrium" between the state and private sectors required that the state *anticipate* its production needs over the foreseeable future and then *consciously* take steps *in the present* to accumulate the resources that would enable it to meet future demand.

A number of commentators have correctly pointed out that a significant fraction within the Stalin group was moving toward acceptance of much of the Opposition's economic argument for industrialization. However, the differences that separated Opposition from majority were far broader than a simple review of economic events and policies would reveal. It was not industrialization *per se* that Preobrazhensky and the Opposition were after, although this *was* the basis on which Preobrazhensky changed his position in 1929 (see my article in *Critique*, cited in note 2, above), but industrialization as part of the general historical tasks facing the proletariat in a backward country. Thus the theory of primitive socialist accumulation was premised on propositions of a more general political-methodological nature that were common to the Left Opposition as a whole.

First, industrialization was not an end in itself, but a means to other ends. It was the mechanism for regrouping increasingly large sections of the population around collective production relations, which form the basis of any socialist economy and society. Though a general objective, this had a special meaning in the USSR, where there was already large-scale urban unemployment (itself a testimony to industry's weakness) and rural overpopulation. Absorption of this overpopulation required sufficient *absolute* industrial growth to more than offset the labor-saving effect of reequipping existing industry.

Second, as a new proletariat was created it would have to assume control over the political apparatus of the Party and the state,[17] which required that the proletariat be numerically and politically strong enough to assert its own interests. To create such a working class, however, the country had to be able to provide its working population the leisure time and resources to educate itself, adequate social provisions (for instance, communal canteens and laundries, child care facilities, etc., to enable women to leave the home and take an active part in political life), and in general, a rising standard of living. There also had to be a maximum of

Party democracy, including an erosion of bureaucratic privilege and the incorporation of proletarian elements into the political leadership. Industrialization was a precondition (but not in and of itself a necessary condition) of each of these objectives; in short, it was a precondition for mass participation by the working class in political life. Yet, like industrial policy, this "primitive political accumulation" had to be consciously planned for; this is why the industrialization program was *specifically* linked to the program for Party democracy.

Third, these arguments were equally premised on the Opposition's hostility to the Stalinist dogma of socialism in one country. It would be a grave mistake to conclude that the question of "socialism in one country" was a doctrinal issue divorced from the substance of the debates of the Soviet twenties. Trotsky in his theory of permanent revolution had laid a theoretical basis for the internationalization of the Russian revolution long before the idea of socialism in one country had ever been voiced. In doing so Trotsky had been traveling fairly uncontroversial ground. Marxists, at least up to 1914, had taken it as an article of faith that socialism could only be established on a world scale. In the Soviet Union, where the country's isolation lay like a dead weight on all its problems and impasses, the issue attained tremendous urgency. From the Opposition's point of view, either the USSR would use its leading position within the international workers' movement to encourage revolution in other countries, or accepting its isolation as a *fait accompli* it would become increasingly conservative in its foreign policy, sacrificing its own and the world's socialist future. Preobrazhensky's early formulations of his theory of Soviet crises had consistently accented the country's reliance on the world division of labor and argued that economic backwardness would drive the revolution into a dead end in the absence of proletarian revolution in the West.[18]

It is important to stress the place of the issues of Party democracy and internationalism in the Left's political program, because by 1927 a large fraction of the ruling group had come to accept the basic outlines of the Opposition's economic argument for industrialization. While the two sides had differences over the rates of accumulation and the extent to which it should be financed at the expense of the prosperous kulak strata of the countryside, far more crucial were their divergences over the type of society to be built through industrialization. In the article "Economic Equilibrium in the System of the USSR" Preobrazhensky argued that industrialization would prove impossible if the country remained isolated: the social tensions engendered by a drive for rapid industrialization would be so severe as to threaten the continued existence of the Soviet state. The Party majority by contrast, grudgingly inching toward some sort of industrialization policy since 1925, very much saw industrialization as part and parcel of the doctrine of socialism in one country and an affirmation of the country's self-sufficiency.

To ignore these issues, as many historians and economic historians of the Soviet twenties are prone to do, is to make it appear that the only questions that separated the Left from the ruling group and the emergent Soviet elite were those of economic policy. Though these divergences over economic program were important, especially the Stalin group's failure to take up the problem of industrializing the country before the crisis had become unmanageable, we need to keep the other points of difference in mind when assessing the coherence of Preobrazhensky's theory and the attacks that it provoked.

The Application of Marx's Reproduction Schemes to the Soviet Economy

When Preobrazhensky concretized his analysis of the law of primitive socialist accumulation and its application within the Soviet economy, it must have seemed almost automatic for him to turn to the schemes for simple and expanded reproduction developed by Marx in vol. II of *Capital*. This part of *Capital* has come to be the genuine stepchild of Marx's economic theory, which is odd since Marx's use of the schemes, far from being technical or an attempted objectification of concrete capitalist conditions, is rich in insights into both the regularities behind capitalist production and exchange and the inherent instability of the capitalist system. Though the schemes no longer receive the attention from students of Marxist economics that the first and third volumes of *Capital* do, they were at one time a major focus of controversy, to which we shall return shortly.

First, however, we would do well to provide a quick and simple description of the mechanics of the schemes. Though some of this ground is covered by Preobrazhensky in the first of the three articles on "Economic Equilibrium" ("The Problem of Economic

Equilibrium Under Concrete Capitalism and in the Soviet System"), it will greatly facilitate the reader's grasp of Preobrazhensky's argument if she or he is already familiar with the basic outlines of the reproduction schemes and so can devote primary concentration to the details of the piece.

Marx noted that the total product of society could be broken down into two basic categories: means of production and means of consumption. If we collect together all the industrial enterprises that produce each of these types of commodities, we will get, as Marx said, two "great branches of production, that of means of production in the one case, and that of articles of consumption in the other."[19] He designated the department producing means of production as department I and that producing means of consumption as department II. Marx then set out to define the regularities of capitalist production with regard to exchange between these two departments. Here he examined two cases: first, that of simple reproduction, where society consumes all of its surplus value and undertakes no accumulation. Such a situation does not exist in capitalist society, except as a transient moment in certain periods of crisis. Its major importance is that, as an abstract, hypothetical moment in the process of accumulation and economic expansion, it allowed Marx to lay down the basic patterns of economic life before proceeding to a more concrete level of study. The second case examined by Marx is what he called reproduction on an extended scale, or expanded reproduction. Here society takes part of its surplus value and devotes it to augmenting its productive forces. Some goes to increase the means of production, that is, machines, raw materials, and auxiliary products. The rest goes to increase the supply of labor power to work with these means of production. This, in turn, can take place in two ways: either by hiring more workers, or by increasing the subsistence of workers already employed so as to establish a work force of higher quality and skill, that is, a work force with a greater productivity of labor.

Marx studied simple reproduction in great detail. The process of accumulation, however, received only one chapter in vol. II of *Capital*, and even that abruptly breaks off. This aspect of his study was, therefore, incomplete.

Let us first take up simple reproduction. Marx used the following figures for his scheme:

I. 4,000*c* + 1,000*v* + 1,000*s* = 6,000 means of production
II. 2,000*c* + 500*v* + 500*s* = 3,000 means of consumption

Department I produces means of production whose value equals 6,000. All of department I's product exists physically as means of production, and so the question arises, How will this product be used? Four thousand of it can go directly to replace the used-up means of production that have worn out in the course of production. The capitalists of department I exchange them among themselves, well enough, but in terms of their use they remain within that department. The other 2,000 means of production cannot be used as they are. Neither the workers nor the capitalists of department I can use them as means of production, for workers must use their wages to purchase means of subsistence and, under the assumptions of simple reproduction, the capitalists use their surplus value to do likewise, although the quality of their "subsistence" will be considerably higher than that of the workers. The result of all this is that department I must exchange these 2,000 in means of production for an equivalent value in means of consumption. Since there is no other department of production than department II, it is with the latter that department I must exchange this part of its commodity-product.

If we look at department II we see a similar case. This department produces means of consumption with a total value of 3,000. Of this it can directly use 1,000 in their existing physical form: 500 will go to support the workers of II (II*v*), and 500 will go to sustaining its capitalists (II*s*). However, department II will then have 2,000 of its product left over in a nonusable form. It cannot take means of consumption (food, textiles, toasters, and so on) and use them to replace the part of its means of production that were used up in the previous year's production—they cannot serve as a replacement for the used-up constant capital in II. Therefore, department II must also enter into exchange, and it must do so with department I.

The basic condition of simple reproduction is, then, that the part of the product of department I that it cannot use in its existing physical form (and hence must exchange with department II) must have a value equal to the part of department II's product that the latter cannot directly use (and, therefore, must exchange with department I). In other words, the equivalent of I($v + s$) must exchange against the equivalent of II*c*. In Marx's scheme this exchange is possible: $\mathrm{I}(v + s) = \mathrm{II}c$.

The process of accumulation, though more involved, is still not difficult to follow. Marx started with the following scheme:

$$\begin{array}{l} \mathrm{I.}\ 4{,}000c + 1{,}000v + 1{,}000s = 6{,}000 \\ \mathrm{II.}\ 1{,}500c + 750v + 750s = 3{,}000 \end{array}$$

Here we must remember that the surplus value of each department is now divided into two portions. One is for capitalist consumption, and the other is for accumulation. Marx assumed for the sake of exposition that half of the surplus value in department I would be consumed and half would go for expanding production, making I*s* divide up into 500 for capitalist consumption and 500 for accumulation. This automatically changes the conditions of exchange with department II. Department I needs only 1,500 means of consumption, rather than the 2,000 we saw under simple reproduction. Thus, Marx adjusted the distribution of productive capital within department II such that II*c* would still equal the consumption fund of department I. But in keeping the total volume of II's production the same, the organic composition of capital (the ratio of constant to variable capital, or c/v) in department II is reduced from a ratio of 4:1 (the same as in department I) to 2:1. The problems this brings with it will be discussed in a moment.

To show how accumulation takes place, Marx began with department I. It takes the 500 surplus value intended for accumulation and divides it up in proportion to the existing ratio of constant to variable capital. Four hundred goes to augment the supply of means of production; 100 goes to increase the amount of labor power. Thus after accumulation we have for department I:

$$\mathrm{I.}\ 4{,}400c + 1{,}100v + 500 \text{ capitalist consumption}$$

Department II, however, has a II*c* of only 1,500. But it, too, must accumulate, and Marx assumes that it does so in line with the needs of department I, that is, it expands its production only as much as is required for it to supply department I with the latter's increased demand for means of consumption.

If we do this, department II must take out of its total surplus value 100 to increase II*c* to 1,600. But, in order for the technical structure of production in II to be maintained, this rise in II*c* demands a proportional rise in II*v*. Therefore, the organic composition of capital being 2:1, II raises IIv by 50. As a result, II winds up taking a total of 150 from its surplus value, which in turn leaves 600 for consumption by II's capitalists. After accumulation in both departments the total scheme looks like this:

I. 4,400c + 1,100v + 500 capitalist consumption
II. 1,600c + 800v + 600 capitalist consumption

After the year's production, assuming a rate of exploitation of 100 percent (that is, a Iv of 1,100 produces a Is of 1,100, and a IIv of 800 produces a IIs of 800), we have:

I. 4,400c + 1,100v + 1,100s = 6,600
II. 1,600c + 800v + 800s = 3,200

These schemes as they stand are not without limitations. These are of two kinds. The first is methodological: Even at the most detailed level to which Marx carried them, the schemes must still be accepted as extremely abstract representations of capitalist reality. For Marx, as Preobrazhensky quite correctly noted, this level of abstraction was essential, for it allowed him to deal with the basic patterns of capitalist production and circulation before moving onto a more concrete examination of capitalist economy and society. But they are not, and indeed cannot be, "real" descriptions of the day-to-day workings of the capitalist economy. Rather, the schemes must be seen as part of Marx's overall theory, residing at a stage of analysis still very general and yet to be built upon in vol. III of *Capital.*[20]

The second type of limitation inherent in the schemes derives precisely from this abstractness, and it is these limitations that proved the subject of such controversy at the end of the last century and the early decades of the twentieth. As we do not wish to involve ourselves in a historical review of these debates (this has been done far better in other works than we could hope to do here[21]), we will concentrate on the observations made by Rosa Luxemburg. Her framework was perhaps closest to the one from which Preobrazhensky was working, both in the sense that her criticisms of Marx's schemes were made from a politically revolutionary perspective (as opposed to the critique developed by the Austro-Marxists), and in the sense that she too was taken up with the problem of how the capitalist and precapitalist economies interrelate.

The first problem that Luxemburg noted arose from Marx's assumption—through all four volumes of *Capital*—that capitalist production was universal. His schemes claimed to represent the regularities of a "pure" capitalist economy, without any of the complications that would be introduced by a study of the way in which capitalism interacts with noncapitalist modes of production. Yet such a capitalism does not exist in the real world: Its relations with noncapitalist sectors is a historical fact, and the theory of reproduction, Luxemburg claimed, must take this into account.

In fact, Marx himself, in vol. II of *Capital*, anticipated the need to incorporate capitalism's relations with noncapitalist production into the theory of reproduction:

> Within its process of circulation, in which industrial capital functions either as money or as commodities, the circuit of industrial capital, whether as money capital or as commodity capital, crosses the commodity circulation of the most diverse modes of production, so far as they produce commodities. . . .The character of the process of production from which they originate is immaterial. They function as commodities in the market, and as commodities they enter into the circuit of industrial capital as well as into the circulation of the surplus value incorporated in it. It is therefore the universal character of the origin of the commodities, the existence of the market as world market, which distinguishes the process of circulation of industrial capital. . . .
>
> . . .As soon as act M-MP [the exchange of money for means of production—DF] is completed, the commodities (MP) cease to be such and become one of the modes of existence of industrial capital in its functional form of P, productive capital. Thereby however their origin is obliterated. They exist henceforth only as forms of existence of industrial capital, are embodied in it. However, it still remains true that *to replace them they must be reproduced, and to this extent the capitalist mode of production is conditional on modes of production lying outside of its own stage of development. But it is the tendency of the capitalist mode of production to transform all production as much as possible into commodity production. The mainspring by which this is accomplished is precisely the involvement of all production into the capitalist circulation process.*[22]

The problem, then, had already been posed. It remained, however, to concretize Marx's schemes so that the regularities—and points of crisis—of these interrelations could be studied.

Luxemburg pointed to a second difficulty when she showed that the schemes contained several simplifications that Marx dropped elsewhere in his analysis of capitalist production, and which, if removed, would disturb the regular patterns of accumulation and overall equilibrium. If we look at Marx's scheme for accumulation, we see that he adjusted accumulation in department II to that in department I. Department I accumulates 50 percent of its surplus value, but department II does not. It accumulates only as much as is needed to bring II*c* into line with the consumption fund of I (I[$v + s/x$], where s/x is the notation Marx used to designate the part of surplus value that went for capitalist accumulation). In the first year this amounts to 150 out of a surplus value of 750, or 20 percent. If we work out accumulation over a number of years, we see that as long as department II adjusts its accumulation to suit the demand of department I, it will accumulate exactly 30% of its surplus value against the 50% in department I.[23] In reality, however, there is no reason to believe that the capitalists in department II behave any differently than those in department I. The schemes should allow for equal rates of accumulation in both departments.

Another simplification is that Marx does not allow the organic composition of capital to rise in either department. This is clearly an abstraction that would have to be dropped in a more detailed and concrete analysis of capitalist reproduction, since the rise in the organic composition—i.e., the secular tendency toward technical progress—is one of the central pillars of Marx's theory of capitalist development, including his law of the tendency for the rate of profit to fall.

Finally, by adjusting accumulation in department II to that in department I, Marx obscures the effect on accumulation of the unequal organic compositions of capital. If both departments were allowed to accumulate independently, department II would grow faster than department I. We can illustrate this simply by taking the scheme for the first year of accumulation. We already know how department I would look. If department II were to accumulate half its surplus value, the same percentage as department I, this would come to 375, rather than 150. If it divided this up according to its organic composition of capital, it would devote 250 of this to increasing II*c* and 125 to raising II*v*. We would have

I. 4,400c + 1,100v + 500 capitalist consumption
II. 1,750c + 875v + 375 capitalist consumption

And after the year's production:

$$\text{I. } 4{,}400c + 1{,}100v + 1{,}100s = 6{,}600$$
$$\text{II. } 1{,}750c + 875v + 875s = 3{,}500$$

Here $\text{I}(v + s/x)$ = 1,100v plus half the new surplus value (1,100/2, or 550), making 1,650 in all. IIc = 1,750. There is an overproduction in II by 100; II has 100 in means of consumption it cannot sell. By the same token there is an underproduction in I, also of 100; I cannot supply II with 100 in means of production needed by the latter for the renewal and augmentation of its constant capital.

Luxemburg did not use this example, but she did recognize that overproduction would ensue in department II if it had a lower organic composition of capital than department I and if both departments accumulated the same percentage of their surplus value. Likewise, she noted that allowing for a rise in the organic composition of capital would also produce overproduction in II relative to I, since it would reduce the quantity of Iv (and hence also Is) while raising the size of IIc.

Finally, Luxemburg pointed out that under these conditions, where there was a tendency for department II to grow faster than department I, the balance could only be redressed by the transfer of capital out of department II into department I. This transfer, she argued, would encounter tremendous difficulties, since the physical form of the means of production used by department II would not allow their ready use in the production of means of production.[24]

Although Luxemburg highlighted these various problems with Marx's schemes, she did not actually use the reproduction schemes to work out a systematic exposition of her own theory of capital reproduction, incorporating the necessary modifications. In many respects this was unfortunate, for her theory of the interconnection of the capitalist and precapitalist modes of production readily lends itself to the type of two-sector scheme that Preobrazhensky was to use in his three articles on economic equilibrium.

Although we do not wish to involve ourselves in the controversy over the correctness of Luxemburg's theory of capitalist accumulation, it is worth giving a brief summary of it, especially since it should highlight just how similar her approach was to that of Preobrazhensky (a closeness that Preobrazhensky does not himself appear to have fully appreciated). Essentially, Luxemburg maintained that in a pure capitalist system consisting only of capitalists and workers, accumulation would be stifled because of inadequate effective demand. The accumulated part of surplus value is to be consumed productively, not individually. Therefore, neither the capitalists nor workers can provide the effective demand for this new investment through their own personal consumption. Similarly, the capitalists cannot simply "swap" their surplus products *in natura*, since under capitalist conditions what is produced must first be realized on the market for money. How, then, was exchange to be initiated? Luxemburg argued that under "pure" capitalism there were no holders of revenue who could provide this necessary demand, and so accumulation would have to presume that capitalists accumulate merely for the sake of accumulating—something unrealistic in an economy where the driving force of production is the realization of profit. Put another way, it may be possible on paper, within the bounds of the reproduction schemes, to pose the problem of accumulation under capitalism (with its atomized production units) without posing the motivation for accumulation and demonstrating the possibility that this accumulation will find purchasers on the market. But this does not accurately reflect the real world, where what is produced must first be sold on the market and the surplus value realized as money capital before accumulation can actually proceed.

The source of the effective demand needed to break the impasse, Luxemburg argued, came from outside the capitalist system, from noncapitalist strata either within capitalist countries or in the colonies. Luxemburg, therefore, claimed that the surplus value to be accumulated in at least one of the departments must first be realized in the noncapitalist sector in order for accumulation to proceed. At the level of description this was certainly correct—capitalism did realize part of its surplus value in the noncapitalist sector. But Luxemburg went on to deduce a quite rigid relationship between capitalism and its petit bourgeois periphery, not recognizing the extent to which her deduction was itself conditional upon the abstractness of the reproduction schemes, even after her modifications. (For example, they failed to incorporate the functions of the modern credit system in assisting capitalism to effect precisely that internal demand she considered impossible.)

Preobrazhensky, while acknowledging the brilliance of parts of her work, basically did not accept the way in which Luxemburg had posed the problem of accumulation.[25] Certainly it is impossible to surpass those sections of *The Accumulation of Capital* that detail and expose the methods by which capitalism penetrates and subordinates noncapitalist production in real life. But in addition to describing the actual relations between capitalism and its noncapitalist periphery, Luxemburg maintained—and thought she could theoretically prove—that it was impossible for capitalism to accumulate on the basis of its own resources and that its expansion was dependent on realizing an increasing share of its product in the noncapitalist sector. This approach establishes an *absolute* dependence by capitalism on the noncapitalist sector, such that once capitalism has completely subordinated and eliminated noncapitalist production, accumulation will be impossible and the automatic collapse of capitalism must follow.

It was with this part of Luxemburg's argument that Preobrazhensky most profoundly disagreed. He considered that the significance of the precapitalist sector was not in its absolute role in realizing part of the capitalist product, but rather in its existence as a buffer that afforded capitalism an indispensable elasticity both in finding markets and in acquiring the necessary *in natura* elements of production. Without this extra flexibility, Preobrazhensky argued, the disproportions that naturally arise in the course of capitalist reproduction would lead to crises of greater severity and frequency than is actually observed.[26]

The different approaches of Luxemburg and Preobrazhensky to the question of accumulation are probably best explained by the respective natures of the problems each was trying to solve. Luxemburg, of course, was concerned with imperialism and the ever more intense and competitive assault by capitalist countries on the noncapitalist world. Her task in these circumstances was to explain what drove capitalism to extend its grasp over other economic formations, and she believed she had found the theoretical foundations for doing so.

Preobrazhensky, on the other hand, was confronted by an altogether different problem: How could the Soviet Union industrialize in a backward country whose economy was dominated by peasant agricultural and craft production? When Preobrazhensky modified and elaborated Marx's schemes of reproduction he was not engaging in some baroque algebraic exercise in search of a hypothetical but historically extraneous solution to the problem of capitalist accumulation. Insofar as he was dealing with *capitalist* production, his modifications were intended to point to the manifold possibilities for crisis within the imperialist system, as well as to indicate the extent to which capitalism utilizes its relations with the precapitalist economy to try and smooth over some of its worst disproportionalities.[27] Insofar as Preobrazhensky was working out analytical tools for analyzing the commodity-socialist system of the *Soviet Union*, his modifications of the schemes were an attempt to determine what *consciously chosen policies* the proletarian state would have to carry out if the state sector were to predominate in its struggle against private production and exchange and to guarantee the socialist development of the country. We know that Preobrazhensky had been thinking about how to apply the reproduction schemes to this problem for some time prior to publishing his articles on "Economic Equilibrium." Already in 1923, in *Economic Crises Under NEP* (*Ekonomicheskie krizisy pri NEP'e*), he had stated that in order to properly analyze the Soviet economy and to understand the sources of its crises and disproportions it would be necessary to add a third department to the two Marx had used in his study of simple and expanded capitalist reproduction:

> In general, for us to carry out the necessary analysis of all the conditions of the exchange of goods in our commodity-socialist system of economy, we will need not two schemes, with which Marx operated, but three. It is necessary to introduce a third scheme, which will characterize the exchange of goods and the numerical regularities and proportions of this exchange between state industry and the peasant economy.[28]

Preobrazhensky must have soon realized that just an additional "third scheme" or third department would not do. The problem was another entire system of economy, as he had already pointed out. Thus, an analysis of expanded reproduction would necessitate the introduction of a new *sector*, which itself produced both means of production and means of consumption. This is what Preobrazhensky did.

It was Preobrazhensky then, and not Luxemburg, who actually worked out the pattern of accumulation in a mixed industrial-precapitalist economy. The object of such an investigation was to analyze the economy of the USSR, but before doing that it would first be necessary to study in some detail the regularities of accumulation under what Preobrazhensky called "concrete capitalism," that is, capitalism as it exists in its constant and evolving interrelation with noncapitalist modes of production. The result was the first of the three articles on "Economic Equilibrium," published in *Vestnik Kommunisticheskoi Akademii* (*VKA*) 17 (1926).

In the first part of the article Preobrazhensky presents a scheme for simple reproduction under concrete capitalism. Although no accumulation takes place in either the peasant or capitalist sectors, he shows that there is a definite pattern of interdependence between these two modes of production. This interdependence is hierarchical: The peasant sector is subordinate to the capitalist sector—disproportions in the latter call forth a new division of labor in the former, which in turn allows the imbalances in the capitalist sector to be overcome. Preobrazhensky's initial scheme reads as follows (the letter K designates the capitalist sector, the letter P the precapitalist one):

$$\begin{aligned} \text{KI. } 4{,}000c + 1{,}000v + 1{,}000s &= 6{,}000 \\ \text{KII. } 1{,}500c + 375v + 375s &= 2{,}250 \end{aligned}$$

$$\begin{aligned} \text{PI. } 750c + 1{,}500 \text{ consumption fund} &= 2{,}250 \\ \text{PII. } 2{,}000c + 4{,}000 \text{ consumption fund} &= 6{,}000 \end{aligned}$$

KII*c* is 500 less than KI(v + s) and so cannot provide the full complement of means of consumption to department I of the capitalist sector. However, *c* of department II of the precapitalist sector is 500 greater than the consumption fund of PI. Neither sector's exchange is internally in balance. Equilibrium does, however, exist for the system as a whole. Department II of the peasant sector can obtain 500 in means of production from KI that it could not get from PI. Similarly, it can sell to KI 500 in means of consumption that it could not dispose of in PI. Thus, Preobrazhensky established that there is a reciprocal relationship between the two sectors. Shortfalls in production in one of the capitalist departments can be made up if the equivalent department of the peasant sector has a surplus in its own intradepartmental exchange.

Preobrazhensky's choice of figures in this illustration is unfortunate, since total production is equal in the two sectors, whereas production in KI equals that in PII and production in KII equals that in PI. Thus, it may at first appear as if his result is an artifact of the symmetry he has established in his figures. The subsequent analysis in the article makes it clear, however, that this is not the case.

Another point that Preobrazhensky is at pains to emphasize—and to which we will return in the next section of this Introduction—is that the relationships he defines here apply solely to the value magnitudes of each department's production. In reality, in a concrete study of a specific economy, such as Preobrazhensky offered in the final article of this volume ("Economic Equilibrium in the System of the USSR"), account must be taken of the *in natura* composition of the different branches of social production. It may be, for instance, that although PII can make up the shortage of means of consumption within KI in value terms, they may not be the kinds of means of consumption that the workers and capitalists in KI need to purchase. In that case equilibrium cannot be restored, and a crisis must ensue—at least on the assumptions we have made here, which exclude the prospect of foreign trade.

The second section of the article returns to the schemes for pure capitalism. Here Preobrazhensky drops the simplifying assumptions made by Marx. He keeps the organic composition of capital lower in department II than in department I, as this corresponds to the division of social labor under modern capitalism. But he then allows for equal rates of accumulation in the two departments, and when he does this he derives a tendency for department II to grow more rapidly than department I because of the greater addition to its variable capital—and ultimately to its surplus value—with each period of accumulation. Likewise, Preobrazhensky traces the effects of a rise in the organic composition of capital. This, too, leads to a relative overproduction in department II, for the reasons we have stated above.

As Preobrazhensky is here assuming a pure capitalist economy, with no peasant sector on which to fall back, the only solution left open is the transfer of capital from department II to department I. This transfer must ensure that the overall size of I is sufficiently great that, even with its higher organic composition of capital, the sum of its $v + s/x$ will equal the now-lower IIc. Preobrazhensky shows that this transfer cannot eradicate the tendency toward overproduction in department II in ensuing production periods, and hence such transfers must take place systematically, with each and every year. Finally, in this section Preobrazhensky tries to demonstrate how capitalism overcomes the physical obstacles to such capital transfers, which had been one of Luxemburg's objections to the rigidity of Marx's schemes. This was a problem that Preobrazhensky did not fully take up, however, until his book *The Decline of Capitalism*.

The last part of this article provides a synthesis of the analyses of the two preceding sections. Given the tendency for a capitalist economy to suffer from periodic underproduction of means of production, how do its relations with noncapitalist strata help it to overcome this disproportion? Clearly there must be a corresponding tendency for precapitalist production to alter its division of labor in such a way that it produces more means of production and fewer means of consumption that its own internal demand would call for. If the peasant sector absorbs the shifts in the social division of labor in this way, capitalism can be spared the potential disruptions and possible crises that transfers of capital within the capitalist sector would entail.

It is no secret that Preobrazhensky is here talking about the situation actually confronting the Soviet Union. The argument in this first of the "Economic Equilibrium" articles implicitly previews that in the final article, which deals specifically with the USSR. The Soviet Union suffered a pressing shortage of means of production. This shortage could only be overcome if the peasant sector could produce a surplus of means of production, which could either fill gaps in state production directly or be exported for foreign currency, which could then be used to buy needed machinery and raw materials on the world capitalist market.[29] Already Preobrazhensky shows the pattern of mutual dependence that characterized the Soviet Union under NEP. Department I of the peasant sector had to produce a surplus of means of production. In so doing it would also increase its dependence on department II of the state sector for means of consumption. Conversely, the state's department II could use this surplus of peasant means of production to make up the shortages of means of production that the state sector was not capable of supplying.

This argument applied to the Soviet Union only in its most general outlines. There were further complications that the Soviet economy's poverty of fixed capital and other means of production would impose on this process of growth. But the analysis in this first article provided the analytical tools that Preobrazhensky was to use later on to develop his theory of crisis in the Soviet economy. The implications of the argument were clear enough in their own right. The dictates of proportionality in an industrial or industrializing country demanded accelerated growth in the department producing industrial means of production. Where this could not be done except at the risk of generalized crisis, an equivalent *value* of these means of production had to come from the peasant periphery. The contradiction facing the Soviet economy was that this presupposed the prior production of industrial means of production, without which agriculture could not expand at the rate and volume required. And these means of production Soviet industry could not supply.

Preobrazhensky's Concretization of the Schemes and His Theory of the Soviet Crisis

For Preobrazhensky to extend his analysis he had to solve two additional problems that were closely related. First, he had to incorporate into his analysis and, to the extent possible, into the reproduction schemes the differentiation in the *in natura* composition of production in all four departments of the two major sectors. The nature of this problem and the inadequacy of confining a study of reproduction simply to the analysis of the exchange of values have already been touched on. Secondly, Preobrazhensky had to allow for the fact that the various elements of productive capital are reproduced differently *in time*. Both of these problems were really different dimensions or aspects of one single problem, namely the fundamentally different processes through which fixed and circulating capital are reproduced. In addition, it is one thing to study the basic mechanisms behind these differences within a developed capitalist system, where we can expect to find a general pattern of regularity in the whole process, and another thing completely to examine them within the context of the Soviet system, where the entire economic organism had been disrupted by the Revolution, World War I, and the Civil War, not to mention the drastic alterations in production and exchange relations that had occurred with the transformation of the social system. With the second and third of the articles on "Economic Equilibrium" (which deal with capitalist Europe and the Soviet Union, respectively), Preobrazhensky began to make the necessary modifications in his theory of reproduction, although he did not manage to really complete this part of his study until 1931, with *The Decline of Capitalism*.

Marx had noted in vol. II of *Capital* that the specific properties of fixed capital presented special problems for the study of simple and expanded reproduction. Unlike circulating capital, which is used up and demands replacement in the course of a single production period (assumed to be one year), the functioning of fixed capital is of longer duration. While it is purchased *in toto* in a certain year, its value passes into the products it helps produce only little by little, over several production periods. This opened up for Marx a whole new area of potential disturbances and crises for capitalism. Not only could imbalances result from the inability of the two departments to produce commodities in the right value proportions, but they could also arise from *temporal* discontinuities in the replacement of fixed capital. If the fixed capital already purchased and functioning was not replaced at exactly the right *moment in time*, this too would disrupt the division of labor within department I and the pattern of exchange between the two departments, and would in consequence precipitate a crisis.[30]

Unfortunately, except for a few scattered passages in vols. II and III of *Capital* and in *Theories of Surplus Value*, Marx discussed the difficulties engendered by the reproduction of fixed capital only within the context of simple reproduction. Even here, however, Marx's analysis foreshadowed the work Preobrazhensky was to do later on. For from this work, as from Marx's analysis of the breakdown of the product of department II into articles of luxury and necessities, we can derive the need to "disaggregate" the reproduction schemes not just into different departments but into different sectors, each of which produces qualitatively different types of commodities. If anything, it is more essential to do this with the production of means of production than with department II. Means of production serve as both circulating and fixed capital, and the different use forms acquired by particular means of production must be taken into account in analyzing either simple or expanded reproduction.

It is not surprising that Preobrazhensky would give this relationship special attention, since in the Soviet Union the differentiation between fixed and circulating constant capital largely corresponded to the separation of the economy into state and petty-commodity production sectors. While state industry's department I would produce means of production that would serve as both kinds of constant capital, this was not true of the peasant sector. Its production of means of production, at least insofar as they were produced for sale to the state sector, would be virtually entirely devoted to commodities that would function solely as circulating capital, mainly raw materials. Thus, any analysis of the interrelations between the two sectors had to take this material distinction into account.

The problem of fixed capital proved important also because of its temporal aspect. It is not just that fixed capital *wears out* over a period of years, giving rise to temporal discontinuities in the reproduction process. The *production* of fixed capital also has a time dimension that must be allowed for if economic growth is to proceed smoothly. Investments in fixed capital, as all new investments, require the prior existence or construction of plant and equipment. That is, they demand the prior production of fixed capital. These investments have a relatively long gestation period, that is, once an investment project is initiated it is usually several years before it yields any result and itself begins to produce commodities. Such investments in the production of fixed capital, therefore, entail a one-way withdrawal of means of production and labor power from society's production apparatus without giving any value in return for some years. In this way, investment in fixed capital would actually lower the supply of commodities coming from department I of the industrial sector that was available for exchange, either within that department itself or with the other three departments of the economy. Society gets around this problem by having on hand substantial reserves in the form of idle plant and equipment, raw materials, and auxiliary products, as well as reserves of labor power and means of subsistence needed to sustain new workers. When new investment projects are undertaken, these reserves are brought into play to tide society over until the new plant and equipment are completed and are themselves employed in production. It is clear from this that society must arrive at a fairly fine balance between the investment projects it initiates and those that are just coming to fruition if it is to maintain proportional growth of all departments. This growth must also maintain a balance between current production on the one hand and reserves of all kinds (means of production, means of subsistence, and labor power) on the other, so as to allow both for periods of expansion and for "normal" disruptions in the material proportions between the productive forces or for imbalances in the latter's times of production.[31]

It is not hard to see that the Soviet Union could fulfill none of the economic preconditions for the relatively crisis-free accumulation of fixed capital. This was true regardless of the angle from which we approach the problem. On the one hand, the balance between retirements of expired fixed capital and that portion of fixed capital stock still capable of functioning in production was completely disrupted by World War I and the Civil War. Many factories were using machinery that should have been scrapped years before: Once the process of recovery was under way and the maximum expansion that could be realized simply by bringing idle capacity back into use had been reached, the amount of fixed capital renewals would vastly exceed that of a normal capitalist economy during a comparable period of time. (This was the "transition from recovery to reconstruction"; in the second "Economic Equilibrium" article, dealing with declining reproduction, Preobrazhensky shows that post–World War I Europe faced a very similar though far less chronic problem.) The difficulty was simultaneously exacerbated from the other end. The Soviet economy's initial poverty, inherited from backward capitalist Russia, and the destruction of its fixed capital base during the war and postrevolutionary years meant that it did not have at its disposal the plant and equipment required to produce the fixed capital it would demand to restore Soviet industry. Consequently, its output of fixed capital was to prove seriously deficient.

Secondly, the investment required to produce the fixed capital that would subsequently provide means of production for both departments of the state sector and for agriculture would withdraw resources from the economy—means of production and labor power—without yielding any output for a certain number of years. Therefore, *in the short run* the existing famine of means of production in the state sector would deepen, since means of production had to be diverted to heavy industry to provide an adequate supply of means of production *in the future.* But this meant that the current annual product of department I of the state sector would be severely retarded. The Soviet Union's future needs came into sharp conflict with its present capacities, a contradiction rooted in the fundamental temporal disequilibrium inherent in the backward structure of the economy.

Preobrazhensky noted that, as in the case of disproportions in the *in natura* composition of the product of the various departments, this disequilibrium could be partially ameliorated by recourse to the foreign market, where ready-made means of production could be purchased and where the prior investment in the plant and equipment essential for their production could be avoided. But this could not solve the problem. Politically the capitalist West was not prepared to deal with the Soviet Union on an adequate scale. Economically, it merely begged the question: to purchase on the world market, the Soviet Union had to sell; and peasant production, which was tied to its preindustrial technique, could not keep pace with the demands of industrial accumulation, which would proceed much more quickly. Preobrazhensky could demonstrate that access to the world division of labor was indispensable both for ironing out disproportions in the physical make up of peasant and industrial output and for overcoming certain aspects of the temporal disequilibrium plaguing the economy; but for both economic and political reasons he could also demonstrate that so long as the world division of labor was *capitalist*, the Soviet economy could not escape from its impasse. What was needed was *assistance*, and that would come only from other countries where the dictatorship of the proletariat had triumphed.

Herein lies the true *tour de force* of the 1927 article "Economic Equilibrium in the System of the USSR," for in it Preobrazhensky showed more clearly than in any other of his writings the deeply contradictory nature of Soviet society. It was true that if the dictates of the law of primitive socialist accumulation were ignored, disruption would result. But it followed equally from his analysis that implementation of the policies demanded by this theory would bring with it further conflicts and distortions in the economy and in the "equilibrium of social forces" within the country. The underlying reasons were the backwardness of the Soviet economy and society and the fact that the needs of industrialization could not be met with the paucity of economic and human resources at the Soviet Union's disposal. As such the contradictions were not strictly economic but also political and social, being bound up not merely with the poverty of the country but with the political character of the Soviet regime. It was not Soviet backwardness alone, nor the simple fact of its isolation from the world division of labor, that structured the USSR's development, but rather that these were factors in a conflict of class forces *both inside the country and on a world scale*. Here was "proof," if such was needed, of the impossibility of socialism in one country.

Preobrazhensky's Attack on the Five-Year Plans

In 1929, as we have mentioned, Preobrazhensky broke with Trotsky and the Opposition and made his peace with Stalin over the latter's "left turn" towards industrialization. The "peace," such as it existed, was short-lived. In 1931 Preobrazhensky was again expelled from the Party. Although we have not as yet done the detailed archival research that would perhaps fully explain the exact reasons for Preobrazhensky's second expulsion, two events seem to provide all the explanation we are likely to require.

The first is Preobrazhensky's own literary activity during 1931. In that year he published his book on capitalist crises, *The Decline of Capitalism.* Also in 1931, he submitted an article to the journal *Problemy ekonomiki*, entitled "On the Methodology of Drawing Up the General Plan and the Second Five-Year Plan" ("O metodologii sostavleniia genplana i vtoroi piatiletki"). This was an attack on the way in which the industrialization drive then under way was being conducted, and appears to be Preobrazhensky's only attempt after 1927 to write directly about the Soviet economy. The article given to *Problemy ekonomiki* was never published, but to judge from the attacks that it provoked and the quotations that the latter provided, Preobrazhensky seems to have based his critique of Stalin's industrialization drive on the ideas developed in the 1920s articles on "Economic Equilibrium" and in *The Decline of Capitalism.* Given that in the latter Prèobrazhensky had made it quite explicit that he was continuing the theoretical work begun during his days in the Opposition, it is not surprising that his opponents delved deep into his theoretical and political past to draw the connection between his present "errors" and his political and intellectual association with Trotsky.

During 1932 Preobrazhensky was subjected to a barrage of attacks in various articles and symposia, all of which zealously attempted to link his book on capitalism to his critique of the five-year plans, and to tie the two directly to Preobrazhensky's alleged attempt to bring "Trotskyist contraband" into the Party.[32] For once Stalin's intellectual thugs of the Institute of Red Professors seem to have told the truth. For it is interesting that, though Preobrazhensky had broken with Trotsky just two years before, by 1931 the two were again advancing an identical argument: that the five-year plans were leading to disastrous dislocations and overaccumulation in heavy industry, beyond all bounds of maintaining proportionality with other sectors of the economy. As Deutscher notes this should have been an obvious argument, but "as happens so often, the truisms of one generation were the dreaded heresy of its predecessor; and communists, but not only they, received Trotsky's criticisms with indignation or derision."[33] The concurrence of views reached by Trotsky and Preobrazhensky on this question is in our view the "missing link" that explains the ferocity and speed with which Preobrazhensky was hounded during this period.

Taking the "Economic Equilibrium" articles as his starting

point, Preobrazhensky used them to develop a theory of the capitalist business cycle based on what he termed "the temporal uneveness in the renewal and augmentation of fixed capital." Central to his theory was what he saw as the discrepancy between the demand for new fixed capital (which, given the long gestation period of investments and the massive prior investment in plant and equipment needed to effect them, tended to be covered by bringing reserve capacity into operation) and the moment in time when new investments would be completed and their output thrown onto the market in search of realization.

Suppose, says Preobrazhensky, that there is an extraordinary demand for new fixed capital equal to 100% of society's existing yearly output of these types of means of production. To fill such a demand from scratch would require society to take on the literally impossible economic task of doubling its existing stock of fixed capital, i.e., to undertake the prior construction of plant and equipment equal in value (in Preobrazhensky's example) to some 7.5 times the value of the final output of fixed capital that is required. What is more, since the technical proportions of production in department I must be kept intact, this would also demand a doubling of supplies of raw materials, labor power, and means of subsistence. Clearly no society could ever meet with new orders of such magnitude unless it already had on hand adequate reserves of all types of means of production and means of subsistence. Specifically, it would have to have adequate excess capacity such that no new construction of plant and equipment was immediately needed. If this could be brought into play, the entire accumulation fund could be devoted to constant and variable circulating capital, and the demand covered in a relatively few years.[34]

It is noteworthy that Preobrazhensky bases his example on such an extreme increase in the output of fixed capital, especially since in his actual theory of the investment cycle new demand for these means of production is shown to arise from the upward conjuncture of a recovery-boom-slump cycle.[35] Clearly he is trying to construct his "model" to more closely reflect Soviet conditions. By inference he is at this point in his argument already pointing to the USSR's inability to undertake such a massive reequipment given its paucity of reserves and excess capacity.

To see where Preobrazhensky takes this argument we need to look at his picture of the pattern of the business cycle. Under competitive, classical capitalism such new orders for fixed capital will, in fact, be covered by bringing idle capacity into operation. Given the competitive conjuncture new capital will flow into those branches of production manufacturing fixed capital; but the new investments made with this capital will not complete their gestation for some time after their initiation. By that time the demand for fixed capital will already for the most part have been filled by existing production units. When the new investments are complete there will be overproduction and crisis. Preobrazhensky used this theory to demonstrate the important structural changes in the morphology of the investment cycle that come with the evolution of monopoly capitalism, but this is not our immediate concern here.[36] In his unpublished article of 1931, "On the Methodology of Drawing Up the General Plan and the Second Five-Year Plan," he drew what conclusions he needed from this theory to make his attack on the five-year plans and Stalin's industrialization drive.

Although the Soviet Union was driven to attempt to overcome industrial backwardness by its isolation and by the fact that its productivity was drastically below that prevailing in the world capitalist market, the policy pursued by Stalin involved a disproportionately massive investment of resources in heavy industry. Department I would find at the end of this process that it had outstripped the ability of the other sectors of the economy to keep pace with it. Heavy industry would end up with neither adequate supplies of raw materials nor sufficient output of means of subsistence. This was inherent in the fact that the one sector of the economy that had to be modernized as a prerequisite for general industrial development was large-scale industry. The problem was that this had been done without regard to the needs of proportionality: "In drawing up the second five-year plan," warned Preobrazhensky, "the amount of pig iron or coal must be *the end result*, and not the beginning."[37] The crux of the argument resided in the temporal unevenness of the accumulation of fixed capital. Preobrazhensky noted that while huge investments had been made in the latter, the rate of consumption of the total output of the economy had remained stable despite an actual growth in the size of the work force (i.e., real per capita consumption had fallen). This investment, however, had not yet come to completion and hence had not begun to yield any output. Following his analysis of the capitalist cycle, it seemed clear to Preobrazhensky that once the gestation period of this investment was over there would be a sudden swelling of department I, with no compensating or proportional growth in either department II of the state sector or in agriculture (which had to provide certain raw materials, and more importantly, means of consumption). Preobrazhensky logically called for a shift of resources *back into department II* and an increase in individual consumption. This may at first seem an odd conclusion to be reached by a person once labeled a "superindustrializer"; but not when we recall that this appellation was but an epithet attached by the Stalinists at a time when intra-Party struggle demanded that the Left Opposition be portrayed as the pillagers of the working class and the countryside. Within the context of Preobrazhensky's overall theory of the Soviet transition, and especially in terms of the argument put in "Economic Equilibrium in the System of the USSR," the warning against a hypertrophy of heavy industry was perfectly consistent.

We do not know the specific conclusion that Preobrazhensky reached in this article. M. Mekler indignantly imputed to him the view that such difficulties could have been avoided only by, in Mekler's words, "the victory of the proletarian revolution in other countries and state aid from their victorious proletariats."[38] Mekler then goes on to specifically link Preobrazhensky's article to Trotsky's statement of the mid-twenties, "The contradictions in the position of a workers' government in a backward country, with an overwhelmingly peasant population, can only be resolved on an international scale, on the arena of the world-wide proletarian revolution."

It is our own view that the subsequent history of the Soviet Union has amply borne out the validity of Preobrazhensky's warning. On one level this is empirically verified in the immediate experience of industrialization in the 1930s, where the bottlenecks of supplies and labor power and the squeezing of working-class and peasant living standards have been detailed by so many first-hand and secondary accounts that it would be superfluous to reproduce them here. On a deeper and more enduring level, however, it is worth noting that even in Stalin's time there were—and there have continued to be—countless plans that called for a more rapid growth in consumer over producer goods, and yet the end result has been an utter failure to carry out the plan: when all is said and done it has been "Group A" that has yet again swollen out of proportion to "Group B."[39] The root cause, in our view, lies in the bureaucratic nature of Soviet planning, to which the fetish of "Group A" and the vulgar equation of heavy industry with "Marxism" must ultimately be laid. Nevertheless, in light of what we have said in this Introduction and of the articles presented in this collection, we must point out that from an economic point of view a genuine transfer of emphasis in favor of the development of consumer goods in the Soviet Union would require the massive *prior* construction of a consumer goods industry. In an economy where the social and economic mechanisms are such that the plan is always "taut,"[40] such investment is simply out of the question, and will remain so until these mechanisms themselves undergo a fundamental upheaval.

NOTES

[1] The reader should be aware that we are able to provide here only the most general historical background to the events of the Soviet twenties, and have made no attempt to take up the ideas of Preobrazhensky's individual opponents in the debates over industrialization. We refer the reader instead to such standard works as E. H. Carr's multi-volume *A History of Soviet Russia*, published by Macmillan; Isaac Deutscher's three-volume biography of Trotsky, *The Prophet Armed, Trotsky: 1879-1921* (London: Oxford University Press, 1954), *The Prophet Unarmed, Trotsky: 1921-1929* (London: OUP, 1959), and *The Prophet Outcast, Trotsky: 1929-1940* (London: OUP, 1963); Alec Nove's *An Economic History of the U.S.S.R.* (London: Allen Lane, 1972); and Alexander Erlich's *The Soviet Industrialization Debate* (Cambridge, Mass.: Harvard University Press, 1960). Nicolas Spulber's anthology, *Foundations of Soviet Strategy for Economic Growth* (Bloomington: Indiana University Press, 1964) is a valuable collection of documents by the leading economists of the 1920s. It also contains a translation of most of Preobrazhensky's article "Economic Equilibrium in the System of the USSR" (included in the present book), important passages of which, however, have unfortunately either been omitted or inadequately translated.

[2] For specific references to Preobrazhensky's role in the Left Opposition of 1923 and the United Opposition of 1926-27, see Deutscher, *The Prophet Unarmed*, pp. 113-34 and chapters iv and v; Carr, *The Interregnum* (London: Pelican, 1969), chapters 13 and 14, plus the "Note," pp. 374-80, giving the text of the "Platform of the 46," as well as the various reservations expressed by its signatories; David S. Law, "The Left Opposition in 1923," in *Critique*, No. 2, pp. 37-52; Carr, *Socialism In One Country* (Pelican, 1970), vol. I, Part II, and vol. II, ch. 19; and scattered references in E. H. Carr and R. W. Davies, *Foundations of a Planned Economy*, 2 volumes (London: Macmillan, 1969-71). See also Alexander Erlich's early article, "Preobrazhenski and the Economics of Soviet Industrialization," *Quarterly Journal of Economics*, February 1950, and Richard Day's "Preobrazhensky and the Theory of the Transition Period," *Soviet Studies*, April 1975. Both my own article, "Preobrazhensky and the Problem of the Soviet Transition," in *Critique*, No. 9 and this Introduction should be taken as an implicit rebuttal to Day's treatment of Preobrazhensky, especially in regard to the issue of Preobrazhensky's attitude towards socialism in one country. Finally, much of the biographical information on Preobrazhensky has been drawn from Preobrazhensky's autobiographical

sketch and the accompanying note by Jean-Jacques Marie, in Georges Haupt and Jean-Jacques Marie, *Makers of the Russian Revolution* (Ithaca, N.Y.: Cornell University Press, 1974), pp. 191-201.

[3] We will not give detailed bibliographical references to Preobrazhensky's works cited in the Introduction, but instead refer the reader to the bibliography of Preobrazhensky's major writings at the end of the book. To assist the reader, textual references will be to the English titles, with the original Russian given in parentheses.

[4] See Donald A. Filtzer, "Preobrazhensky and the Problem of the Soviet Transition," *Critique* 9, where we discuss the political conceptions behind Preobrazhensky's economic theories.

[5] Lenin, *Selected Works*, in three volumes, vol. 2 (Moscow, 1970), pp. 43-47. See also Trotsky, *History of the Russian Revolution*, vol. I (London: Sphere, 1967), pp. 284-89.

[6] The "Theses" of the Left Communists, "On the Current Situation," have been published as a pamphlet in English translation by the journal *Critique* (Glasgow, 1977). Preobrazhensky and Bukharin were coauthors of the well-known *ABC of Communism*, an exposition of the Party's 1919 program.

[7] Preobrazhensky's writings on inflation are a notable contribution to the Marxist theory of money, the literature on which is not overly abundant. See in particular *The Reasons for the Fall in the Exchange Rate of Our Ruble* [*Prichiny padeniia kursa nashego rublia*] and *A Theory of Depreciating Currency* [*Teoriia padaiushchei valiuty*]. His other works on finance are cited in the Bibliography.

[8] Carr, *The Interregnum*, pp. 374-80.

[9] This was a constant theme in Preobrazhensky's writings in these years. See in particular *On Morality and Class Norms* [*O morali i klassovykh normakh*], pp. 105-07.

[10] These will be discussed below, in the final section of the Introduction.

[11] Nove, Introduction to *The New Economics*, pp. xiv-xvi.

[12] "Sotsialisticheskie i kommunisticheskie predstavleniia sotsializma," *VKA*, 12-13 (1925).

[13] *The New Economics* (English translation by Brian Pearce), p. 2.

[14] "Economic Equilibrium in the System of the USSR." See pp. 230-31 of this volume.

[15] For Preobrazhensky's other discussions of capitalist crises see *From NEP To Socialism* (English translation by Brian Pearce), pp. 1-9 and 97-104; *The New Economics*, English edition, pp. 150-60; *The Theory of Depreciating Currency* [*Teoriia padaiushchei valiuty*]; and *The Decline of Capitalism* [*Zakat kapitalizma*].

[16] Preobrazhensky's own references to the continuity between *The Decline of Capitalism* and his articles on "Economic Equilibrium" appear in *Zakat kapitalizma*, pp. 54ff., 61-62, 70-71, and 82-83. We discuss this point further in the final section of the Introduction.

[17] It should be remembered that the most politically aware sections of the working class had been annihilated during the civil war, so that the proletariat, a minority of the population in any case, had lost its most capable elements.

[18] This is discussed in Deutscher, *The Prophet Unarmed*, pp. 277-78 and in Trotsky's *The Third International After Lenin* (New York, 1957), specifically

dedicated to this issue. Preobrazhensky, in his early theory of Soviet crises, noted that even if industry were to undertake expansion at the partial expense of peasant surpluses this would have the contradictory effect of holding down the growth of agricultural supplies to industry and to the export fund. At a deeper level, so long as the economy contained two different modes of production which produced with nonequivalent techniques, at a certain point industry's growth would outstrip the ability of agriculture to finance such industrialization or to maintain supplies of technical crops. "It began to become clear that the rate of development of agriculture was beginning to lag behind the rate of development of industry and the demands of foreign trade.... Such changes were needed in the entire technique of the peasant economy as would signify a rapid and decisive increase in the agricultural basis for Russia's industry.... This huge task was beyond the power of the Soviet Republic alone. Here the development of Russia's productive forces necessarily depended on proletarian revolution in the West and a re-grouping of productive forces on the European scale." (*From NEP To Socialism*, English edition, pp. 84 and 87). Jean-Jacques Marie (*op cit*, pp. 198-99) cites the following incident of a confrontation between Preobrazhensky and Stalin over this question at the Sixth Party Congress in 1917:

> Stalin read a report on the political situation which contained a resolution declaring the task of the Russian people to be "the seizure of power and, in alliance with the revolutionary proletariat of the advanced countries, its direction towards peace and the socialist reconstruction of society." Preobrazhensky objected to this formulation and proposed the following version: "...its direction towards peace, and, in the event of a proletarian revolution in the West, towards socialism." Stalin refused this version, saying that one "cannot rule out the possibility of its being precisely Russia that will open the path to socialism."

[19] *Capital*, vol. II, English edition (Moscow: Progress Publishers, 1967), p. 399.

[20] See the recent and extremely welcome publication in English of Roman Rosdolsky's *The Making of Marx's Capital* (London: Pluto Press, 1977), which contains an excellent discussion of the methodological relation between Marx's schemes and Marx's method of abstraction (pp. 63-72 and chap. 30).

[21] In addition to Rosdolsky, chap. 30, see Rosa Luxemburg, *The Accumulation of Capital* (New York: Monthly Review Press, 1968), sec. 2. Luxemburg's book, along with her *Accumulation of Capital—An Anti-Critique* (London: Allen Lane, 1972), were, of course, themselves major contributions to the debate.

[22] *Capital*, vol. II, English edition, p. 113 (emphasis mine). Neither Luxemburg nor Preobrazhensky cites this passage, although it has direct relevance for the discussion in "The Problem of Economic Equilibrium Under Concrete Capitalism and in the Soviet System."

[23] In *The Accumulation of Capital*, p. 122, Luxemburg mistakenly maintained that arranging accumulation in this way meant that department II accumulated varying proportions of its surplus value in each year. Her conclusion, however, was based on a number of simple errors in addition and subtraction. The fact that the equations for accumulation are linear should have told her that if department I accumulates 50 percent of its surplus value each year, the percentage of II*s* accumulated, though lower than department I's, would also have to be constant from year to year.

[24] For Luxemburg's discussion of the contradictions within Marx's schemes, see *The Accumulation of Capital*, pp. 120-26, and chap. XXV, especially pp. 336-47. On the possibility of transferring capital between departments, Preobrazhensky takes this point up in some detail in the first article on "Economic Equilibrium."

[25] *Zakat kapitalizma*, p. 14. Mention should also be made of Bukharin's reply to Luxemburg, *Imperialism and the Accumulation of Capital* (London, 1972; the same volume contains Luxemburg's *Anti-Critique*). Independently of Bukharin's rather specious polemical methods in this work it is often overlooked that it was written with a dual political purpose in mind: one, to bolster the attack on the so-called "Luxemburgism" of the Polish Communist Party of the time (1924), and two, to counter any negative implications that Luxemburg's theory might have for the "theory" of socialism in one country or for the idea that the USSR could industrialize without accumulating at the expense of the peasant economy.

[26] *Zakat kapitalizma*, pp. 14, 15, 77.

[27] The objection will inevitably be raised that Preobrazhensky's modifications of the reproduction schemes are subject to the same critique as Rosdolsky has made against the Austro-Marxists: that the latter's neat mathematical solutions to the problem of accumulation are only possible if one denies the essential premise of the problem, namely, that we are dealing with *capitalist* production, for which the instability of the schemes—once concretized in the manner Luxemburg (and Preobrazhensky) had suggested—reflects the real instability of the system in its day-to-day existence. Suffice it to say that Preobrazhensky, though not accepting the breakdown hypothesis as formulated by Luxemburg, was still attempting in his concretization of the reproduction schemes to develop a theory of crisis based, in this case, on the temporal unevenness in the reproduction and accumulation of fixed capital. The modifications he made in the articles on "Economic Equilibrium" were thus necessary steps along the way to developing the theory of crises contained in *The Decline of Capitalism*.

[28] *Ekonomicheskie krizisy pri NEP'e*, p. 16.

[29] It is interesting that this was also the pattern of industrialization under tsarist capitalism, where exports of peasant grains were used to finance foreign loans and foreign investment in capitalist industry. To the extent that domestic resources were inadequate for indigenous capital accumulation, the problem was "solved" at the expense of peasant living standards.

[30] *Capital*, vol. II, English edition, chap. XX, sec. X, pp. 453-73.

[31] "Once the capitalist form of reproduction is abolished, it is only a matter of the volume of the expiring portion—expiring and therefore to be reproduced in kind—of fixed capital . . . varying in various successive years. If it is very large in a certain year (in excess of the average mortality, as is the case with human beings), then it is certainly so much smaller in the next year. The quantity of raw materials, semi-finished products, and auxiliary materials required for the annual production of the articles of consumption—provided other things remain equal—does not decrease in consequence. Hence the aggregate production of means of production would have to increase in the one case and decrease in the other. This can be remedied only by a continuous relative over-production. There must be on the one hand a certain quantity of fixed capital produced in excess of that which is directly required; on the other hand, and particularly, there must be a supply of raw materials, etc., in

excess of the direct annual requirements (this applies especially to means of subsistence). This sort of over-production is tantamount to control by society over the material means of its own reproduction. But within capitalist society it is an element of anarchy" (*Capital*, vol. II, English edition, p. 473).

32 These are Grigory Konstantinovich Roginsky, ed., *Zakat kapitalizma v trotskistskom zerkale (o knige E. Preobrazhenskogo, "Zakat kapitalizma")* [*The Decline of Capitalism in the Trotskyist Mirror (on E. Preobrazhensky's Book "The Decline of Capitalism")*, Moscow, 1932]; K. Butaev, "K voprosu o material'noi baze sotsializma" ["On the Question of the Material Basis of Socialism"], *Problemy ekonomiki*, No. 1 (1932); and V. Balkov, "Kapitalisticheskoe vosproizvodstvo v trotskistskom osveshchenii" ["A Trotskyist Interpretation of Capitalist Reproduction"], *Problemy ekonomiki*, No. 6 (1932). The Balkov article (subtitled "A Critique of the 'Theory' of E. Preobrazhensky") states that it was to be followed by another article, but unfortunately, the series of *Problemy ekonomiki* available to us at the time of writing was incomplete, and so we do not know the contents of this later piece. Balkov also cites part of his "Critique" appearing separately in *VKA*, No. 7-8 (1932). The Roginsky collection—the same Roginsky who was co-prosecutor at the infamous "Menshevik Trials" of 1931-32, among whose victims was the eminent Soviet economist I. I. Rubin—was the outcome of a symposium organized by the Institute of Red Professors to attack Preobrazhensky's book. Among its contributions is an article by M. Mekler, "Obshchii krizis kapitalisma i bor'ba dvukh sistem v svete teorii Preobrazhenskogo" ["The General Crisis of Capitalism and the Struggle of Two Systems in the Light of Preobrazhensky's Theory"] attacking the unpublished article by Preobrazhensky, "On the Methodology. . . ." The latter article was also the object of Butaev's attack, and it is from these two sources that we know of its contents. The first person to note the existence of this article by Preobrazhensky and its importance was Erlich, *Soviet Industrialization Debate*, pp. 178-80.

33 Deutscher, *The Prophet Outcast*, pp. 93ff., where references to Trotsky's criticism of the first five-year plan are given. Trotsky was to express this position throughout the years 1929-1933, and in fact, the references in the various volumes of his writings are too numerous to list. In addition to the references cited by Deutscher, see in particular "The New Course in the Soviet Economy," in *The Writings of Leon Trotsky, 1930* (New York: Pathfinder Press, 1975), pp. 105-19, and "The Five-Year Plan and World Unemployment," *ibid*, pp. 123-29. This analysis was by no means confined to Trotsky and Preobrazhensky: we should not lose sight of the extent of the turmoil caused by collectivization and industrialization and the opposition this provoked within the Communist Party itself (and not simply among former members of the Right Opposition). See Tibor Szamuely, "The Elimination of Opposition Between the 16th and 17th Congresses of the CPSU," *Soviet Studies*, January 1966, pp. 318-38. I am grateful to Michael Cox, Queen's University, Belfast, for calling these references to my attention.

34 *Zakat kapitalizma*, pp. 66-71.

35 At the Sixteenth Party Congress (1930) Kuibyshev announced that the country's stock of fixed capital was to be doubled in three years.

36 This part of Preobrazhensky's argument bears a certain similarity to that of J. Steindl in *Maturity and Stagnation in American Capitalism* (New York: Monthly Review Press, 1974). The transition was characterized, according to Preobrazhensky, by the greater use of reserves in the monopoly period and concomitantly by investment in and construction of new fixed capital coming at a later phase in the cycle. This in turn worked to create a secular tendency toward stagnation, with deeper, more prolonged crises and briefer, less pro-

nounced periods of boom. Although he based his theory on these disequilibria in the *the natura* output of the different branches of the economy and their temporal dimensions, it must also be said that Preobrazhensky consistently stressed the impossibility of a strictly monist theory of crisis, noting that one purpose of his book was to bridge the alleged gap between the theories of crisis derivative from vol. II of *Capital* and Marx's repeated statements, especially in vol. III, to the effect that the primary source of crises lay in the contradiction between capitalism's drive to extend the development of the productive forces and its need to restrict the basis of social consumption.

[37] Pig iron and coal were two of the worst bottlenecks in the early years of industrialization, with construction sites and factories lying idle for lack of these two basic means of production. What Preobrazhensky means here is that the eventual output of pig iron and coal had themselves to be determined on the basis of existing capacities, rather than have the quite unrealistic *targets* for pig iron and coal production serve as the starting point for calculating production in those sectors dependent on them.

[38] Mekler, in Roginsky, ed., p. 56. In his book Erlich argues that Preobrazhensky's conclusion predicting over-accumulation was unrealistic, since the economy did not have the means to augment heavy industry to the extent that Preobrazhensky had posited in the rather extreme hypothetical illustration on which he had predicated his conclusion. We would suggest, however, that Preobrazhensky was deliberately using hyperbole here, and that he was addressing the economic situation as it actually existed. The question for Preobrazhensky, after all, was one of proportionalities of expanded reproduction and not absolute volumes. It is a fact that the legacy of Stalin's industrialization has been a more or less rigid and unrectifiable hypertrophy of heavy industry in the Soviet economy.

It is interesting that in the article "Economic Equilibrium in the System of the USSR" Preobrazhensky makes the statement that overaccumulation in the state sector was in his view impossible, since the internal market presented an almost limitless demand for the products of state industry. We should remember, however, that he was here attacking those of his opponents who were cautioning against a "too rapid" growth of industry. The statement is equally premised on the assumption that peasant incomes would be systematically *rising* (though a portion of this rise would be siphoned off into the fund of socialist accumulation), an assumption rendered completely inoperative by the destruction of agriculture during collectivization.

A modern discussion of the issues raised here that uses data from the period appears in Michael Ellman, "Did the Agricultural Surplus Provide the Resources Needed for the Increase in Investment in the USSR During the First 5-Year Plan?," *Economic Journal* (December 1975). Ellman's conclusion is that industrialization was indeed carried out by raising the degree of exploitation of the industrial workers, and not through drawing off supposed surpluses from agriculture.

[39] "Group A" and "Group B" in Soviet parlance correspond essentially to Marx's department I and department II. Statistics on the discrepancy between planned growth in departments I and II and the increases actually achieved can be found in Alec Nove's *An Economic History of the U.S.S.R.* Hypertrophy here should not be taken simply as a matter of the relative standing of producer and consumer goods, since Soviet economists still complain of the productive capacity of heavy industry having outstripped the creation of a suitable infrastructure upon which any pattern of "balanced" growth must depend.

[40] This is by now so well documented in both Marxist and non-Marxist literature on the Soviet Union that it hardly needs elaboration here. For a very good and readable description of the dysfunctionality of current Soviet planning, see Robert Kaiser's *Russia, The People and the Power* (New York: Atheneum, 1976), chap. 9. From a theoretical standpoint, the most provocative analysis of Soviet planning to appear in recent years is in our view to be found in two articles by Hillel H. Ticktin: "Towards a Political Economy of the USSR," *Critique*, No. 1 (1973), and "The Contradictions of Soviet Society and Professor Bettelheim," *Critique*, No. 6 (1976).

PART ONE

The Economics of NEP

The Outlook for the New Economic Policy

1921

In the preface to the first edition of *Capital*, Marx wrote the following words, which have been cited many times since: "One nation can and should learn from others. And even when a society has got upon the right track for the discovery of the natural laws of its movement . . . it can neither clear by bold leaps, nor remove by legal enactments, the obstacles offered by the successive phases of its normal development. But it can shorten and lessen the birth-pangs." And a few lines earlier in the same preface, Marx said: "The country that is more developed industrially only shows, to the less developed the image of its own future."

Alas, on both the European and American continents we have countries that are much more developed industrially than Russia, but unfortunately, not one of these countries is in a position to show industrially backward Soviet Russia the image of its immediate future. The unexpected zigzag that history has taken by virtue of the victorious establishment of the dictatorship of the proletariat in just such a backward, agrarian European country as Russia, whereas capitalist relations still prevail in the economically more advanced countries, has made the situation in Europe incomparably more complex (in the sense of backward countries learning from the advanced nations) than the one in which Marx wrote the words cited above. Of course, if one takes the Menshevik position that

In the pages that follow, Preobrazhensky's notes accompany the text. The editor's notes appear at the end of each article.

there was no socialist revolution in October, but merely a bourgeois democratic revolution clothed in socialist slogans and complicated (unhappily for the Mensheviks and the bourgeoisie) by the preeminent and leading role played by the proletariat, if one is of the conviction that that revolution merely cleared the ground for capitalist development in Russia much more thoroughly than a bourgeois revolution led by the capitalist class could have done, then things are quite simple. In that case it is indeed capitalist Germany, Great Britain, and especially America that in all major respects have to show us the image of our own future, and all that is left for Russia is to "shorten the birth-pangs" of normal capitalist relations in the country—a task to which our Mensheviks and SRs have as a matter of fact applied themselves with appropriate zeal, though they stubbornly refuse to admit it. Indeed, it may be true that we have nothing to learn from the Mensheviks; that *capitalist* relations in the advanced countries do not show us the image of our future; and that, on the contrary, *our* October should stand as a lesson for the advanced class of the advanced countries—that is, the working class—on how to carry out a proletarian revolution. It is likewise true that in the area we should like to presently consider—the area of industrial development and technology—we still have much to learn abroad.

Of much greater relevance for us, particularly in the period when we are implementing the New Economic Policy and trying to calculate its future prospects, are Marx's words that a society that has got upon the right track for the discovery of the natural laws of its movement cannot leap over the obstacles presented by the successive phases of its normal development. In the twentieth century, the century of capitalism's downfall, of proletarian revolutions, and of socialist wars, the proletariat has broken through its capitalist shell and established its revolutionary dictatorship in Russia, and it is thanks to these circumstances that human society is now able to dimly perceive the "natural laws of its movement" in the upcoming period. This is what is most essential for understanding the fundamental process now taking place in Soviet Russia. But we also have to remember that our petit bourgeois encirclement, too, follows a natural law of development: with all the elemental mass of its forces, the petite bourgeoisie weighs heavy upon the young socialist sprouts—bending some down to the very ground, twisting the stalks of others, totally preventing still others from even breaking through to the light. And most important of all is that this petite bourgeoisie, driven by iron necessity and by the laws of its own development, will be compelled to strive to close the breach in the capitalist system that has been opened by October and our victories in the Civil War. The next few years will provide us with the opportunity of observing and studying two different "natural laws of development" in the Soviet republic—two laws that are centuries apart on the scale of history but, by the irony of fate, are operating in the same country and at the same time: (1) the natural law of development of petty commodity production, establishing capitalist relations anew or reestablishing capitalist processes and bonds sundered by October, and (2) the natural law of development of socialist society, its roots firmly implanted in large-scale industry, and geared toward widening the breach that October has made externally, and striving to gradually extend it internally at the expense of the petit bourgeois and (if we may be permitted to use this term) middle-capitalist encirclement. We know the natural laws of the commodity economy well enough from the entire past history of capitalist countries and from our own prerevolutionary past. Here we face a repetition of processes that have already been studied, processes that promise no surprises if we make proper and timely adjustments for the unique features of the situation as a whole. The natural laws of socialist accumulation and development of socialist relations, on the other hand, have barely been adumbrated. History teaches us very little here, because it is we ourselves who are now making it. We can study only the little that has been achieved up to now—and even this has been achieved in extremely complex circumstances, by no means characteristic of the future development of socialist relations in the West. Herein, of course, lies our weakness. At the same time, our strength consists in the fact that our petit bourgeois encirclement, even in the person of its political ideologues, does not know what surprises await it from the socialist isle within. In our struggle with the petite bourgeoisie we shall be in the position of a military command that, while hampered because it has only a rough idea of what it will itself do in the future, is compensated by its dead certain knowledge of what its opponent will be forced to do.

What, then, is the outlook for the next few years?

For a rough, schematic answer to that question, one that by no means claims to be prophetic, let us begin by examining how relations in Russia would develop if the petit bourgeois encirclement were to advance with maximum success along the line of its "natural law of development." We shall then look at the prospect of an ideally rapid development of socialist relations. And, finally, we shall take these two processes as they interact—that is, as they will actually have to develop and collide.

Let us begin with the countryside. Before the revolution the productive forces of agriculture developed along two lines: on the one hand, capitalist, land-owner, kulak, and merchant economies were organized and consolidated, and on the other hand, vigorous kulak holdings of the capitalist farm type began springing up in the territory of peasant agriculture. These new farms began using fertilizers in working the soil; they introduced new crops, and they built up animal stocks of better breeds than did the rest of the peasant masses. While the poor peasant economy deteriorated and the middle peasant economy was at best stagnant, only kulak agriculture showed any progress. The kulaks awaited a brilliant future with the victory of the bourgeois revolution: the large-scale peasant farm would have become the dominant form not only within the peasant economy but within the country's agriculture as a whole. The October Revolution, which eliminated feudal land tenure, also disrupted the evolution of the new type of peasant holding. Not only did it arrest the process of accumulation in the kulak economy, but during the period of the Committees of Poor Peasants it was largely, albeit not fully, successful in bringing the kulaks down to the same level as the middle peasants. From the stage they had attained on the way to a capitalist economy, the kulaks were thrust back to the level at which they had been when that process had first begun in earnest, that is, to approximately where they had been in the 1870s and 1880s.

Under the conditions of the New Economic Policy, which means freedom to enrich oneself, to accumulate, and to employ wage labor in both urban and rural petty production, the evolution of a capitalist farmer class—a process that had been interrupted by the revolution—will begin anew. It has already started in regions of good harvest no less than in those suffering from famine. In a good harvest the well-to-do peasant earns greater profits than the others, because he has sown more acreage and cultivated it better (perhaps even using an extra allotment or two left behind by a horseless peasant who moved away). In provinces struck by famine the kulak remains on his farm, whereas the poor peasants emigrate. He buys up their livestock and implements for next to nothing, and by 1922 he will already have sown areas larger than those he would have even dreamed of a year ago. As far as wage labor is concerned, the poor peasants who have been forced from the ranks of the active farming population by poor harvests and lack of working stock will provide as much wage labor as is needed so long as there is a demand. And the demand is already there, particularly in the outlying districts, and it will grow.

The development of the kulak class under the new conditions also must inevitably lead to a regrouping of forces in the countryside. First, the number of poor peasants, which was reduced to a minimum after the expropriation of the kulaks and the leveling in the countryside, will increase; the countryside will begin to lose its homogeneity and assume once more a differentiated character. We cannot exclude the possibility that the kulaks will exert a political pull on the stratum of the poor peasantry that will be economically dependent on them. And there is absolutely no doubt that the kulaks will find a following among a number of the middle peasants who will lie awake many a night thinking about the successes of the kulaks and who will feel themselves preparing, as it were, for primitive accumulation. But, on the other hand, those peasants who are sinking into poverty will undoubtedly end up clashing sharply with the kulak upper strata on three issues—land, the tax in kind, and local taxes and obligations—and they will inevitably force Soviet power to intervene in the struggle *on their side*. But regardless of that, the kulaks will on their own collide directly with the dictatorship of the proletariat, inasmuch as the workers' government will through its tax policy dampen the ardor of kulak accumulation and will block the way of the kulak class as it moves toward capitalism. Banditry is ceasing; the last flames of the previous period of open war against Soviet power are dying out. Instead of lending his support to banditry—that is, to a hopeless and unprofitable cause—the kulak will now turn toward a more profitable business: accumulation within the limits laid down for him by the New Economic Policy, with the reservation that when those limits prove uncomfortably narrow, the *rushnitsa** will again be the order of the day.

As regards the town, the "natural law" of development in the capitalist direction in its ideal form (for the bourgeoisie) and with ideal speed takes the following shape. Petty merchant capital occu-

*A sawed-off rifle commonly used by bandit gangs in the Ukraine.—Trans.

pies all positions in the sphere of state and cooperative distribution. As a result, all surpluses from the peasant economy—with the exception of the tax in kind and state and cooperative compulsory deliveries, all production from craft industry and from medium-size enterprises leased by private persons, and part of the output of state enterprises, since part of their products end up on the free market—is distributed through the petty trading system. Competition within petty trade will end up strengthening many commercial enterprises and concentrating considerable wealth in the hands of a few people. As for merchant capital as a whole, it will very quickly exceed the volume required for commodity exchange, within the limits imposed upon it by insufficient production, and will spill over into production. The rush to lease enterprises will be incomparably greater than now, when trade offers enormous profits at no expense. Organization of new petty and medium-size production units will also increase. As a result, both the urban merchant class and the medium-size capitalist enterprises are turning into a serious factor in economic life. Already they are the suppliers to millions of people and the employers of tens of thousands of workers. This stratum too is moving toward inevitable conflict with Soviet power, since the workers' government bars its way through the further development of taxation and railroad policy, does not provide suitable guarantees for free exploitation of labor power, and does not reestablish the necessary legal framework for accumulation.

Foreign capital is at first enlisted as an ally of large-scale socialist industry to help raise the productive forces on the basis of large-scale production and combat the barbaric backwardness of petty production. But once it has entrenched itself at several points and is forced to use the domestic market both for a variety of purchases and for the sale of part of its products, it will establish business connections with the bourgeois encirclement and at a certain point will shift its orientation. No accumulation within the bourgeois encirclement is capable of amassing such an amount of merchant capital that it could in a historically brief period take control of production in our large-scale industry. The only candidate for seizing that control is foreign capital, which could place itself at the head of a petit bourgeois encirclement with its large-scale capitalist orientation—which, in terms of the type of production it promotes, is of a similar order. Consequently, the unnatural alliance between the socialist state and large-scale foreign capital will be broken and replaced by the natural alliance between foreign capital and all the bourgeois forces of Russia. The time will arrive for combat between this alliance and the socialist state, and the outcome of that struggle will be decided by the relationship of forces within the country and on an international scale.

Let us now imagine an ideally rapid development at the other pole—in the area of socialist production and distribution. Now that it has begun to restore the economy in the most vital branches of large-scale industry and transportation, the socialist island is expanding simultaneously through the development of its own intrinsic forces and by systematic deductions from the income of the petit bourgeois encirclement. Now that it has begun to reestablish the economy's food base through the tax in kind and a limited commodity exchange, Soviet power is in a position—thanks to the successes of its large-scale industry—to expand from year to year a second source for the procurement of agricultural products for industry. At the same time, successes in coal mining, petroleum production, and peat harvesting, together with the electrification of St. Petersburg, Moscow, and other districts, is creating a steadily increasing fuel base for developing industry.

Deductions from the income of the petit bourgeois encirclement will increase as that income steadily grows. The tax in kind is being maintained at its old level during the first years of industrial recovery, or even decreasing with fluctuations in the harvest (and, with the general advance of the peasant economy and expanded acreage, there is no *economic* barrier to such a development).[1] Taxes on handicrafts, cottage production, trade, and private industry, on the other hand, will grow steadily, which is also economically possible given the growth of productive forces in these areas. At first, these branches will be taxed to such a degree that expenses for the state apparatus and maintenance of transportation, the army, and so on fall on them to the same extent as they fall on socialist industry. Later on, these taxes will be raised until the lessee is left with a profit corresponding to the income of a good specialist, and the bulk of what otherwise would have gone into the capitalist accumulation fund will be taken from petty production. As a result, the surpluses of the kulak economy and private industry will spill over primarily into the socialist accumulation fund. At the same time, the republic's foreign trade will play an increasingly greater role, and socialist commercial profit, a new economic category, will appear. As the peasant economy gets back on its feet, grain will be the most important article of trade. By selling grain abroad and selling the products of large-scale foreign industry to the peasants, the Soviet state will realize a substantial and ever-increasing profit, beyond what it needs to cover its own organizational expenses. As production and large-scale industry increase and the possibilities for commodity circulation with the countryside grow, the Soviet state will evolve a stable currency through taxes, the curtailment of currency emissions, and the expansion of commodity exchange on the free market. Later on it will use the issue of new currency (as long as it does not endanger the ruble's exchange rate) to draw out of circulation and into the socialist accumulation fund that quantity of *commodity resources* of the petty economy that corresponds to the volume of *money accumulation* in the private economy.[2]

Capital held as foreign-run concessions in Russia is another point in question; as its own industry begins to recover in earnest after the Soviet state, having started to attract foreign capital into production, will come to realize that this method of attracting foreign capital is economically unprofitable and politically dangerous as compared to the system of commodity loans. In a period of general industrial collapse, commodity loans are impossible because of the great risk involved for the capital that is loaned. But now, during a period of upswing of socialist industry, they will become the preferred form for using foreign capital in Russia, and, despite extortionate interest rates, they will serve as a highly effective stimulus for the advancement of all our industry and agriculture.

As a result of the rapid recovery of large-scale industry and the creation of favorable material conditions for the proletariat, and with the prospects of an industrial crisis or crises abroad, unemployment, and persecution by bourgeois governments, masses of foreign workers will stream into Russia; this proletarian colonization of Russia will provide support to our developing industry to compensate for Russia's own lack of skilled labor. Not only will the proletariat as a class grow continuously in number, but its qualitative composition will also improve.

The success of industry will hasten the process of socialization of agriculture. The state farms will be able to stand on their own feet. State farms attached to factories will grow in number and quality. Urban communal plots will grow. The horse will gradually be replaced by the tractor and electric plow, thus enlarging the islands of collective economy in the countryside. Along with this slow process, another much more rapid development will occur. The state will begin organizing a new type of state farm on the idle lands of outlying regions, using tractors and foreign workers. As an outgrowth of the renewed stratification of the countryside, more intense and more conscious efforts toward the formation of communes will be initiated among the poor peasantry. This will occur in a period when proletarian power will be much more capable than previously of encouraging that process by supplying communists with machines, fertilizers, and agronomic expertise.

Thus, whereas on the one hand the proletarian base of Soviet power will grow from day to day, on the other socialist large-scale production will acquire increasing dominance over petty production in the country's economy. At first, both large-scale and petty production will expand, without coming into sharp conflict. Then large-scale production will begin not just to grow but to do so at the expense of petty production. In this period, the Soviet state will, as a rule, not only cease to lease out certain medium-size enterprises but will already have begun to feel burdened by present lessees and, instead of renewing existing contracts, will run the medium-size enterprises itself. The petty trade that exists along with the cooperatives will already be subordinated in considerable measure to large-scale production. It will receive products for sale in cases where the state finds it more profitable to use the apparatus of petty trade than that of the cooperatives or when use of both apparatuses is required. The state will control not only trade but also petty and medium-size industries that have been granted credit by the state bank and in this way drawn under the wing of the Soviet state. This process of systematic ouster of private petty and medium-size industry, continuous pressure on the kulaks, higher taxes, and so on will incite rebellion among that part of the petit bourgeois encirclement that is steadfastly trying to get its hands on the means for unrestricted capitalist accumulation. A bourgeois-kulak counterrevolution will break out, which, given the relationship of forces existing at the time, will be easily routed. After this defeat, there will be—if we can use this expression—a period of socialist reaction. The New Economic Policy will be partially abolished; after a period of partial denationalization, there will once again be intensified nationalization of the areas that are profitable for the Soviet state to nationalize. The critical period will have passed. Socialism will have triumphed across the board.

This is how we can imagine the "natural law" of capitalist accumulation and growth, the "natural law" of socialist accumulation, and development in the ideal form for each process.

Let us now take both these processes in interplay with one another, including all the factors that can complicate the course of their development. That is, let us try to imagine how it will really look as socialist production develops alongside the commodity economy. We can take the second half of 1921 as our chronological starting point.

The first period, through whose initial stages we are passing now, in the fall of 1921, is characterized by the relatively peaceful coexistence of the two processes. The kulak—expropriated in the period of the Committees of Poor Peasants, deprived of electoral rights in the Soviets, regarded with general suspicion, especially as concerns speculation, the use of hired labor, and accumulation—is now in the position of a man who has escaped from prison. Introduction of the tax in kind to replace the requisition suits him completely, at least in the first period. Right now he could not wish for anything better: the tax in kind gives the kulak more than he could expect, at least as long as Soviet power exists. The kulak is extending his sown acreage, he uses his accumulated monetary resources to improve his livestock and to replenish his stores of implements, and he is beginning to heal the sores that he suffered from the policy of the Committees of Poor Peasants. The medium-sized kulak also welcomes the tax in kind as a replacement for the requisition, and he willingly hands over to the state the payments demanded of him by the tax.

At the same time there is emerging from the middle kulaks a stratum that is not content with remaining on the level of a consumer economy that barely makes ends meet, with nothing left over. This stratum strives to develop production to such a degree as to have some surpluses for accumulation. If one does not consider the currency emissions that form part of the peasant economy's income as some sort of tax in kind, then the present economic policy presents no obstacles to that process. As regards urban trade, the stratum of urban merchants is on a honeymoon of "primitive accumulation." The change from a ban on almost all forms of trade to unhindered commodity circulation, the enormous profits reaped during the first stages of the revival of commodity exchange, while competition is still small, compel the merchant class to seize the time while it is ripe.

In this period, this class has no interest in politics. It has for the time being reconciled itself to the existence of Soviet power; it has ceased its underground and malicious agitation against us. It has no time for such activities now. Feverishly, it carries out the formula *M-C-M*, which in a period of the ruble's falling exchange rate leaves no time for extraneous activities.[3] This stratum willingly pays all its taxes, which for the time being are modest, and immediately passes them on to the consumer. It is even happy that, by the very fact of taxation, Soviet power is in practice legalizing its business activity. As regards the lessees of medium-size enterprises, they have just begun to regard themselves as bosses, and, of course, in this period they do not represent a particularly sizable force in the country's economy. But, on the other hand, there are not at the moment any points of collision either. The prospects unfolding before the resurrected Kolupaevs and Razuvaevs are so unexpectedly pleasant that they too have no time for conflicts at this point.

The same thing must be said of the grouping of petit bourgeois forces that is taking shape within and around the cooperatives, particularly the producers' cooperatives. The cooperatives cannot move an inch without state support. In a period when severing one's ties to the state and assuming a hostile attitude to it means severing the ties between one's own meager purse and the state till, it is, of course, highly unlikely that the cooperatives will make a sharp break with the proletarian state. This is all the more true since before the petit bourgeois forces in the cooperatives decided to move into sharp opposition to Soviet power, they would have to organize themselves and do battle with and defeat the Soviet forces within the cooperatives themselves. This class alignment of the cooperatives—that is, the necessity of allying with the proletarian state on an important issue (the struggle with private trade) and the advantage of union rather than a break with the state for many other reasons—hinders antiproletarian forces from abruptly turning the cooperative apparatus against the state in defense of the interests of the well-to-do peasantry. But nevertheless, since during the revolution the cooperatives were rallying points for anti-Soviet forces from the ranks of the so-called specialists, this leading stratum of the cooperatives has already begun to draw the line for a split with the state; that is, they have jumped ahead and are already trying to enter the second period, the period of conflict between the two processes we are examining.

The consolidation of the positions that the socialist state has reserved for itself and the development of socialist production will encounter a number of obstacles, which can be foreseen even now. A factor that will come to play an extremely important role here is Mr. Harvest. A good harvest can give a powerful impulse to the development of the productive forces in large-scale industry, just as a series of poor harvests can severely retard their advance. A good harvest means half a billion extra poods of grain. It will ensure full payment of the tax in kind even in instances when the peasants have begun to forget about the requisition and have started to trade with the state even on the basis of the tax in kind.

Furthermore, a good harvest means that grain will become cheaper in relation to industrial products—and, hence, that the proletariat can obtain more agricultural products for its commodity-exchange fund. A good harvest means that the state can receive more income from currency issues at the same time that the issue of paper money will have less harmful effects on the ruble's exchange rate. Finally, a good harvest will enable us to begin, albeit only modestly at first, to export grain and increase our imports of machinery for the peasant economy. The influence of good harvests on the expansion of our prewar industry was established long ago by economic research. That influence ought to be even greater now.

We cannot yet foresee how things will develop with the use of capital from foreign concessions. It may be that things will proceed as we described them above in the ideal development of socialist industry. But it is also a possibility that our first attempts at concessions will prove unsuccessful and that the socialist organism will not digest them but spit them out, even vomit them up. In the same way, the commodity loan projects may be held back. Finally, it is impossible to predict all kinds of external complications that might not only sever our economic ties with the capitalist countries but will also most effectively retard even that part of socialist construction that is based on the domestic resources of the Republic.

But no matter how great the deviations from the ideal pace of socialist progress that may result from these causes, this first period of existence of the two different and inherently hostile developmental processes will be marked by one dominant feature throughout—the peaceful evolution of both processes. Regardless of whether the process of development and restoration of capitalist relations in the next few years outstrips the process of socialization and the initiative of attack comes from the side of the petit bourgeois and bourgeois forces or whether the development of socialist industry outstrips the first process and the initiative comes from the proletarian state—in either case the conflict will require some time to grow and mature. But how long?

For a Marxist, it is always more advantageous to refrain from answering this insidious question and to limit oneself to an analysis of the economic tendencies and their political consequences. But the realities of life and struggle demand an answer, even if only an approximate one. It seems to me that two or three years in which capitalist and socialist relations develop peacefully side by side are probable, if not assured, and that it would be more correct to lengthen than to shorten that period. All this is providing that the conflict is not speeded up from outside, that is, by a proletarian revolution in the West to the advantage of the socialist offensive or by intervention of the foreign bourgeoisie to the advantage of the capitalist reaction.

The Republic is currently engaged in developing its productive forces in all branches of its national economy under the slogan of maximum increase in the number of products, by whatever means and methods available. This increased output, which at the same time means increased income and consumption by groups not directly engaged in production and trade, not only does not serve psychologically to stir up conflicts but, on the contrary, helps dampen those that may already exist. For a better picture of how capitalist and socialist relations will develop side by side, and to determine the moment when they begin to conflict with one another, we might look at the whole process like this: picture two truncated pyramids placed alongside one another with their bases pointing up, and imagine that these figures are growing upward. Up to a certain point, both pyramids can grow without colliding. But sooner or later a collision is inevitable, and one of the two will have to yield.

We can draw another important conclusion from this analogy. The more rapidly both processes unfold, the sooner the conflict will occur; but it will happen later if there is stagnation or progress is slow.

At what point can we expect the peaceful coexistence of the two laws of development to break down?

It seems unlikely that the conflict will break out in the towns. Neither petty urban production nor urban trade, and especially not the medium-size capitalist industry based on factory-leasing, could provide the ground soil for the decisive conflict. These branches of industry do not account for a large enough share of the entire economy, and the social weight of the classes associated with this economic milieu is not significant enough, for a decisive conflict to begin here. Although under the New Economic Policy we can no longer say that only two classes—the workers and the peasants—have survived in the Republic, these two classes are still now, as before, the ones that will decide the outcome of any future struggle. It is precisely from the countryside that we have to expect the outbreak of the conflict that will be brought to a head by the New Economic Policy. Specifically, this conflict can develop as follows.

Under the new conditions, the process of stratification in the countryside, a process interrupted by the revolution, is beginning again. Since the kulak benefits both from good harvests and from famines—in the good harvest because he has more grain left over to exchange and in famine because he can buy up more of the poor peasants' livestock and implements for next to nothing—he will retake, one after another, all the positions he had lost earlier. No matter what the price level on agricultural products, the kulak will be the first to make use of all the advantages offered by those market conditions, for it is the kulak, above all, who will begin and has already begun improving land cultivation and soil yields. On the other hand, the strata of rural poor, who have been hard hit by the poor harvests, will to a large extent find themselves back where they were before the Committees of Poor Peasants came into being. The greater the growth of kulak wealth, the greater will be the irritation of the rural poor. A struggle will develop in the countryside on the land question (because the kulak will rent out land allotments to those who have no farms), on the question of wages for hired agricultural workers, and on questions of the use of kulak livestock and implements for working the land of poor peasants, the families of Red Army soldiers, and so on. The poor peasants will demand a reduction of their share of the tax in kind and higher rates for the kulaks. Beginning on a local or *volost* scale, this struggle will then spread over all Russia. It will then move to the cooperatives, and cause a split within them, which, depending on local conditions, will either be converted into a weapon in the hands of the poor against the well-to-do strata of the countryside or vice versa. The Soviet state will have to intervene in the struggle, and its main task will not be to clip the kulaks as happened in 1918 but, on the contrary, to create an economic basis for the poor peasants by intensifying the formation of collective economic units among them. This inevitable intervention of proletarian power into the struggle will in turn force the kulaks to seek their own allies in the cities. They will find some of these allies in the cooperatives, where there are enough SR–Menshevik elements, but they will also find them in the newly emerging merchant-industrial class and the bourgeois intelligentsia. It is not inconceivable that the kulaks themselves might take the offensive, beginning a struggle to rescind the tax in kind, and trying on that basis to enlist the support of the majority of the peasantry.

The grouping of forces then might take place roughly as follows. On the side of Soviet power will be the working class of the socialized enterprises, the rural poor, and the state apparatus. On the kulaks' side will be all the new capitalist groupings and the part of the middle peasantry that is gravitating toward the upper strata of the countryside, plus those groups of the urban population whose existence is bound up with the free market and developing capitalist relations. The majority of the middle peasantry will most likely remain neutral, because the New Economic Policy has enabled them to improve their holdings and raise their income, whereas a kulak victory would not lead to any significant improvements in their situation. Therefore, the outcome of the struggle will depend largely on the degree of organization of the two extreme poles, but especially on the strength of the state apparatus of the proletarian dictatorship. It is possible, of course, that the capitalist forces of the town and countryside will display great willingness to adapt to proletarian power and that during the conflict they will follow the line of least resistance, limiting themselves to passive means of struggle on a purely economic basis. The likelihood of such a development will increase depending on how rapidly the entire socialist system is consolidated in the period before the conflict and on how well socialist production manages economically to subordinate to itself the commodity economy (transportation, the state bank, state orders, foreign trade, etc.).

After all that we have said, it is not difficult to understand the essence of the struggle being waged abroad between the two factions of the Constitutional Democrats: the *Poslednie Izvestiia* group headed by Miliukov and the orthodox Cadets from Rul'. After the Cadet party had lost its class base in the person of the capitalist bourgeoisie and part of capitalist agriculture, the *Rul'* group was condemned to play the role of coffee-house ideologists, cut off from their social roots in Russian life, since those roots had been wrenched up by the October Revolution. Neither urban trade nor medium-size capitalist industry, which is beginning its gradual revival, can form a stable base for the old Cadet party, and the *Rul'* group is doomed to become a political nonentity. Miliukov, on the other hand, is seeking a base in the countryside. He wants to revive the Cadet party on a kulak base, that is, on the base of the one social group that has a serious role to play in the country's economy and could represent a powerful force in the political struggle. And since in order to succeed in the struggle the kulaks have to enlist the support of the middle peasantry, their new ideologists have to do everything possible to dainty up their capitalist-landowner faces, sprinkle themselves with SR *eau de cologne* in order to cover the Kolchak–Denikin odor that envelops them, and then, after all these preliminaries, step into the role of leaders of the rural bourgeoisie. It is quite obvious that in this debate it is Miliukov, and not Gessen and Nabokov, who is right, because if bourgeois power is to triumph in Russia, it can do so only if the rural bourgeoisie enters the battle. And Gessen and Nabokov will never be able to enlist that group with their historical memoirs. We do not know if Miliukov can enlist them either; for the moment it looks like they have enthralled him with the bracing smell of kulak black earth. But that Miliukov is searching in the place where every serious counterrevolutionary and serious political opponent of proletarian power has to search—that fact cannot be contested.

Let us end our discussion by drawing a few conclusions from all that we have said so far. The first conclusion is that the next few years will not offer favorable soil for a mass counterrevolutionary movement in the Republic, with the possible exception of sporadic and uncoordinated actions in outlying regions. Insurrection attempts and conspiracies on the part of SR–White Guard elements will not only be purposeless but will also be proof of these groups' bankruptcy and total inability to understand the political and economic situation in the country. The concentration of counterrevolutionary forces is currently taking place through peaceful expansion of the underpinnings of neocapitalist relations. The task of Soviet power consists in using this expansion to develop the productive forces of the country without letting our political opponents use it to overthrow Soviet power. And this in turn means that in this peaceful period proletarian power must not only not relinquish a single political position—that fact is self-evident—but it must also not give up a single decisive economic position, especially not key positions such as large-scale industry, banking, foreign trade, and wholesale trade in monopoly and foreign commodities, and must reject all proposals for widening the zone of retreat. Such positions must be regarded as objectively counterrevolutionary. In view of the fact that in this period the main forces of the counterrevolution are taking shape in the countryside, it is essential that we begin organizing the rural poor as a counterweight to the kulaks. In large-scale industry, we must begin to restore the most important branches with utmost haste, outstripping the construction of the nonsocialist part of industry. Finally, we must consolidate the state apparatus and make maximum use of it in all areas—such as education—to prepare for everything that will ensure victory in the inevitable class battles that are to come.

EDITOR'S NOTES

[1] That is, so long as agriculture is expanding the incidence of the tax in kind can fall and total government collections will still increase.

[2] The state is able to increase its purchase of peasant commodities simply by printing more money. So long as the volume of new currency emissions remains equal to the volume of private peasant savings (which are thus drawn out of circulation), the total volume of money in circulation will stay the same and the currency will not depreciate. As Preobrazhensky noted in other writings, the state could achieve the same objective by using peasant savings held in the State Bank to purchase the peasants' own commodities.

[3] This is Marx's formula for the simple circulation of money capital: Money (*M*) is exchanged for Commodities (*C*), which are then sold and transformed back into Money (*M*).

The Economic Policy of the Proletariat in a Peasant Country
1922

The vast majority of comrades who belong to the Comintern see Soviet Russia's New Economic Policy as merely a tactical maneuver on the economic front, a maneuver to which Soviet power has had to resort under pressure from the peasantry and in order to retain power in the hands of the proletariat.

This point of view is wrong, although it must be confessed that Russian Communists have done very little to provide a more correct interpretation of NEP.

NEP is, assuredly, a slow outflanking tactic on the part of the proletarian government of a country that has not been supported by proletarian revolution in other countries and that has been obliged to build socialism in isolation within a hostile capitalist encirclement.

But it is at the same time the economic policy of the proletariat of a *peasant* country that finds itself in this situation. In analyzing what NEP is today and what it promises for tomorrow, we must therefore take both of these aspects into account.

Had it been an industrial country rather than a petit bourgeois agrarian country that found itself in a position of socialist isolation, then the economic policy of that country, which also would have been obliged to dodge and maneuver, would have of course been different—if indeed such a country could have held out for long in a situation of capitalist encirclement without an adequate internal agricultural base. We can arrive at the same conclusion from the other direction. Suppose that a proletarian revolution were to occur right now in Germany and in the smaller countries of Central Europe (Czechoslovakia, Austria, Hungary). Could we then completely do away with our New Economic Policy and replace the present economic system as a whole with "true" socialist organization of labor in state industry and with socialist distribution of the production of town and countryside? It is enough to pose the question in that way to answer it in the negative. A revolution in Germany would radically alter the international political and economic situation for Soviet Russia and open up enormous possibilities for much more rapid socialization of the whole economy. It would eliminate all the tactical and maneuvering elements in NEP, but it would not do away with NEP altogether.

What would be left of NEP would be its *organic part*, that is, the economic policy of the proletariat in a peasant country.

It is precisely these elements of NEP that must be revealed in all clarity, for in them Soviet power is moving along the path that lies ahead of every economically backward country where the proletariat will find itself in power.

Let us see what the interrelations are between large-scale state industry and the nonsocialized sector of the economy—above all, the peasant economy—and the direction in which economic relations here will inevitably have to develop.

Under "War Communism," Soviet power made a mighty attempt to impose upon its petit bourgeois encirclement a compulsory system of planned *distribution*, at a time when that encirclement still used a petty individual mode of *production*. The name for the system of distribution that existed in our country under War Communism can be debated: semisocialist, precapitalist, planned–*in natura*, and so on. The name is not important. In essence, our requisition was a system of compulsory loans in kind shouldered by the peasantry, because the state could not fulfill its promise to pay for agricultural products with industrial products. The peasantry repudiated that system not only because *as a class* it did not receive from the town the equivalent of the products it had delivered in the requisition but also because a system of appropriation along the lines of a requisition and equalized distribution of the products of urban industry killed every incentive to expanded production in independent petty holdings. The period of War Communism convinced us that such a system of equalizing distribution does not even benefit the workers, that is, the class that would have to carry out socialization (*see below*). What then could one ask of the mass of independent petty producers? This whole system of compulsory distribution was abolished at the end of the Civil War, which, owing to the depreciation of the currency and the shortage of grain in the country, had made this necessary—if not in its entirety, then at least in its principal features. The peasantry forced the state to return to the old system of market distribution.

In this situation the tasks of the Soviet state were altered as well. These tasks can be stated as follows: (1) How to increase the output of large-scale industry on the basis of a system of distribution that, *given the present level of culture and socialist consciousness of the working class*, will ensure maximum productivity of labor; (2) how to increase the country's agricultural output, using the motive forces of petty production itself, and at the same time gain control over petty production in the way that capital has always done so, namely through trade and credit; and (3) how to move on to the next stage, when the technological base of petty peasant production must be transformed.

The plan for carrying out the first of these tasks has already been outlined in full. The level of culture and socialist consciousness of the working class today is such that there can be no talk of equalizing distribution within the state sector. Under War Communism we experimented with the principle of equalization of distribution through rationing. The results were deplorable. In that period the working class as a whole demonstrated a magnificent heroism and self-sacrifice that history will not forget. Hungry, with his hungry children behind him, the worker stood at his machine; often, he would faint from exhaustion, but he did not stop working. Some detachments, some plants and factories, performed miracles on the economic front. But all that was done in the upsurge of general revolutionary enthusiasm, not because of the principle of equalization of distribution—and possibly in spite of that principle. In that period it was a heroic feat to work at all, and we were not able to demand of the worker even half of his prewar productivity. When the need arose to raise the productivity of labor at all costs, especially in certain highly important branches, we had to bid farewell first to the principle of equalization and then to monthly wages: piece rates were used more and more extensively. It was in keeping with their character that Soviet power and the trade unions had partially rejected the idea of equalization essentially even before the transition to the New Economic Policy. NEP hastened the transition to a new wage system, and at present that system is for the most part based on the same principle as wages under capitalism: the more an individual turns out, the more he gets paid. The principle of equalization through rationing that operated under War Communism may have been a "step forward" as compared to the wage system under capitalism, but the form wages take under NEP is a step backward as compared to the years of War Communism. It has been said that equalization of distribution through rationing, though imperfect, was nevertheless "a bit of socialism," but it is doubtful whether it was even that. The new form of wages has yielded positive results. It has served everywhere as the strongest incentive to raising the productivity of labor, which in many plants has reached the prewar level. And if we keep in mind that it has reached this level at a time when wages are extremely low (one-half to one-third, on the average, of what wages were before the war), then this success speaks for itself. Socialism in the area of distribution means greater equality on the basis of greater productivity. When productivity is falling or standing still, the equalization principle is poor consolation. In the present case the rise in the productivity of labor has to a considerable degree (though not entirely) been due to an abrogation of the principle of equalization in distribution. This fact in itself answers the question of whether Soviet Russia has gone very far toward socialist distribution within the state sector. It has not gone very far from capitalism. But it would be wrong to deny that there has been some progress. On the one hand, this progress consists in a more or less planned distribution of the wages fund of state workers and employees[1] (for which there is a special central agency that sets wage rates); the system already contains the seed of more complete planned distribution in the future. On the other hand, the elements of collectivism that have already taken root also constitute a definite step forward. In a number of enterprises a worker is paid not only according to his individual output but also according to the output of the entire enterprise. How will things develop from here?

Nowhere in socialist literature has it been precisely established what form of distribution within a socialized economy is characteristic of *socialism as such*, and whether there is any difference between capitalism and socialism in this respect. To take a specific example, Karl Kautsky, in his brochure *On the Day After the Social Revolution*, allows room not only for the existence of wages of the capitalist type but also for the variation of wages between different branches depending on the supply of and demand for labor power of various levels of skill. However, a historically transitional stage of distribution is bound to lie between the system of wages under capitalism, with which we all are acquainted, and the system of purely communist distribution based on the principle of "from each according to his abilities, to each according to his needs," since socialism itself is a transitional stage from capitalism to communism. It is wrong to think that socialist distribution must differ from capitalist distribution only in that under socialism the entire product of the socialized sector of the economy is distributed in planned fashion, whereas the wage fund (whose volume is determined under capitalism by the correlation of forces between workers and capitalists and under socialism by calculating all the resources of the economy) will be distributed in about the same way as under capitalism. This means that even under socialism the worker will be rewarded according not only to his skills but also to the amount of his individual output (in cases where it can be calculated). If matters stood thus, it would mean that the incentives for production remain the same under socialism as under capitalism, and it would be impossible to see how mankind can ever make the leap from individual work incentives to a communist system of organization of labor. In reality there must be here a whole series of gradual transitions offering forms of reward and incentive that are just as imperfect, undeveloped, and logically incomplete as socialism itself—that unfinished communism—is incomplete and illogical. Socialism must begin where capitalism has ended: with individual payment of a worker's labor plus an occasional share of the profits of the enterprise (that is, in the present case, bonuses for extra output). But it creates the conditions for the gradual replacement of individual payment of labor with collective payment: "The more I turn out, the more I earn," says the worker under a piece-rate system. "The more my factory or trust turns out, the more I earn," says the worker under a system of collective pay. And from here the next step is the slogan "The more society as a whole turns out, the more *everyone* receives." At first, collective pay will exist side by side with individual pay: a worker's earnings will depend on both his individual output and the collective output of the whole enterprise. Gradually, the part of each worker's wages that he receives from the collective bonus fund will grow, and at the same time the percentage of the general wages fund to be set aside for collective bonuses will also grow. The moment when the majority of workers under a socialist regime have made the step forward from individual to collective incentives for work will be no less important to the struggle for communism than, perhaps, socialization of the instruments of production. This transition will occur mainly because individual incentives prove *inadequate* for socialist production; they are backward and obsolete, especially since technological development (electrification, transport, etc.) *decreases*, rather than increases the possibility and the expediency of individually calculating the labor performed by each worker. On this basis young people will be more rapidly reeducated in the spirit of the demands that the new method will place on the workers' mass psychology, their collective instincts, and their socialist consciousness and habits. Soviet power has already advanced slightly in this direction under NEP. This was the experiment of "collective supply," which was used in a number of our largest enterprises and gave satisfactory results from the standpoint of production. This form is admittedly no longer obligatory, but it can be used with the voluntary agreement of the trade unions and the economic organs. In one or another form, collective wages will (after a spell of capitalist reaction under NEP) develop and become the dominant form of wages under the dictatorship of the proletariat. Of course, in a peasant country, where a petit bourgeois psychology is strong even among the proletariat, we could not advance significantly beyond the methods of the capitalist wage system. But from the very outset industrially advanced countries under the dictatorship of the proletariat will be able to advance further along the path toward socialist distribution.

One of the most important tasks for the proletariat after taking power is swiftly to send out its vanguard to seize control over science and the command posts in industry and in the entire state apparatus and if not to outstrip, then at least in the first decade to compare favorably in the field of culture with the vanquished foe. In this respect there is a fundamental difference between a bourgeois and a proletarian revolution. During its struggle for power the bourgeoisie was not an oppressed class but rather a class that competed with the nobility from a position of power. As an exploiting class, as a minority possessing all the good things in life, wealth and leisure, the bourgeoisie could and did attain a higher cultural level than its opponents, the landed aristocracy and the clergy. Not so with the proletariat. The proletariat is able to seize state power before it has assimilated the culture of the age and begun to create a culture of its own. In this respect it does not overtake the vanquished bourgeoisie *until after the conquest of power*. And in a country like Russia, where the proletariat in general is on a lower level even than the proletariat of other countries, this problem is even more important, if not portentous, for the very existence of workers' power.

This problem confronts Soviet power under NEP just as it did during the period of War Communism. Moreover, under NEP the threat to the proletariat posed by the cultural superiority of the vanquished bourgeoisie and bourgeois intelligentsia is even more serious. For this reason, Soviet power is currently making even greater efforts than before to proletarianize higher education and to aid the proletariat in its striving to appropriate science for its own use. As yet our accomplishments in this respect are still modest, but they surpass anything that the proletariat was able to attain in a whole century of bourgeois rule. We have a network of workers' colleges with 50,000 proletarian students. In the last two years the introductory levels in higher education have been considerably proletarianized. Within three or four years a majority of students in all the institutions of higher education (with the possible exception of the arts academies) will be from the proletariat or socialist-minded peasant youth. This is not to mention the Communist schools, our party schools, from the local district level to the highest institutes (for example, Sverdlov University) as well as the military schools, which have long had students drawn exclusively from the working class and peasantry.

As regards a rise in the productivity of labor, an increase in the number of commodities, and a corresponding increase in wages, things are considerably worse at the moment than under capitalism. Industrial production stands at no more than about one-fifth of the prewar level. The productivity of the individual worker is on the whole lower than before the war: the prewar level is still an ideal we have yet to reach. But at the same time we can state that both the absolute volume of output and output per worker have risen in the last year and a half. But the devastation of industry caused by the war and the revolution is so great that, in the opinion of most economists, Soviet industry will not reach prewar levels for four to five more years, and only after that will it be possible to move beyond the levels reached by capitalism. The only major branch of industry where we have gone further than capitalism is electrification. The question of wages is intimately bound up with this point. During the Civil War, wages fell so low that normal production was altogether impossible. But now wages are rising steadily, albeit slowly. This rise does not promise to be particularly rapid in the next few years either, because industry, after accumulating circulating capital (which is still in extremely short supply), will begin restoring fixed capital and resume urban construction, tasks that will require "primitive socialist accumulation," not only at the expense of the petit bourgeois classes through taxation but also at the expense of wages.

The task of restoring industry and wages to the prewar levels and then advancing further is a task common to every proletarian state. Nor can it even be said now whether a victorious European proletariat will restore industry starting from a relatively higher level with respect to the prewar level than we are having to do, because no one can predict the extent of devastation that the inevitable civil war will inflict on the European economy.

But on the other hand the task of economic subordination of the peasant economy to large-scale state industry is posed in unique fashion in Russia, as an agrarian country; it is posed in a way in which it will not be posed for Germany, Austria, or Czechoslovakia.

It is only the Balkan countries and Poland that will find themselves in a position somewhat similar to Russia's under a proletarian regime. To understand NEP—not its tactical aspect but its organic aspect, its genuinely lasting elements—we have to understand the economic relations between state industry and the peasant economy as they exist now and as they will take shape in the immediate future.

The essential prerequisite for subordinating the peasant economy to large-scale state industry and state banking centers by capitalist methods is, above all, sufficient economic power on the part of large-scale industry itself.

How do matters now stand in this respect?

According to S. N. Prokopovich's calculations,* the entire national income of European Russia for 1913 was 11,805 million gold rubles (rounded off to the nearest million) and came from the following sources (in millions):

Agriculture	5,630
Forestry and fishing	729
Industry	2,566
Transportation	1,055
Construction	842
Trade	980

*S. N. Prokopovich, *Opyt ischisleniya narodnogo dokhoda 50 gubernii Evropeiskoi Rossii* [*A Rough Calculation of the National Income of the 50 Guberniias of European Russia*, 1918].

If we add to the income from industry, transportation, and construction the income from trade in industrial products, which from a methodological standpoint is more correctly regarded as a certain part of the income of industry allotted to trade, and add to the income from agriculture the income from trade in agricultural products, we would have to concede that the Russia that entered the war was not the totally agrarian country that we imagined her to be.

If we then take the ratio of *large-scale* industry to agriculture, we have to exclude from the income of all types of industry the income from craft production (611 million) and cottage industry (289 million) and part of the income of petty producers in the fishing and lumber industries. But even after that deduction, the ratio between large-scale capitalist production and agricultural production would be about 4:7, and with petty production added to agriculture, about 4:8.

In general, industrial, banking, and especially merchant capital played a dominant role in the prewar economy; they occupied the main command posts within the economy as a whole and subjugated agriculture to themselves. And if the proletariat were to take possession of *all the positions of capital* in the Russian economy in *its prewar proportions*, it would exercise complete sway economically over the whole territory of petty, nonsocialized production. But, unfortunately, during the years of war and revolution the relationship of forces between the large-scale and petty economies, in particular between large-scale industry and the peasant economy, shifted sharply in favor of the latter. Large-scale and petty production suffered to quite different degrees during the war and revolution. In 1921 the net national income of the whole country was very roughly estimated at 5 billion gold rubles in *prewar prices*. Our economists calculate that the net income of industry was 500 million (about 1 billion in gross income) and that of transportation about one-fourth the prewar figure, that is, about 350 million. And these figures are probably somewhat exaggerated. Peasant income is currently more than 3.5 billion, whereas the income of craft and artisan workers has fallen to half its prewar level. In any case, the ratio of net output of large-scale industry and transportation to peasant income is approximately 1:5, which is a dreadful step back from the prewar proportions. True, industrial production has risen this year (and production costs have dropped), but thanks to the good harvest the peasant economy's output has risen *even more*, and the ratio between industrial income and agricultural income has become even more unfavorable for the former.

These, then, are the conditions under which the Russian proletariat must undertake the task of economically subordinating the peasant economy to state industry. This task is extremely difficult given present proportions in the economy, but it can unquestionably be managed once industry is restored. There are two ways to subordinate the peasantry to large-scale production: first, through trade and credit, that is, through exchange; and second, by transforming the basis of the peasant economy through electrification of agriculture and mechanized farming, that is, through production. For us the second alternative still lies in the future; the first already has been started, although our success in this direction has been extremely modest.

Our task as far as trade with the countryside is concerned consists in the gradual elimination of private middlemen; in the elimination of private merchant capital from the relations between large-scale industry and the peasantry; in reliance on the cooperatives; and in the creation of a state monopoly not only over trade in products of large-scale industry with the countryside but also in the sense of controlling the bulk of agricultural products that are poured onto the big market. Here and there we are already enjoying success. For example, in the *guberniia* of Orel 60 percent of all trade is now carried on through organs of state trade, whereas workers' cooperatives dominate the market in certain factory centers. Thanks to the foreign trade monopoly, the state will be able to maintain control over the country's entire trade with foreign capital in grain and agricultural raw materials.

As regards credit, its main form must be long-term ameliorative credit; credit-sales of agricultural machinery, improved seed grains, and artificial fertilizers; and cash loans from the State Bank (Gosbank) for the purchase of horses and the restoration of agriculture in general. Long-term agricultural credit has an enormous future in Russia. This is the easiest way for the proletariat to subordinate agriculture to the dictatorship of large-scale industry. Here the State Bank has the chance to grant credit to the peasantry not only in the form of money but also—and principally—in kind, in the form of agricultural machinery and other commodities needed in the countryside. By receiving payments and interest on loans *in natura*, that is, in the form of grain and raw materials for export, the State Bank can gradually guarantee the state a considerable share of all surpluses of agricultural production, which together with its resources from the tax in kind will constitute a stable foodstuffs and raw materials fund not only for Soviet industry but also for foreign trade. Later the state will easily be able to switch from its role as chief buyer and sole creditor of the peasantry to the *role of order-placer and inspector of peasant production.* By adopting the appropriate price policy and issuing statements as creditor (that it will accept certain products, and not others, as payment for loans), the State Bank can influence the extension of one type of crop, encourage the development of another, and eliminate a third, thereby subordinating in a capitalist manner the individual peasant economy to the requirements of its general economic plan. This method can also provide a rather precise accounting of all rural production, since the creditor has to know all the economic resources of the debtor. And socialism is above all, accounting.

If we keep in mind that the state also possesses another powerful means for redistributing the national income, namely, by levying taxes that should fall in increasing measure on the more well-to-do strata of the countryside and on private merchant and industrial capital, then the combination of all these methods provides Soviet power with the means to divert the flow from the channels of primitive (or, more accurately, secondary) NEP accumulation to the mill of primitive socialist accumulation, thus transforming the victories of revived capitalist economic relations into a form that is lower than and subordinate to the forms of large-scale socialist economy.

EDITOR'S NOTE

[1] The Russian phrase *rabochie i sluzhashchie* is used to differentiate manual, usually waged workers (*rabochie*) from salaried employees (*sluzhashchie*), such as office and other so-called "white collar" workers.

PART TWO

Strains in NEP: The Problem of Capital Accumulation

Economic Notes I. On the Goods Famine
1925

Everyone recognizes that the goods famine is the result of an excess of effective demand over supply. Likewise, everyone realizes that this excess is an indication that production is not keeping pace with demand, at least not *for the moment*—that is, that the goods famine is a function of insufficient accumulation in industry. But apparently not everyone understands that the goods famine is not a seasonal phenomenon. Yet it has in fact lasted a year and a half in all: its most recent exacerbation set in before the harvest and is stubbornly holding on four months after the harvest, despite the limited deliveries of peasant grain to the market—deliveries that are incommensurate with the volume of the harvest. In essence, this view of the seasonal nature of the goods famine has but a short time left to live, because the crucial test is approaching inexorably: if the present episode of the goods famine lasts a year, the explanation will be worthless. However, practical refutation of the "seasonal theory" will certainly not wrap up the season for all the theories that are, in the final analysis, inclined to regard present levels of industrial production and the current rate of industrial expansion as normal. Therefore, we feel that even now it would not be unwarranted for us to share with the reader some figures from an investigation dealing with this whole problem.

According to the Gosplan control figures, gross agricultural production in 1924–25 was 9.15 billion rubles, or 71 percent of the prewar figure. Total industrial production was 5 billion rubles, or 71.4 percent of the prewar level. Apparently, there is a superficial arithmetical proportionality.

Let us look at the relative proportion of agricultural and industrial output that was sold on the market, that is, the relative percentages of marketability of agriculture and industry. Gosplan's control figures provide us with the following information on this point. In 1924–25, agriculture marketed products worth 2.857 billion prewar rubles, as opposed to 4.498 billion in 1913—in other words, 63.7 percent of the prewar figure. Goods marketed by industry amounted to 7.011 billion rubles in 1913 and 4.450 billion in 1924–25, that is, 63.5 percent of the 1913 sum. Here too, we see the full arithmetical proportionality of the two sectors' marketability, so to speak.

The question now arises, why, *in even one of the prewar years that corresponded to 1925 in level of production and marketability* (that is, in one of the years in the decade 1900 to 1910), *did we not see a goods famine in Tsarist Russia*?

Merely posing the question in this way is enough to lead us to seek an explanation above all (although not exclusively) in the different structure of the expense budget of the countryside and the workers, as well as, perhaps, in the different distribution between producer and consumer demand in the country. In the present report I will take up only the first basic, decisive problem.

From the standpoint of the conditions of realization and the condition of distribution, the portion of prewar rural output that was sold on the market was divided into two main parts: (1) goods subject to *compulsory sale*, for which the peasantry did not receive an equivalent return; and (2) goods on which the peasantry earned money, which (not counting the part that went into money accumulation) it then used for acquiring industrial goods or goods within peasant exchange.

Let us take a closer look at the first part of marketed peasant output—that is, the share that the peasant was forced to sell. It had to cover three main items of expenditure:

(1) central and local taxes

(2) rent that the peasant paid on land hired in addition to his allotted lands

(3) usurious interests to kulaks, buyers-up, and landowners, as well as maintenance of the clergy and other lesser payments. This latter class of expenditures exists even today in some measure, although presumably less than before the war. We shall not examine this item here, but will rather go back to the first two. If we divide the total income in the 1913 Tsarist budget obtained from direct

taxes, indirect taxes, customs duties, and royal monopolies by a population of 175 million, we get a state per capita income of 12 rubles 78 kopecks, or 11.2 percent of the gross national income. The 1924–25 budget from the same sources as the prewar budget (hence, omitting income from transport and from the People's Commissariat of Postal and Telegraphic Services, in particular), divided by the total population, yields 7 rubles 66 kopecks per capita, or 7.7 percent of the gross national income. In particular, the peasantry in the fifty *guberniias* of European Russia paid 10 rubles 54 kopecks in direct and indirect taxes in 1912–13, whereas in 1924–25 they paid 3 rubles 56 kopecks (in prewar rubles).* Thus, in 1924–25 the peasantry paid, in absolute figures, 815 million prewar rubles, or 1.4 billion chervonets rubles,[1] less than they did before the war (assuming a rural population of 116.8 million in 1924–25). Despite the overall reduction of agricultural income, the peasantry now pays proportionally much less in state taxes than it did before the war. Hence, on this point a considerable portion of rural commodity output has been released from forced sales.

As regards rental payments, according to Karyshev's well-known study,** about 49.8 million *desiatinas* of all types of lands were being rented out to peasants in addition to their allotted lands in the late 1880s (these included lands belonging to the rural gentry, imperial estates, state lands, church and monasterial holdings, and urban land—cultivated as well as uncultivated pastureland and hayfields).[2] The average rent in the 1880s was 6.3 rubles per *desiatina*. Later on, the number of titles to peasant lands grew considerably, but this tendency was countered by higher rents for smaller plots, especially in the Central Black Earth Zone and in the Ukraine. If we take into consideration first that the peasant did not pay for the land lying fallow under the three-field system of cultivation and second that he had to pay rent on pastureland and hayfields, then the total rent paid annually by the

*According to preliminary calculations by the TsSU (Central Statistical Administration) for 1925–26, the peasantry will pay per capita 4 rubles 64 kopecks in prewar rubles, or about 44 percent of the 1912–13 level of tax.

**Karyshev, *Krest'ianskie vnenadel'nye arendy* [Peasant nonallotment leases] (Dorpat, 1893). A. I. Chuprov places the area of nonallotment leases at 40 million *desiatinas*. See *Melkoe zemledelie v Rossii i ego osnovnye nuzhdy* [Small-scale agriculture in Russia and its basic needs] (Moscow, 1906), p. 17.

peasantry before the war was *at an absolute minimum* 200 million prewar rubles per year, or about 360 million of our chervonets rubles. If we recall that according to the 1925–26 budget estimate the entire single agricultural tax will bring in only 235 million rubles, it should be clear how important it was for the peasant budget that rental payments on landowners' lands be eliminated. But right now we are interested in another aspect of this question—the aspect of exchange of goods, the aspect of exchange of commodity output between town and country. Eliminating land rental payments of 200 million prewar rubles, or 360 million chervonets rubles, means eliminating a second major component of forced sales of the marketed portion of peasant output—with all the ensuing consequences of that fact.

Just what are the consequences of the data we have presented on tax cuts and elimination of land-leasing for the exchange of goods between town and country in 1924–25 (and hence in 1925–26 as well)?

The first conclusion is that, in view of the reduction in forced sales, the peasantry has considerably more freedom now than before the war in choosing the dates and the terms under which it disposes of its surpluses—indeed, greater economic freedom in general. This applies not only to the well-to-do sector of the peasantry, which has always enjoyed a certain degree of economic freedom, but in even greater measure to the broad rural masses. This fact is of enormous significance in explaining why the peasantry is in no hurry to sell grain.

The second conclusion is that, given the same agricultural income as before the war, the reduced number of forced sales must lead to increased rural consumption of foodstuffs.

Finally, the third and most important conclusion is that out of the total commodity output cited above—that is, out of 2.857 billion for the last economic year and 3.639 billion for 1925–26 (or out of other figures, if Gosplan's statistics on marketability are incorrect)—a much smaller sum than before the war went to forced sales without equivalent return. And this in turn means that, given the same conditions of realization, there must be a corresponding increase in the peasantry's effective demand for industrial commodities and products within peasant exchange.

The enormous importance of this last conclusion for our topic is quite obvious. *Maintaining the equilibrium between the marketed share of industrial and agricultural output at prewar proportions last year and this year means sharply upsetting the equilibrium between the effective demand of the countryside and the commodity output of the town.* And herein lies the key to understanding why we now have such a persistent goods famine. Our current goods famine is the result of the positive changes in the structure of the peasant budget that have been effected by our October Revolution. As long as the Civil War continued and requisitioning was in effect—and later on, as long as the general level of peasant output was much lower than before the war—these consequences of October did not make themselves felt, and it is quite obvious why not. But the more closely we approach the prewar proportions of production in industry and agriculture (90 percent this year), the more *Soviet conditions of agriculture* are making themselves felt and the more forcefully, as compared to the prewar situation, the formal arithmetical proportionality has to be, and is being, transformed before our eyes into an unhealthy, protracted, and by no means seasonal disproportionality in the distribution of productive forces between industry and agriculture.

But that is still not all. Disproportionality is lying in wait for us from the other end as well, although here it has not yet been able to manifest itself in due measure. I am referring to the progressive change in the very nature of wages under the Soviet system on the one hand and the change in the nature of expenditures of the former surplus value on the other. Since wages are less subject now than before the war to the law of value of labor power and will be even less so in the future, to the advantage of the working class (this applies especially to wages for unskilled workers), then this circumstance plus a reduction of tax deductions from wages is bound to mean a relatively greater consumer demand from the working class from year to year and, consequently, the necessity of a more rapid pace of expanded reproduction to that end. As regards the different nature of the expenditure of surplus value, one must remember both *the nonproductive consumption of the prewar bourgeoisie in the form of foreign imports of means of consumption* and the fact that a considerable portion, probably the major portion, of dividends obtained by foreign capital from foreign industrial enterprises in Russia ended up abroad. (According to the calculations of P. V. Ol', a total of 2.243 billion rubles was invested in Russia. If we assume an 8 percent dividend, then the profits on imported capital would have been about 180 million rubles annually.)

All this must lead to an expansion of our domestic market for industrial products. The significance of this rise in worker–peasant demand as a stimulus to the pace of expanded reproduction in industry quite different from the prewar rate is not, from the standpoint of our national economy, *currently* the result of a different degree of development of the entire economy; rather, it is the result of a different system of distribution of the national income and of the change in the balance of payments with foreign countries. The state takes less for nonproductive purposes; less goes to nonproductive classes, especially those who squander funds abroad or on imports of consumer goods; *nothing* goes to pay foreign debts and nothing as profit to foreign capital invested in our industry. If we add up all the sums we have listed, minus the growing consumption in natural form, then we get the total amount of extra effective domestic demand that has resulted from October.

The reader has probably already noticed that I do not say that effective demand within the country has increased by anywhere near the entire amount of the reduction of parasitic consumption for the state income budget. The point is that the national consumer budget, the budget of the exchange of commodities of the country, and the expenditure budget of individual classes from the standpoint of distribution of the national income, are two different things. If, let us say, the peasants do not pay rent to the landowners, if the whole country pays much less into the budget of the parasitic classes or for maintaining the state, then that does not mean that with the elimination of these nonproductive expenditures the domestic effective demand of the country is increased by the full amount of those expenditures. True, the nobility, the bourgeoisie, and the state bureaucracy also consumed, but only at the expense of the workers and peasants. When the same amount of domestic effective demand, satisfied by domestic production, is today divided among five classes, and tomorrow among only three, then the demand of those three is increased, but the demand of the country as a whole can remain the same. From the standpoint of exchange between town and countryside, from the standpoint of proportionality between the masses of commodities of industry and agriculture and the proportions of distribution of productive forces, the important thing is not simply the elimination of parasitic income, but the elimination of the part of that income that was spent outside the country, *or within the country but for the import of consumer goods.*

To make all the special features of precisely the present moment in the development of our economy especially clear in the area we are examining, I shall recapitulate the discussion thus far and illustrate it with a numerical example using figures that are arbitrary but are, in general, close to the actual situation.

Let us take a prewar year with a gross output close to what we have today—a year, let us say, with an output of 18 billion prewar rubles. Let us assume that of this 18 billion, 6 billion goes to restore constant capital, 1 billion goes to accumulation (and of this accumulated sum, that 250 million leaves the country), 1.5 billion goes to the state apparatus (in addition to the personal consumption of state employees) and to payments abroad, 7 billion to peasant consumption, 1.5 billion to the consumption of workers and craftsmen, and 1.5 billion to the consumption of nonproductive classes. Let us now take the same volume of production under Soviet conditions. How will the exchange of this mass of commodities differ? (1) Of the 2 billion consumed by parasitic classes, the part spent to purchase imported articles of consumption, plus the part spent by the bourgeoisie and the nobility abroad, will be released; (2) the amount previously used to pay foreign state debts and a number of other expenses of the old state apparatus that we do not have in the new system of the Soviet state will be released; (3) there will be a release of the surplus value of foreign capitals.[3] If we assume that the total amount thus released is 1.5 billion rubles, then this sum will go, first of all, to increase the peasantry's consumption in natural form—which will result in a corresponding drop in our exports of agricultural products. The workers, who will have more to spend, will increase their demand for products of the countryside and commodities from the city. Provided that conditions for the realization of their output are normal, the peasants will increase their demand for industrial commodities, provided that the same proportions prevail between industrial and agricultural production as before the war. And here precisely is the source of the chronic goods famine that has developed, even with a substantial drop in agricultural exports as compared to the prewar figure.

Consequently, even if all other economic conditions in the Soviet Union were the same as before the war, that is, if we had, above all, the prewar *import of capital* invested annually in industry and transportation, then even in that case, given a change in the nature of the distribution of the national income and a curtailment of the flow of values out of the country, we would have a goods famine caused by the inadequate development of industry. And just look at our present situation, when there is almost no import of foreign capital into the country, if we disregard the negligible influx of concessionary capital. Thus, if we add to the abovementioned reason for the goods famine this second reason—the elimination of the import of capital—then the disproportionality between industry and agriculture is thrown into even sharper relief.

True, the reduction in parasitic demand has been partly offset during these years by the accumulation of circulating capital by the trading apparatus, which relatively reduces the intensity of the extra worker and peasant demand. But this intensified accumulation of circulating capital in trade is bound to return to normal proportions in the future.

Very briefly, then, these are the considerations on which we base our assertion that the present rate of accumulation in industry—that is, the rate of expanded reproduction—is quite insufficient in relation to the additional domestic market that the October Revolution has created for us in a situation where capital imports have ceased. The closer the entire economy comes to the prewar level of production at the prewar proportions between industry and agriculture, the more noticeable will be the realization of that domestic market. *This additional demand now has, and will continue to have, the same effect as if, let us say, prewar Tsarist Russia had annexed a vast new agrarian territory that manifested an additional demand for the products of the industry of that time.*

The conclusions to be drawn here are obvious. If we pursue the line of least resistance, that is, a sharp increase in imports of articles of mass consumption (which admittedly can be done without upsetting the trade balance, but only to the detriment of imports of means of production), if we do not turn the line of greatest NEP support into the line of least socialist resistance, then we have to recognize three things: (1) the projected expansion of industry is insufficient; (2) the budget allocations for industry are insufficient—and, I would venture to say, downright disgracefully small for a socialist state; and (3) the financial plan for renewing fixed capital, and especially the financial plan for new plant construction, is insufficient and is retarding the development of the entire national economy.

On the basis of everything I have said, I can make the firm prediction that the insufficiency of the development of our industry, the insufficiency of accumulation of new capital in it, the lack of correspondence between its expansion and the development of agriculture will be universally recognized as an obvious fact. And I strongly fear that, when that fact is universally recognized, there will be those among us who will propose that we extricate ourselves from this situation by the *path of least resistance*: they will not propose that we intensify accumulation in our industry at the expense of the entire national economy; they will not suggest that we satisfy our domestic demand with the products of our own industry; rather, they will propose that we sharply increase our imports of consumer goods as a perpetual system of relations between our economy and world capitalism. Every worker understands that this will be a system destined to undermine socialist industry.

EDITOR'S NOTES

[1] Over the period of the Civil War and its immediate aftermath the ruble experienced a near-disastrous depreciation which threatened the reestablishment of commodity exchange premised by the New Economic Policy. In October 1922 the ruble was replaced by a new currency, the chervonets ruble, equal to the prewar 10-ruble gold coin. The chervonets and the ruble continued to exist side by side until well into 1923, the former being a stable currency, the ruble continuing to depreciate. The fact that Narkomfin tied the chervonets to gold (even though it was not convertible for foreign exchange) was a major bone of contention between Preobrazhensky and the finance commissariat for the better part of the 1920s, mainly because Preobrazhensky saw it as a reinforcement for Narkomfin's financial conservatism with regard to industrial credits. For a detailed empirical study of the financial history of the Russian ruble from the period of World War I through to the currency reform of 1922/23, see Preobrazhensky's *Theory of Depreciating Currency* [*Teoriia padaiushchei valiuty*].

[2] One *desiatina* equals 1.09 hectares (2.7 acres). Nonallotment leases refer to rented holdings outside the land allotted to the peasants, and held in common with periodic redistributions, after the 1861 reform. N. A. Karyshev was a Narodnik statistician who published a number of works on the Russian economy during the last part of the nineteenth century. He is frequently cited—and attacked—in Lenin's *The Development of Capitalism in Russia*, English edition (Moscow: Progress Publishers, 1967).

[3] That is, the surplus value on foreign capital, which in tsarist times would have been repatriated to its country of origin, now remains within the domestic Soviet economy.

Economic Notes II.

1926

In an earlier article* we discussed the long-term causes of the goods famine. We now want to inquire into the consequences of the goods famine, the problem of equilibrium in our economy, and the question of the economic course dictated by the current economic situation.[1]

An imbalance in the distribution of productive forces in an economy with commodity–money exchange will be reflected first and foremost in prices. Likewise, in the goods famine that we have been experiencing for the past two years, this disproportion in the economy also shows up in prices, although under our economic system price movements display characteristic features of their own. Before going into the specific price movements determined by the structural features peculiar to this economy, let us pose the following question. Suppose that socialized industry and transportation did not exist in Russia. How could we attain equilibrium in the economic system if there were a shortage of industrial commodities, that is, if the country were underindustrialized? Through the operation of the law of value, equilibrium would be attained as follows. A long-term rise in the prices of industrial commodities would have to lead, on the one hand, to increased imports of the commodities in short supply and, on the other hand, to a redistribu-

---

**Pravda*, December 15, 1925. Incidentally, in a feuilleton published in *Pravda*, Comrade Guloian has taken, without citing his source, all the main conclusions of my first article and presented them to his readers as his own views. But, most importantly, he has presented them as a polemic against the main theses of my feuilleton. I would ask Comrade Guloian to have someone with a literary background tell him what the usual name is for that sort of thing.

tion of productive forces between town and countryside through the influx of fresh capital into branches with underproduction of commodities. Thus, production would adjust to the country's expanding effective demand through the spontaneous operation of the law of value. But under our conditions, where industry has been nationalized, equilibrium cannot be attained in the manner outlined above. We ourselves run our industry, and if in our planning we do not ensure the necessary level of accumulation in it, we ourselves lend force to the goods famine. By nationalizing industry we have restricted the operation of the law of value in the state economy, yet we are not replacing the operation of that law by a requisite rate of planned socialist accumulation. That is, we are not following a conscious planning policy of distributing labor power and material resources in the country in such a way as to ensure economic equilibrium. In this case, rather than annulling the law of value, we are creating conditions for its operation in its most distorted and, for us, most unprofitable form. In the sector of private trade—that is, above all in retail and wholesale-retail trade—prices of commodities in short supply are rising sharply. Yet instead of leading to a spontaneous redistribution of the country's productive forces in the interest of industrialization, that rise is leading only to the rapid accumulation of private capital. Private capital is raising prices to the limits of effective demand and is diligently profiting from the economic disproportion.

Underaccumulation and too slow a rate of expanded reproduction in industry are thus inevitably leading to a drop in the purchasing power of our money in a particular sphere of commodity circulation. But in addition to this cause, the depreciation of the currency has two other causes, whose analysis will make it much easier to understand the economic difficulties we are presently experiencing. These causes are the following.

By lowering the single agricultural tax, we tipped the balance of payments between town and countryside in favor of the latter. That tax cut alone would have had appreciable consequences in terms of the relative increase it caused in the monetary resources within the peasant economy. Added to this is the circumstance that 1925 was, first of all, a year of good harvest; second, there was a general increase in sown acreage that year; third, the peasantry continued to expand its production of industrial crops and industrial raw materials in general; and fourth, prices in the private economy began to rise. The combined result of these factors, compounded by an undersupply of industrial commodities on the market, was that the peasants received more money than they could spend. The balance of payments between the town and the countryside showed a deficit. Had the currency exchange rates been normal, that would have had to lead to an increase in the amount of paper money accumulated in the countryside. The peasants would have accumulated money for future purchases, deposited their excess money in state savings banks, and so on. But with a depreciating or simply fluctuating currency, the peasants abstained from money accumulation for reasons that are fully understandable. Selling 100 poods of grain for 100 rubles, depositing those 100 rubles in a savings bank, and after one year withdrawing 104 rubles plus interest—all this while the price of grain was on the rise—means perhaps being able after one year to buy no more than 80 or 90 poods of grain for those 104 rubles. With the market moving in that direction, it is more profitable for the peasants to sacrifice a few percent of their grain to the mice and rats than to be seduced by the 4 percent interest on the money they deposit in a savings bank.

Moreover, grain prices were much higher last spring than they had been in the autumn of 1924. The peasant who sold his grain at the fixed prices in the autumn was clearly a loser compared to his neighbor who held on to his grain and sold it for twice the price the next spring. All year long the unfortunate fellow's wife nagged at him for "being a poor businessman," for "not knowing how to make a deal," and she would point to the example of their neighbor who held back his grain and got twice as much for it. The memory of all that is undoubtedly etched very deep in the peasant's mind, and this year he will be very cautious in selling his grain, waiting for prices to rise in the spring. All this has reduced the peasantry's paper-money accumulation to a minimum. The peasant knows quite well that when prices are rising, it is more profitable to keep your surpluses in commodities rather than in money. He knows that the only time it is more profitable to keep your surpluses in money is when prices are falling and when 100 rubles deposited in the bank in January 1925 will buy more commodities when it is withdrawn in January 1926. It is quite obvious that the conditions that have now developed—that is, a halt in paper-money accumulation in the countryside—are also going to upset, at least for the coming year, all plans based on using that accumulation in the interests of industry.

The second cause of the instability of our currency is the mistake made by Narkomfin in the issue of paper money. If we take the volume of money in circulation at the end of 1924 and compare it with that at the end of 1925, we see that the total amount of money in circulation has increased by 70 percent at the same time that the output of our state industry has increased barely 40 percent, and total commodity circulation by even less. Obviously, this too has contributed to inflation. And although the exchange rate of the chervonets ruble (taking the average of the wholesale and retail indexes) fell by only 8 percent during the same period, that merely proves how stable our currency is in general and how slowly it still reacts to the experimenting being done with it.

It is evident from the previous remarks that there have been more than enough causes for the depreciation of our currency. Now we have to ask what is so unique about the price movement of which we spoke earlier. Let us assume that as a result of all the causes listed above we have a total of 15 percent more money in circulation than the minimum. How is currency equilibrium attained in such a case if no artificial measures are taken to reduce the volume of money circulating in the country? A balance is normally reached spontaneously, by price rises on *all* commodities, at *all* levels of commodity circulation. If commodity circulation in the country remains constant, a 15 percent price rise (and, consequently, a 15 percent drop in the purchasing power of all money in circulation) would lead precisely to currency equilibrium. The entire volume of money would be devalued by the percentage by which that volume of money exceeded the necessary minimum of circulation. But for us this entire process assumes unique forms, which are highly unprofitable for the state economy. Our trusts have fixed and stable disposal prices; consequently, currency equilibrium cannot be attained spontaneously in the territory covered by our state economy. *But this entire process is thereby artificially transferred to the private economy*, whose price movements are outside our control or are subject to our control to only a negligible degree. Thus, the private economy is obliged to achieve currency equilibrium by raising prices. Or, in other words, *we are granting the private economy a monopoly on price rises*. The result is quite obvious. Grain prices are rising in the private economy; prices are increasing for industrial raw materials over which we have little control; and the private economy is getting more in paper money for its entire output. The state economy, on the other hand, is selling its entire output at fixed prices, that is, at a fixed total amount. And that means that the balance of payments between the state and private economies is being tipped sharply in favor of the private economy and against that of the state.

It is also quite obvious that under existing market conditions not only the state economy as such loses, but state workers and employees lose too, to the extent that they buy their food on the free market. Hence, real wages are falling, and in the cases where we carry out planned wage increases, they are only capable of maintaining the old real minimum wage.

* * *

What, then, are the conclusions to be drawn from this situation for our economic policy?

Here we have to distinguish between measures *of a purely conjunctural character*, which we have to adopt for the immediate future, and the long-term measures that are associated with the general line of our economic policy.

As regards immediate measures, we must first of all see to it that the state economy recovers all the losses it has incurred because of the depreciation of the currency. We have to adjust the balance of payments in the interests of the state economy, recover its losses, and ensure it against losses in the future. In practical terms, we can imagine two main ways to attain that goal: first, by increasing taxes on private economy (which is, of course, the most difficult method to apply), and second, by raising the disposal prices of the trusts on those consumer items that are in shortest supply and that yield the greatest profit for private capital. As undesirable as this second operation is, it remains the only way out of the situation if we want to limit accumulation by private capital and stop the flow of values from the state economy into the private economy. Of course, we are talking about a price rise that cannot be reflected in higher retail prices. On the other hand, this is the only way we can obtain the necessary resources to reimburse the working class for what it lost because of price rises in private trade, and it is the only way we can guarantee the working class a particular level of real wages for the future.

As regards long-term measures, we must pose for ourselves clearly and firmly the task of attaining a level of accumulation in state industry that will ensure equilibrium within the entire economic system. We must draw up our state budget for the coming economic year in such a way that industry *first and foremost* will be ensured that portion of the funds necessary for new construction that it itself is unable to raise. Our budget must be the budget of a *socialist* state; that is, the interests of socialist accumulation must stand in the forefront. Second, our policy on the disposal prices of the trusts must be such as to ensure socialist accumulation from that quarter. If the currency is stable, this will mean at first a stabilization of wholesale prices and then a careful lowering of those prices so as not to threaten in any way either the necessary proportion of accumulation or the growth of wages.

Third, we must reexamine the question of tax increases, above all, tax increases for the well-to-do elements of the countryside. From this standpoint, Narkomfin's planned rates for direct taxes are patently insufficient.

Fourth, we must begin immediately to work out an import plan that will completely guarantee industry all the necessary equipment and raw materials in the year in question. *Not until all of industry's needs have been met in full* can we begin discussing how to meet other claims upon the import plan.

If we do not take all these vital measures, of whose urgency the goods famine is the most telling witness, we will not only fail to eliminate that famine for next year, but we will in 1926 already be preparing the ground for a goods famine in 1930. It must be pointed out that we have already fallen far behind in our new construction. Within a year we will no longer be able to increase the output of our metal industry on the basis of the equipment of old factories. And yet, new factories cannot begin to turn out goods for another three years, even if we begin their construction immediately. The socialization of industry and transport is not to be taken lightly. If we limit or eliminate the operation of the law of value—that spontaneous regulator of capitalist production relations—then we have to replace it with planned socialist accumulation *in the proportions dictated to us by the entire national economy*.

The idea that we can limit our capital expenditures and concentrate on developing light industry is a reactionary utopia. That idea lives on mainly through analogy with 1921, that is, with the period when our industry had just barely begun to get on its feet again after its unprecedented collapse. When a man is lying on the ground and has to get up, it makes sense to ask whether he should get up on one arm or one leg at a time. But when a man has gotten up and is walking along at full stride, you do not recommend to him that he put his left foot down faster than his right unless he is lame or paralytic. And yet, people are recommending that our industry today, which is moving along at full stride, put down one foot, light industry, faster than the other, heavy industry. Such advice is either economic illiteracy, which is more easily laughed at than refuted, or a cover for a repressed thought of something else. That repressed thought can only be the following. If our agriculture displays an effective demand in excess of the productive capacity of our industry, then, given the current level of accumulation, equilibrium can only be attained by increasing the import of ready-made consumer goods, that is, by following the line of least resistance. This path is not the path of industrialization of the country, but *the way to bind our effective demand for consumer goods to foreign industry*. If we continue for long to postpone rapid industrialization, if we content ourselves for long with the systematic underdevelopment of our heavy industry and with a deficit in the area of socialist accumulation, if we stubbornly close our eyes to the economic and political dangers of such a situation, then the argument about more rapid development of light industry and about a moderate pace of capital construction makes sense. But in that case we should also be forthright enough to foresee all the consequences that such a path of development will have for our economy. As our harvests grow in size and quality, and as our possibilities for export grow, we will inevitably have such pressure from private economy on our tariff system and on our foreign trade monopoly (that is, on the barriers with which we paralyze the operation of the law of value of the world economy), that our artificial barriers will be shattered to their very foundations and our import plan will not be drawn up in accordance with a plan for industrializing the country, but will be rather like Trishka's caftan, in which patches in the form of exports[2] of consumer goods will play an ever-growing role from year to year. We agree that such an economic policy makes sense in its own way, but it has no relationship whatsoever to the decisions of the Fourteenth Party Congress regarding the industrialization program, and it is dictated by petit bourgeois pressure on the economic policy of the proletarian state. This line is leading us right where the capitalist countries want us, namely, to abolition of the foreign trade monopoly, abolition of socialist protectionism, integration of the USSR into the world system of division of labor based on the workings of the law of value, and *maintenance of the present level of industrialization of Europe by making our country relatively more agrarian*. The party must decisively and categorically repudiate not only such an economic policy, if someone presents it quite consciously, but also any policy of vacillation and opportunism in the area of industrialization that would *unconsciously* lead to the same, objectively inevitable result.

* * *

I would now like to present my objections to Comrade Stetskii's feuilleton "Economic Difficulties," in *Pravda* of February 6 this year [1926]. It contains many true statements, but it makes no clear distinction between the immediate conjunctural tasks and the central problem of our economic policy over the long term. Similarly, in explaining the causes of our present economic difficulties, Comrade Stetskii does not draw a precise distinction between the consequences of economic disproportion and the consequences of currency fluctuations. Comrade Stetskii's article is a rather typical example of the policy of balancing between two stools.

Comrade Stetskii holds that the main cause of our present economic difficulties is "the complexity of the task of establishing and discovering the proper relations between the socialist nucleus of our economy and the petit bourgeois encirclement, between large-scale state industry and the peasant economy."

What, then, was the specific mistake we made in "discovering the proper relations between large-scale state industry and the peasant economy?" Comrade Stetskii answers this question as follows: "In analyzing the present situation we cannot in any way disregard our 'miscalculation' of last autumn, or rather last summer, for it played a major role in the development of the difficulties now facing us. . . . We cannot deny that underlying our present difficulties is a disproportion between industry and agriculture. But neither can we forget how our grain procurement policy has aggravated that disproportion. . . . *The attempt to disregard this circumstance is an attempt to avoid recognizing and analyzing our errors by recourse to general, empty discussions about the disproportion between industry and agriculture.*"

There can be no question but that last autumn's miscalculation had a very harmful effect on our economic construction; in particular, it contributed to the depreciation of the currency, since the volume of the currency issue was calculated on an assumed commodity circulation that turned out to be unjustified. One of the conclusions to be drawn from this experience is that Narkomfin's policy on currency issue has to be discussed by all planning organs, and discussed five times more carefully than has heretofore been the case. But all this is just one side of the matter, and not its main side at that. We had a goods famine *even before last autumn's miscalculation*; therefore, to shift the center of attention to that last concrete miscalculation means "to avoid recognizing" some other miscalculation that *preceded* that of last autumn. And that leads us to the general necessity of maintaining a rigorous distinction between conjunctural miscalculations and a more fundamental one with more far-reaching and more profound consequences.

The underestimation of the growth of the effective demand of the peasantry and the city is just such a fundamental miscalculation. This underestimation was made as early as 1923–24; in economic policy it led to the slogan "Industry, don't get ahead of yourself!" and in practice it resulted in systematic underaccumulation in industry. Consequently, the fundamental miscalculation that has been the major cause of our economic difficulties was made in 1924, not in the autumn of 1925. In 1925 we simply reaped the fruits of that fundamental error, which is still having effects even now and for which, apparently, no one is willing to bear the responsibility. And this means that in the debates of 1923–24, and in the later debates on the same topics conducted within the planning organs, it was the "industrializers" who were completely correct, and not those who hoped to establish an alliance with the peasantry by means of industrial underproduction.

Comrade Stetskii admittedly does not deny the role of disproportion between industry and agriculture. In the quote above he writes: on the one hand, "we cannot deny," and on the other hand, "we cannot forget." In short, two "cannot's": we cannot but recognize, and we cannot but admit. But then, Comrade Stetskii, can you not admit that you were not right in the main debate with the industrializers in 1923–24? Is it not obvious that if we had in 1924 prepared the elements for expanding the production of commodities designed to meet peasant demand for 1925, if only for 70 or 80 million rubles more than present production, we could have in 1925 bought 70 million more poods of grain from the peasantry and exported 100 million more poods of that grain abroad? Is it not obvious that we might not have been obliged to cut back our import of industrial equipment and to cut back production and lay off workers in branches that depend on the purchase of foreign raw materials?

Comrade Stetskii formulates one of our next tasks in the area of economic policy as follows: *"The only proper and admissible course for us is to implement a general reduction of prices within the country and to strengthen the chervonets."* I agree entirely with that line of economic policy, insofar as we are concerned with formulating our programmatic tasks with regard to the economy. But Comrade Stetskii's formulation, though correct in general, by no means answers the concrete question facing us right now: if the state economy has already lost, I would think, no less than 100 million rubles from the depreciation of the currency, if the level of real wages has been reduced by the rise in prices in the private economy, then from what sources does Comrade Stetskii propose to cover the deficit in the balance of payments between the state and private economies—*a deficit that is already a fact*? We do not find an answer to that question in Comrade Stetskii's article. It is not a matter of declaring for a stable currency and reduced prices, but one of *showing in practice how, with insufficient socialist accumulation, we can have a stable currency and a normal level of retail markups over the disposal prices of the trusts.*

Somewhat late, Comrade Stetskii is discovering America: he writes that we can use peasant accumulation by developing deposit operations for a part of the peasantry, rather than by means of currency issue, by using peasant savings to help finance industry. The author of these lines discussed that topic back in 1922. The policy of using peasant accumulation is entirely beyond question. But let us hear something more from Comrade Stetskii than pretty possibilities for the future; let him tell us how, with a fluctuating currency and a lack of peasant accumulation in money form, we can ensure the necessary accumulation in industry for expanding production and meeting the necessary capital expenditures. Why, it is clear to everyone that the plan for supplying industry with the necessary resources by using peasant accumulation and new currency issues *has failed—at least for this year*—because it meant resorting to those methods of financing industry at the expense of the budgetary appropriations for, and accumulation within, industry itself. But rotten as it may have been, this abortive plan, which was based on very great optimism with regard to the private economy and great pessimism with regard to the state economy, was nevertheless a *plan*. This plan must be replaced by something; it must be replaced by a proposal of concretely defined measures, and not by dreams of how someday in the future we can make good use of peasant accumulation for financing industry.

I must also comment on the section of Comrade Stetskii's article where he talks about the development of heavy industry. The opinion is rather prevalent among us right now that the large appropriations earmarked to cover capital expenditures in state industry have been an important factor in aggravating the country's goods famine. Rather than rattle off empty arguments on this topic, I have tried to calculate the amount of commodities in constant demand that our industry has removed from the market for its capital expenditures. It turns out that to fulfill a plan for capital expenditures of 800 million rubles, we would have had to withdraw commodities in constant demand worth about 5 percent of the total commodity circulation in 1925–26. That, then, sums up the whole argument about us having overextended ourselves in capital construction. As regards this question Comrade Stetskii writes: "The development of heavy industry is the prerequisite for the development of light industry. However, we cannot squander all our resources on developing heavy industry." No one is proposing anything so economically ignorant as to "squander all our resources on developing heavy industry." *We need a proportional development of both heavy and light industry*. But at the same time we are in dire need of capital construction for combating future goods famines and for lowering prices through technological reequipment of our industry. The thing is to reconcile these two tasks, and not get bogged down in opportunism and make no headway at all toward industrializing the country. Things would have been made much clearer if Comrade Stetskii had answered the question directly: what figure for capital construction does he support? One that will forestall a future goods famine, or one that will perpetuate and aggravate the one we have?

Let us sum up. Comrade Stetskii's article contains many correct ideas, mainly of an academic nature. There is, however, no sign of an understanding—or rather, of acknowledgment—of the fundamental miscalculation in our economic policy that has been responsible for an insufficient volume of socialist accumulation and its inevitable consequence—aggravation of the goods famine. As a result, the economic policy recommended by Comrade Stetskii, though it contains a number of correct proposals on points of detail, means *the continuation of a policy of underaccumulation* (which will become increasingly dangerous for us as time goes on) —that is, *the beginning of a policy of cautious retreat from the decision of the Fourteenth Party Congress on industrialization of the country.*

Without wanting to be a prophet, I am nevertheless tempted to conclude with a few predictions. Judging from past examples, the writer of these lines will probably be accused of overestimating one thing, of underestimating another, and of over-underestimating a third—in short, of a deviation. That is inevitable for the present. However, I have the following comments to make in my own defense. Framers of economic policy like Comrade Stetskii desperately *need* my "deviation." They are looking everywhere for a place to run with their line between the two stools. But to sit between stools one needs a minimum of two, that is, a minimum of two deviations. One deviation, the agrarian deviation, has more or less already been provided for them, both formally and in fact. Now they have to either find the other ready-made or make it up. Then everything will be all right: their work clothes will be ready, sewn together from two deviations, throwing into relief the truth of the golden mean. They can begin formulating and substantiating the arithmetical mean and allocating the proper number of kicks to the right and left.

The only trouble is that in the meantime the country's goods famine will go on. . . .

EDITOR'S NOTES

[1] Unlike the other articles in the "Economic Notes" series, this one bears no subtitle.

[2] The word "exports" here is almost certainly an error. The entire thrust of Preobrazhensky's argument, here and in other writings, is that the private sector's demand for imported consumer goods had to be artificially blunted in favor of using the import fund to purchase foreign-produced means of production.

Economic Notes III. On the Advantage of a Theoretical Study of the Soviet Economy

1926

The published chapters of my work *The New Economics*,* a book devoted to a theoretical analysis of the Soviet economy, have been subjected to bitter critique. Opponents have especially attacked the chapter on the law of socialist accumulation. The chapter "The Law of Value in Soviet Economy" at first met with a much milder reception during the three-day debate in the Communist Academy. A few opponents even paid their compliments to the author. But thereafter it did not take long before the new chapter was attacked just as harshly as the preceding one, in particular in an article by Comrade E. Gol'denberg that appeared in *Bol'shevik* last April 30.** I don't know, it may be that the tone he displayed in that article is a personal trait of Comrade Gol'denberg—former oppositionists often display above-average zeal; in any case, if all our other opponents will just be more objective, the matter cannot but profit. For my own part, I would like to maintain my composure and objectivity. Disagreements exist. What is the use of blowing them up, or of inventing new points of divergence that do not exist? Anyone who engages in this, whether in theory or in politics, permits himself this luxury only because he has not given enough thought to our future.

The value—or, on the other hand—the uselessness of a theoretical construction that we as Marxists and Leninists devise in the

---

*"The Fundamental Law of Socialist Accumulation," chap. 2, and "The Law of Value in the Soviet Economy," chap. 3. The entire book has recently been published by the Communist Academy.

**E. Gol'denberg, "Zapozdalyi refleks" ["Delayed Reflex"], *Bol'shevik* 7–8 [1926].

area of social science is determined, first of all, by the extent to which it is logically consistent with the methodological bases and fundamental propositions of Marxism and Leninism, and second, by the degree to which it helps us correctly to foresee socioeconomic developments and thereby serves the immediate practical goals of our class. This verification is crucial and decisive because both Marxism and Leninism are able to serve as a preliminary logical check of any new construction only because they themselves have *already been verified* by the experience of the practical struggle of the working class. When a dispute arises over whether a given construction is logically consistent with Marxism or Leninism, the debate can continue for as long as you please in the sphere of logic, but, once again, only practice settles that debate conclusively and irrevocably.

It is from this standpoint of a logical and, where possible, practical verification of my theory of Soviet economy that I now intend to examine the most important objections raised by Comrade Gol'denberg and several of my other opponents in respect to the most essential theses of my book. I then will attempt to demonstrate that my opponents have so far not only failed to offer but —as long as they maintain their present positions—never will be able to offer anything resembling a Marxist-Leninist theory of our economy, with all the *practical consequences* ensuing from such a theory.

I will begin with the question of method.

Comrade Gol'denberg faults me for taking a "vulgarly mechanistic approach to the question"; I am accused of failing to grasp the "dialectical nexus between contradictory and conflicting principles"; I have supposedly been engaging in a "scholastic, formalistic exercise in logical definitions"; and so on. Now, where is the proof?

First proof: As I begin the analysis of the manifestation of capitalist categories in our economy, I remind the reader of precisely what is counterposed to these categories in a planned socialist economy. Comrade Gol'denberg pretends not to understand the methodological importance of this contrast and its place in my entire exposition. In his opinion, "Comrade Preobrazhensky's total inability to understand the real role of the law of value in our economy is displayed . . . in this barren contrast. . . . In the final analysis, socialism of course leads to the full elimination of the market and market relations. But there can be no more grievous and harmful error than to mistake the results of a process for the process itself."

Not for Comrade Gol'denberg, who of course knows what I am talking about and who is busy putting together his refutation, but for the benefit of readers who may take these "arguments" of his seriously, let me make the following comments:

(1) No genuinely scientific analysis of a transitional commodity-socialist system of economy is conceivable without understanding what that economic formation is a transition *to*.

(2) It is only by being continuously aware of the two poles of the process—the beginning and the end—that we will be able to understand the historical status of each transitional form, without losing ourselves in details and without sliding back into vulgar economics, which tries to pass off a superficial description of today's situation as a scientific analysis of the present economic system.

(3) The contrast we are talking about here can be found in the works of Marx, Engels, and Lenin. Without counterposing, in principle, capitalism to socialism, even a complete analysis of capitalism itself is inconceivable. The reader will find proof of this assertion in *Capital*, *Anti-Dühring*, Marx and Engels' correspondence, and so on. It was only by counterposing socialism to capitalism that Lenin could offer a theory of monopoly capitalism.

(4) Marx based his study of capitalism on an analysis of abstract capitalism; that is, according to Gol'denberg, he mistook the result of the process for the process itself. And, as we know, in doing so he incurred the bitter attacks of the entire international of vulgar economists and philistines.

(5) Counterposing socialism to capitalism in principle is also a methodological prerequisite for an analysis of each period in the development of the commodity-socialist form of economy. Since the whole process of movement toward socialism is a process of struggle between one economic formation and another, neither the relative importance of the conflicting sides, nor the unique features or recurrent patterns of each period, nor even a whimsical muddling of the process of struggle with its immediate results can be understood if we do not always have before us a notion of what is being transformed and of where this transitional economy is heading. To forget this is, in the area of theory, to slide back to Bernstein, with his famous dictum: the movement is everything; the goal is nothing.

The absurdity of Comrade Gol'denberg's captious objections is too obvious to merit long discussion. However, it is certainly no accident that Comrade Gol'denberg and certain other opponents are irritated by the counterposing of socialism to capitalism in a study of a particular stage of the transitional economy. After all, being able to unite this counterposition with a concrete analysis of a particular period in the development of a commodity-socialist system of economy means beginning an analysis of the struggle between two principles in our economy; it means seeking the general features of that struggle; like it or not, it means, in analyzing the main lines of development of state economy, taking up the question of the law of primitive socialist accumulation. But my opponents do not relish the prospect of doing that. And for that reason they are condemned, on the one hand, to repeat the same old phrase—changing only the words and the expressions—about the struggle between the planning principle and the market, and on the other hand, to put together a blend of a few Marxist terms with a description of the state's actual economic policy, which they then try to pass off as an analysis of our economy. And that happens to be the theoretical tailism that is merely the ideological expression and the justification of tailism in practice.

One only has to read through Comrade Gol'denberg's article to see that it goes nowhere at all, that he only throws out polemical sideswipes at me, often with my own ideas, and then serves this up to the reader as an "analysis" of Soviet economy. Just think of all the riches the reading of that article has bestowed on us! Why, before Comrade Gol'denberg came along we never suspected that "it is necessary that the peasant economy produce more for the market before it can be coordinated with socialist industry," that "the extension of the planning principle presupposes gaining control over market relations," that "this path toward socialism has its dangers and its difficulties," and that we accumulate not only from the surplus product of the countryside but also from industry itself. There you have the kind of profound new thoughts with which Comrade Gol'denberg inundates me in his polemical article.

Imagine, dear reader, that you and I are going from Moscow to Leningrad and we have already passed through Tver'. Up comes Comrade Gol'denberg and starts to prove that it is impossible to travel the road from Moscow to Leningrad without going through Klin.

You're quite right, Comrade Gol'denberg, you have to pass

through Klin, and we've done that. And what next? How do you intend to enrich our knowledge next? But just let me ask of you one thing: when we get to Leningrad, don't break the crushing news to us that you have to pass through Tver' to get to Leningrad, and that you have to pass by the Volga, which empties into the Caspian Sea.

Comrade Gol'denberg reproaches me for not saying anything about "how the relations of the commodity economy grow over into socialist relations, but only about how one formation is ousted by the other." This reproof is clearly designed to take advantage of the fact that not all the readers of *Bol'shevik* are familiar with my works, which Comrade Gol'denberg has undertaken to "crush." In the brochure *From NEP to Socialism*, in two chapters of my book on the theory of the Soviet economy, and throughout *The New Economics*, I repeatedly speak not only of the ousting of some forms by others but also of how historically backward forms are subordinated to and transformed by the working of the dominant mechanism of the socialist sector of the economy. Comrade Gol'denberg's objection is therefore formally incorrect. But, like others of his objections, it does have its logical and social sense. Comrade Gol'denberg is dissatisfied with my analysis because I "split our country's whole economy into two halves—one ruled by planning, and one in which spontaneity prevails. . . ." Nowhere do I state that planning *already* fully governs the state economy: there is more than enough spontaneity here. But I do assert that the initial economic basis for planning, for the socialist principle, and for the development of expanded socialist reproduction—that is, the basis on which the law of primitive socialist accumulation can begin to operate—is our state economy, which is engaged in a struggle with the private economy, completely irrespective of the forms that struggle may take. Coexistence with the private economy by no means excludes struggle, just as the coexistence of the Soviet state with capitalist countries is merely another expression of the proletariat's class struggle with bourgeois society. Is it really not obvious that the transformation of lower economic forms into higher forms—for example, the establishment of producers' cooperatives among the peasantry with the support of state industry—is the product of the struggle between the socialist city and the medieval economy of the countryside? The unity of the whole system in a certain sense rests on the coexistence of these two economic formations in our economy, but the equilibrium of that system is achieved on the basis of a struggle along the entire front. This struggle between the socialist principle and the private economy is being waged abroad, since our links with the world economy have not been weakened but are growing and will continue to grow. This struggle goes on at home, since the state economy's link with the private economy through the market has not been weakened but is growing. The struggle encompasses the entire range of relations: the ousting of some forms by others, the subordination of some forms to others, and the transformation of lower forms into higher ones are the products of struggle and not of "peaceful renewal." For this reason it is impossible to conduct a scientific analysis of our system without making that "split" that Comrade Gol'denberg dislikes. And vice versa. Concealing all the elements of struggle between the two formations (as long as it is not due to simple misunderstanding) is at best a product of a casual stroll along the surface of the socioeconomic phenomena occurring in the Soviet system, and from the standpoint of predicting what will happen tomorrow it promises us some very cruel disappointments; at worst all this can lead to the reproduction, in a new set of circumstances, of the Bernsteinian theory of the blunting of socioeconomic and class contradictions. But this conception alone takes the edge off none of the historical contradictions within our system in the interests of the dictatorship of the proletariat; rather, it simply disorients the ruling working class and its party and prevents it from developing the correct view of the society within which it has to fulfill its historical mission.

It should be pointed out generally that there is a regular muddle of opinions regarding the question under discussion, and this is not the fault of Comrade Gol'denberg. The analysis of our system as the social formation where progress takes place in the form of the antagonistic development of contradictions and the struggle between the law of primitive socialist accumulation and the law of value has been scandalously lumped together with the question of whether or not a blunting of class contradictions is advantageous for us. As regards the first contradiction, a scientific Marxist analysis here reveals only that which is actually the case. To criticize my conception with the reproof that it irritates the country's petite bourgeoisie means to capitulate theoretically before that stratum; it means forsaking the entire intellectual life of our party, as well as the preparation of new cadre, under the prior moral censorship of the countryside.

The only methodologically correct way to pose the question of the blunting of class contradictions within our country is as follows. We, the ruling working class, benefit from the blunting of all those contradictions that might develop against us, and we benefit from the exacerbation of contradictions wherever that process turns against capitalism. The formula of the "worker–peasant bloc" is, first of all, a formula that underscores the union of interests of the worker and the peasant against the bourgeoisie, and second, a formula meant to indicate the blunting of contradictory interests between these two classes, also in the interests of the struggle against the bourgeoisie.

A blunting of contradictions on that *basis* in the present period is attained first, best, and most genuinely by the industrialization of the country, that is, by cheapening the products of urban industry, by intensifying agriculture and reabsorbing the excess labor power in the countryside, by issuing long-term credit to the countryside (which a weak industry cannot do), and by establishing producers' cooperatives among the poor peasantry. This process means at the same time the creation of the conditions for greater coordination and organization of the country's whole economy around the state sector, for tighter links between the petit bourgeois encirclement and the controlling centers of our economy, and for drawing the village closer to the town. From the sociological standpoint, this process means an overall consolidation of Soviet society, its greater internal coherence and ability to resist outside pressure, and, finally, the replacement of loose petit bourgeois peasant patriotism, totally unreliable in the event of a foreign war, by the socialist patriotism of an industrialized country ruled by the dictatorship of the proletariat.

But this process, which will save our class, the Soviet system, socialism, and the socially progressive elements of the countryside, is at the same time a torturous, long, and dangerous one—and the longer it takes, the more dangerous it will be, because our main enemy will inevitably have to try to interrupt it as soon as possible.

On the other hand, the pressure exerted by the law of value of world capitalism on our economy, a pressure that is relatively weak as long as we are linked with the ocean of the world market by the narrow Dardanelles of our present level of imports and exports, will inevitably grow. And the question of the pace of industrialization is thereby transformed into the question not only of internal economic and political equilibrium but also of our existence in the face of our *main* opponent.

But given the negligible influx of foreign capital into the country in the form of long-term credits, the problem of industrialization rests upon the problem of using our domestic resources to ensure at least approximate proportionality in the distribution of productive forces between the town and the countryside. Hence the problem of primitive socialist accumulation, with its equations of proportionality of expanded socialist reproduction, which are dictated to us from without, with seemingly mandatory force. Hence the law of primitive socialist accumulation, which was not invented by Preobrazhensky for polemics with his opponents, but which ensues objectively from the conditions of struggle of our state economy, created by the October Revolution, with the capitalist world. Among other things, this law dictates to us certain proportions of alienation of the surplus product of the countryside for the purposes of expanded socialist reproduction. By objecting to the question being posed in that way, my opponents are not polemicizing here with me personally nor with all of us industrializers; rather, they are essentially grumbling about the objective conditions under which the construction of socialism in one country—one peasant country, at that—is occurring. Their attacks are (and it would not be difficult to demonstrate this point once again) merely the ideological and political reflection of the backward tendencies of our economic development. The notion that my opponents are advocating a cautious policy that is more adequate to our conditions and better able to support the workers' bloc with the majority of the peasantry is fully and totally refuted by the facts.

When there is a goods famine—that is, in our particular situation, when there is insufficient socialist accumulation in industry—and the peasants each year pay out hundreds of millions too much on the difference between wholesale and retail prices to private capital or to the cooperatives, which themselves are often engaged in speculation; when they have unused money surpluses and their unsold grain is being eaten by mice, the appropriation of a couple of hundred million from the reserves of peasant accumulation for the development of industry will of course give rise to certain discontent. But at the same time, such a policy begins to create the preconditions for *allaying that discontent* through the expansion of production, the recruitment of new workers from the countryside, the increase in commodities offered on the market, and the halt in the exploitation of the peasantry by merchant capital. On the other hand, a policy of systematic underaccumulation and goods famine, and the high retail prices that are inevitably associated with those phenomena, gradually builds up peasant discontent, which is then not allayed but continues to grow, so that this pressure from the countryside threatens our system of protectionism and the foreign trade monopoly. All this can have very serious consequences for the whole business of constructing socialism in our country. This policy is one of concession to economic backwardness; it is a policy that is cautious in appearance only: at a certain stage of our economy's development it will be transformed into its opposite.

Comrade Gol'denberg sidesteps the question of nonequivalent exchange between socialist industry and petty production and, in criticizing the way in which I pose the question, he effectively declares for equivalent exchange. We need complete theoretical clarity on this important point, not such attempts to evade a direct and concrete formulation of the whole problem. I suggest that Comrade Gol'denberg and my other critics state precisely what it is they are actually advocating on this point. And if they declare for equivalent exchange—to which they are inclined, to one degree or another—then I shall be obliged to show that they are either demonstrating their economic illiteracy or that, on the point under examination, they have broken with Marxism and have moved over to a position of petit bourgeois populism. I will undertake to prove that, when it comes right down to it, they advocate a tax on socialism for the benefit of petty production.

The extent to which Comrade Gol'denberg does not understand my fundamental point of view in the question of the law of primitive socialist accumulation, although he quite freely expounds and criticizes it, is evident from the following triumphant comment he directs at me. He writes: "According to the prospective five-year plan drawn up by the State Planning Commission (Gosplan), we will, in the next five years, invest 5 billion rubles in our fixed capital, of which 4.4 billion will come from industry itself; that is, the 'transfer' that Comrade Preobrazhensky regards as the main thing, the basic thing, and so on, will account for only slightly more than one-tenth of the total sum of what, according to this plan, will constitute the main type of actual socialist accumulation in the next five-year period."

In formulating what is for him a truly death-dealing objection, Comrade Gol'denberg "forgot" to tell the reader the disposal prices that will be necessary for all this accumulation to take place.

He "forgot" to say that all this will take place at prices very much higher than world market prices, that is, by excepting ourselves from the law of value of world economy—in other words, by means of a much greater nonequivalence of exchange between large-scale and petty production than we see in the world economy,* by retaining the foreign trade monopoly, socialist protectionism, etc., in short, *on the basis of the law of primitive socialist accumulation.* If the worldwide law of value is in operation and our domestic prices take shape accordingly, we not only will not receive this 5 billion but will lose fully half our total fixed capital.

The reader can see from this example what a delightful pursuit it is to engage in polemics with opponents like Comrade Gol'denberg, and how well they understand the things they criticize.

However, Comrade Gol'denberg, who understands everything so well, does admit that there is one point in my exposition he has not quite caught (which does not prevent him from exercising his wit—and not on account of his own lack of understanding). He does not understand "why, actually, Comrade Preobrazhensky says that the law of primitive socialist accumulation is the form in which the elemental regularities of an unorganized economy dialectically grow over into a new form of attaining equilibrium." Why dialectically? What has dialectics to do with all this?

Before I explain to the reader what dialectics has to do with all this, I would like to mention that Comrade Gol'denberg, who reproves me for my "vulgar mechanistic approach to the question," openly awards himself a diploma for skill in dialectically approaching the study of our economy. It is unlikely that the word "dialectics" will ever have any luck with us here. People who have never read Hegel, not to mention those who have read him but not understood him, bend that word in every possible way. With their ceaseless repetition of it they terrorize the reader, who starts to be ashamed of his ignorance and accepts the hawkers of the word "dialectics" as people who have mastered the method of Hegel and Marx to perfection.

Comrade Gol'denberg must have known that by using the polemical methods that he applies against me one can "destroy" the

*There is also no equivalent exchange between these sectors in the world economy, because prices on agricultural products are established on the basis of competition between small-scale peasant production and large-scale and medium-scale capitalist agriculture.

most complete, the most classical study, one that scientifically reproduces the dialectical process of social development, from Marx's *Capital* right on down the line. After all, the dialectical process is first and foremost unity. A description of one or another isolated aspect of that unified process can always be "successfully" counterposed to the whole, if one leaves the ground of dialectical logic and floats about in the sphere of what Hegel calls "simple and particular determinations."

This is all the more easily done since dialectical movement is movement that develops on the basis of an internal contradiction. We have an example of that sort of criticism right before our eyes. Having learned from my exposition that the law of primitive socialist accumulation, as it applies to the distribution of the country's material resources, is the law of transfer of values from precapitalist forms of production to the state economy of the proletariat, my opponent writes: "Such an 'understanding' of the fundamental law of socialist accumulation naturally leads to the assertion that the law of value restricts accumulation." However, my opponent does not feel it advantageous for him to understand that the matter is not limited merely to this aspect of the law. The law of primitive socialist accumulation competes with the law of value not only in the sphere of distribution of the surplus product of the country but also in all aspects of regulation of economic life, above all in the distribution of labor power. I discuss this point throughout *The New Economics*, and also, in particular, in the article "The Law of Value in Soviet Economy," which Comrade Gol'denberg criticizes. The sentence quoted above, which contains the words "dialectical development" that Comrade Gol'denberg apparently has such difficulty in understanding, refers to the struggle of the law of primitive socialist accumulation with the law of value *in the entire sphere of economic relations*, therefore also in the struggle to achieve a unified regulation of the economic system. My critic reveals himself here to be fully one of those hawkers of the *word* "dialectics" of whom I spoke earlier.

Now, for the benefit of Comrade Gol'denberg, if he seriously does not understand my conception—but above all for the reader—I will explain, in a few words and in the most straightforward way I can, what I meant to say in the sentence quoted by Comrade Gol'denberg.

If economic relations in our country were now to develop on the basis of the free operation of the law of value of the world economy, that would lead to a situation where, given present-day prices on the world market and the present overindustrialization of Europe, two-thirds of our large-scale industry would be eliminated because of its unprofitability and uselessness from the capitalist standpoint, *from the standpoint of the world division of labor on a capitalist basis*. Our agriculture, on the other hand, would suffer severely *in the long run* from the transformation of the entire country into an agrarian semicolony of world capital, although it would undoubtedly profit in the first few years because of the much lower prices for industrial articles and because of the much more nearly equivalent exchange on the world market. Since there is no German, American, or Russian law of value, but only a law of value for the world economy as a whole, which is merely manifested with certain variations and aberrations within a particular country or group of countries, then if that law were allowed to extend its workings directly into our territory, under the pressure of the world market from without and as a result of the development of commodity relations within, it could overthrow our whole system. After that the distribution of productive forces would occur here in whatever way would be necessary for the reproduction of capitalist relations *throughout* the world economy (and not in the interests of industrial capitalist development *in our country*, as is the dream of the Mensheviks, who on this point display, in addition to everything else, downright economic illiteracy and a failure to understand the general tendencies of contemporary world economy*). The only regulator in our economy would then be the law of value.

What, then, in our country stands in the way of the law of value, whose intensified operation would mean reinforcing tendencies that would lead toward the overthrow of our whole system?

Every reader can count on his fingers the factors that counteract the law of value in our country: the foreign trade monopoly; socialist protectionism; a harsh import plan drawn up in the interests of industrialization; and nonequivalent exchange with the private economy, which ensures accumulation for the state sector, notwithstanding the highly unfavorable conditions created by its low

*Incidentally, in the struggle with the Mensheviks, we make almost no use of the argument that the elimination of the Soviet power and fulfillment of the Menshevik slogan of "back to capitalism" means in practical terms unemployment for *two-thirds of our working class and, indeed, its most highly skilled segment.*

level of technology. But all of these, given their basis in the unified state economy of the proletariat, are the external means, the outward manifestations of the law of primitive socialist accumulation. In the struggle between this law and the law of value we are able each year (more or less successfully) to distribute the country's surplus product and its productive forces as a whole in a way that on the one hand ensures that social needs are to some extent satisfied and on the other hand creates the preconditions for expanded socialist reproduction for the following year and even for a number of years to come. Equilibrium in the system as a whole is attained on the basis of the antagonistic interplay of the two laws; and in this process the scale on which state industry is developed, and hence the amount of the surplus product of agriculture that is appropriated to further that development (regardless of whether that appropriation takes place through taxes or price policy), is dictated to us with seemingly binding force. The law of value is abolished as regulator of the economy through its replacement by the law of socialist accumulation. Not only does the mode of regulation change here, that is, not only does planning replace spontaneity, but the *material content* of the whole process also changes in the sense that each year a different distribution of the country's productive forces is obtained in comparison with what we would have had if the law of value were to operate freely. The planned distribution of our productive forces is governed by a second objective goal, that of maintaining and developing the socialist sector of the economy, which, on the one hand, must satisfy a certain part of the country's social needs with the output of its own production and, on the other hand, must ensure further growth, that is, ensure a certain level of accumulation. In such a system, of course, the volume of the country's social consumption will also come increasingly under the influence of that law as time goes on. It is quite obvious here that the gradual subordination of the country's system of exchange to regulation by planning within the state economy means that the law of value is gradually transformed through struggle into a historically higher type of regulation: that law is not only abolished, it is transformed into the law of primitive socialist accumulation. All this occurs on the basis of market exchange, and in this process the law of socialist accumulation gradually removes the *content* of market relations, while for the moment not affecting their form, and at the same time this process proceeds much more rapidly within the state economy and develops much more slowly and agonizingly at the junction between the state and private sectors. As it develops, the law of primitive socialist accumulation simultaneously begins to resolve both the problem of proportionality in the distribution of existing productive forces—a problem that faces every type of social production—and the problem of expanded reproduction, but in socialist rather than capitalist forms. At present we still do not know what laws will underlie our state economy when it has caught up with and surpassed capitalist technology, that is, when true socialist accumulation begins. This will also depend on how things stand with the struggle for socialism and the construction of socialism in other countries. Nor can we forsee the things that might hasten or, on the contrary, retard or cut short the process of our socialist construction as a result of our relations with the capitalist world. But for the present period, when our development must take place at a lower level of technology than is the case under capitalism (and, moreover, in isolation from the rest of the world economy), the law of primitive socialist accumulation is the law of our development and self-preservation. Every serious Marxist investigator of our economy discovers that law, however he may formulate it, especially if he is dealing with the problem of economic equilibrium in our system when that system is linked up with today's world market.*

From the foregoing the reader can see how unfairly the author of these lines has been charged with trying to undermine the bloc of workers and peasants or blamed for advocating such slogans as "the transformation of the peasant economy into a colony for socialist industry." I ask my critics, who regard themselves as Marxists and Leninists, and who have advanced these charges, to answer the following questions:

(1) Is it not true that expanded capitalist reproduction requires a certain proportionality between the volume of accumulation and the volume of social consumption?

(2) Is it not true that under concrete capitalism the industrialization of economically backward countries is facilitated and hastened by the import of capital from advanced industrial countries?

(3) Is it not true that technological progress and the rise in the

*In the chapter of my book devoted to this latter topic, I try to express the law of primitive socialist accumulation quite graphically using both abstract and concrete schemes for the distribution of the productive forces under a commodity-socialist system of economy.

organic composition of capital—which means the growth of constant capital both in the branches producing means of production and in those producing means of consumption—requires an ever faster growth in the production of means of production and thus a faster growth of the social capital employed in that department, that is, above all, a proportionately faster accumulation in the sphere of heavy industry at the expense of the economy as a whole?

(4) Is it not true that we are already using all our fixed capital and are now compelled to solve two tasks at the same time: the task of more rapidly satisfying social needs and the task of creating new fixed capital, whose functioning will not start to show results, in the sense of an expansion of the supply of commodities, for several years?

(5) Is it not true that in an economically backward country with a socialist regime, which at the moment has no capital imports and is compelled to struggle against the entire bourgeois world, the rate of internal accumulation must necessarily proceed at a far faster rate than in any capitalist country with the same level of development of productive forces?

(6) Is it not true that the rapid shift of the peasant economy over to commodity production in such a country requires a supplementary growth of industry and, consequently, supplementary industrial accumulation if it is to maintain economic equilibrium?

(7) Is it not true that the industrialization of every country, especially a country with a socialist regime, requires raising the level of culture and professional skills of the working class—which means a systematic growth in wages?

(8) Is it not true that, after deducting what is accumulated on the state economy's own base, the remaining part, which is accumulated at the expense of petty production, cannot drop below a certain minimum, a minimum that is dictated to the Soviet state with rigorous economic necessity?

(9) Is it not true, finally, that underaccumulation in state industry leads to a goods famine, a rise in retail prices, accumulation of private capital, and a broadening of the gap that separates the town and the village?[1]

No Marxist can deny that all this is true. But if it is true, this scientific analysis should be able to furnish us with the correct arithmetic values for economic policy and for drawing up an economic plan for the country.

And at the same time it is quite obvious that if we are plagued by a systematic goods famine and fail to satisfy effective demand, if we have the hoarding of money in the countryside—money with which the peasants cannot buy commodities—and the hoarding of grain surpluses, eaten by mice and rats and lying unmoved for eight or nine months, plus abnormally high grain prices for a good harvest, then we have before us *an unequivocal empirical proof that there has been some sort of mistake in the sphere of distribution of the country's surplus product.* At the present time it is underaccumulation, not overaccumulation in industry, that is the potential underminer of the worker–peasant bloc, since if this situation continues for very long the peasantry will have to seek an alliance not with our industry, but with that of foreign capitalism.

The problem of the worker–peasant bloc has a different content in different periods. Simply repreating the bare phrase about that bloc is of no benefit, nor does it save us from any dangers, and the peasantry itself is irritated because it is so void of content. Leninism here means giving a new content to this slogan at each new stage, one that follows from the economic and political situation, from the domestic and international situation. At the present stage, the policy of industrialization, the policy of increasingly rapid socialist accumulation, is the material expression of the slogans "bloc" and "alliance." For so long as we now have a gaping deficit, so long as we live under the Damoclean sword of a growing pressure on us from the world market, industrial underproduction and our technological backwardness are the most serious threat to the cause of maintaining the worker–peasant bloc.

And when under these circumstances the conscientious attempt to think through the conditions that would be necessary for safeguarding and developing our state economy again and again encounters a repetition of absurd charges about "colonies," then do we not have a right to fear that such a method of polemics can, under appropriate conditions, serve as a rallying cry for mobilizing the country's petit bourgeois backwardness against socialism? Now, while it is not surprising that Comrade Gol'denberg and other of our young self-styled professors who have not accompanied our party through the long school of determined struggle against populism and Menshevism should yield to the moral pressure of the 100-million-strong petit bourgeois mass of the country, and while their political inexperience tends to excuse their various zigzags toward a Kuban, Penza, or Kursk "magnetic anomaly," what can one say about the old comrades, the old Bolsheviks, who encourage these zigzags and who themselves often do not weigh their arguments against their possible political consequences? Is it really permissible in the polemical heat of intraparty discussions to forget the fundamental social and historical ties that unite us?

In conclusion I would like to say a few words about the practical verification of the general theoretical positions that have guided the author of these lines since 1923 and for which he has been so bitterly attacked.

In 1924, when my article on the law of socialist accumulation was written, my opponents most of all feared industrial overaccumulation and industrial overproduction. They mechanically transferred to 1924 and the years following the experience of the sales crisis of late 1923—a crisis that they did not correctly understand and that they exaggerated beyond all measure. Their slogan was "more caution in the development of industry, more caution in accumulating." They called for a reduction in prices, no matter what, with no regard for the problem of accumulation. They even went so far as to talk themselves into accepting as a general guideline for the future the totally false economic thesis of first a reduction in prices, then accumulation, instead of the only correct slogan: first accumulation, on that basis a reduction of cost of production, and then a reduction of prices. At that time doubt was cast upon the very slogan "socialist accumulation," and they saw in it a threat to the continuation of the worker–peasant bloc. The years 1925 and 1926 arrived with their acute goods famine, with the upset of the balance of payments between city and village—the natural consequence of underaccumulation—and it was plainly revealed that the problem of socialist accumulation that I had raised had been a *scientific prediction of the goods famine*, a timely forewarning, an attempt to direct the party's attention to the imminent danger of underaccumulation, while my opponents had been orienting the party in *precisely the opposite direction*. By now there is no way to hide or slur over that fact. My opponents' general theoretical presuppositions, along with their inability to apply the Leninist method to a new set of circumstances, has led to practical mistakes in the area of economic policy. And the theory of socialist accumulation, which was proclaimed anti-Leninist, has by some miracle correctly predicted the difficulties that now are upon us and that have, after a year and a half or two years, become clear to all.

The accuracy of the industrializers' prediction is also borne out in other points of our disagreements. Comrade Trotsky's report to the Twelfth Party Congress was viewed by some as extremely industrialist, and yet the economic policy outlined there to cover a number of years proved to be quite correct.

At the Thirteenth Party Conference, Comrade Piatakov supported the thesis that the trusts should earn the greatest possible profit while keeping disposal prices and wages at their present levels; that is, he defended a policy of utmost economy in the interests of accumulation, whereas the comrades who criticized him launched the slogan of least possible profit. In doing so they irresponsibly confused the slogan of greatest possible profit, *all other conditions being equal*, with the slogan of maximum prices, and in this way were able to celebrate a cheap but quite short-lived victory. Now there is scarcely anyone who would seriously undertake to defend the so-called principle of least possible profit. On the contrary, all the efforts at rationalization—efforts that often take a clearly incorrect, at times even harmful, turn—are nothing other than an attempt to ensure state industry a large profit, while prices remain the same as now or even lower; that is, an attempt to implement the so highly criticized slogan of 1923.

Why did Comrade Piatakov prove to be right and his opponents wrong? Because he, like all industrializers, correctly stood for the most rapid industrial accumulation possible—a position that was a prediction of both the goods famine and of the economic difficulties that arose during the transition from the use of old fixed capital to the creation of new. At the same time he put forward a more correct concept of our economy as a whole and the path of its development than did his opponents. This correct general theoretical approach obliged Comrade Piatakov to raise the problem of running the entire state economy as a unified whole, with all the organizational conclusions that follow from it. Today all this seems like a truism, but at the Thirteenth Party Conference the "realists" derided Comrade Piatakov as a hopeless utopian.

Later, Comrade Trotsky submitted his articles *Toward Capitalism or Socialism*,[2] in which he most fruitfully posed the question of working out dynamic coefficients for comparing our economy with the economic system of world capitalism. This question, whose importance has still not been sufficiently appreciated by our party, could likewise be posed only on the basis of a theoretical conception of our economy that was correct in principle.

A correct theoretical analysis of our economic system is of prime importance for our politics, our practice in general. I would like to underscore with particular force at this point the difference between bourgeois and socialist economics. In capitalist society, economic science plays a very modest role for the agents of capitalist production. Maintenance of equilibrium in the economy, if one may put it that way, is left up to the law of value. In its spontaneous way this law maintains equilibrium in the overall system more intelligently and more reliably than bourgeois science, bourgeois professors, and bourgeois governments. Although this method of regulation costs society a pretty penny, since it gives notice of errors committed in the distribution of the productive forces only *post factum*, there is in bourgeois society nothing that can replace it. And while monopoly capitalism attains a higher degree of organization in one or another branch of the economy within a country, it is unable to eliminate the economic planlessness within the national economy as a whole, much less on the world market.

The Soviet state, on the other hand, relying on nationalized large-scale industry, transportation, credit, and foreign trade, is compelled by the very fact of nationalization to defend itself and to launch a planned offensive, thereby turning a new page in the use of economic science for production. As time goes by, we are increasingly compelled to regulate the economy in a planned fashion by giving increasingly free rein to the law of socialist accumulation. But to plan, we must predict. And to predict, we must unceasingly, on an ever-greater scale, and with increasing thoroughness investigate with scientific searchlights the entire visible range of causes and effects in the economic sphere. Our economy is becoming more complex; regulation is growing more and more difficult and crucial; it is encompassing an ever greater range of economic relations and setting in motion increasing masses of people and material values. As the entire management mechanism becomes more centralized, large mistakes become every more dangerous. The role of the planning organs is continuously growing. Being a good politician is in general becoming more and more insufficient for being a good framer of economic policy, for being a leader of an economy of our type, that is, in the leading ranks of a socialist economy. As time goes by, improvisation and dilettantism are becoming more and more harmful for our economy. A policy of frugality demands—if we go beyond mere details—fewer mistakes by our leadership. And the way to achieve that with the least expenditure of effort is precisely by having a correct theory of our economy, that is, in the most democratic way, the way most accessible to every person who really wants to learn and move ahead.

But what do we see in our country in this area? Since Lenin's death we have had no broad, generalizing conception, continuously subject to testing by fresh facts, that could lay the basis for a scientific theory of our economy. Everything that has been done in this respect by the so-called industrializers has been met with a hail of objections and accusations of anti-Leninism, Trotskyism, petit bourgeois deviation, and so on.

Granted, by now there is no one who believes that latter charge any longer, and people will soon cease to believe the others as well. That does not, however, move things forward at all in the sense of getting our critics to make a positive contribution toward a theory of the Soviet economy. My opponents are quite energetic when it comes to polemics and to inventing all sorts of formulas for their accusations, but the question arises, What do they offer as a positive alternative to my concept? The years go by, new facts are gathered, our experience goes on: but what positive contributions have they made to the party in the sense of being able to draw general conclusions from that experience? After all, we Bolsheviks are a very demanding lot when it comes to theory: we have in our past the monumental works of Marx and Engels; we have Lenin. With that kind of legacy on our shoulders we do not content ourselves with floating on the surface of vulgar Soviet economics.

My opponents have provided almost nothing new in the theoretical sphere. And I venture to predict that as long as they adhere to their present positions of theoretical cowardice and eclecticism, they will not provide anything in the future that—without falling into ridiculous self-conceit—they could pass off as a theory of Soviet economy. That is, they may write a sizable number of articles, brochures, and maybe even books. But all that will not be what our economy and our party needs in the area of theory. By holding to their position denying the law of socialist accumulation, that is, by repudiating the attempt to construct a dynamic, proletarian, Marxist-Leninist concept of our economy, they condemn themselves to theoretical sterility, for you cannot get a theory of Soviet economy by adding a little saliva to well-chewed general statements that everybody has long been familiar with and no one would question.

EDITOR'S NOTES

[1] The nine points enumerated here by Preobrazhensky are by no means as straightforward as he makes out and, in fact, represent the main conclusions that he was to draw from the first and third articles on "Economic Equilibrium" ("The Problem of Economic Equilibrium Under Concrete Capitalism and in the Soviet System" and "Economic Equilibrium in the System of the USSR," respectively).

[2] *Towards Socialism or Capitalism?* (London: New Park Publications, 1976). (Originally published in Russian in 1925 as *K sotsializmu ili k kapitalizmu?*)

PART THREE

The Theory of Economic Equilibrium in the Mixed Economy

The Problem of Economic Equilibrium Under Concrete Capitalism and in the Soviet System

1926

In the second volume of *Capital*, Marx begins with an analysis of *simple* reproduction under pure capitalism, that is, under the economic system that exists when capitalism has subordinated to itself both industry and agriculture, when it has ousted all precapitalist forms and become not merely the dominant but in fact the sole form of production in society. In analyzing the conditions of equilibrium of this pure, abstract capitalism, Marx applied in this area of investigation his customary methodological approach, to which he adhered in all his works on economics. He began with simple reproduction precisely because it is there that the equilibrium between the branches of production of means of production and means of consumption is theoretically reflected with greatest clarity, for it is there that equilibrium in exchange of values assumes the form of a mathematical equality.

Through his analysis of simple reproduction, which in real life can occur only as an exception, Marx elucidated the most important part of the problem, the equilibrium between the exchange of means of production from department I for means of consumption from department II, which in value terms is expressed as the complete exchange of $v + s$ of department I for c of department II. Having completed this analysis of simple reproduction, Marx then proceeds to deal with the much more complex problem of expanded reproduction under pure capitalism, when the whole system is in motion and the theoretically conceivable and actually observed possibilities for disproportion are incomparably greater than in simple reproduction. Even with the same volume of capital in society and all other conditions being equal (the organic composition of capital and the rate of exploitation), an entirely different distribution of productive forces is needed here. Moreover, in the event of even the slightest rise or fall in the rate of accumulation itself, these forces must be redistributed. Falling, stable, and growing rates of accumulation each require special proportions in the distribution of capital through the regroupings and changes in the other conditions of reproduction.

But, as we know, at no time during his analysis of simple and expanded reproduction does Marx ever leave the ground of pure capitalism. And yet, the economist who undertakes a study of actual capitalism and the conditions of its equilibrium is obliged to apply Marx's scientific discoveries to conditions in which capitalist reproduction is interwoven with reproduction in a simple commodity economy.[1] On the one hand, this undoubtedly complicates the whole problem, since the investigator must introduce two new departments, in addition to the two used by Marx, in order to provide for precapitalist economic formations; hence, he must examine the conditions of equilibrium among four sets of figures.[2] On the other hand, however, an analysis of mixed capitalist and precapitalist reproduction also meets with a certain simplification of the problem, since, for example, in *simple reproduction* within the petit bourgeois sector of the economy the entire product is divided into only two parts: the income consumed by the petty producers themselves and the part of constant capital* that is replaced. Conversely, in expanded reproduction within a simple commodity economy the analysis is again complicated, insofar as one cannot in this case assume any constant value of labor power, because the surplus product of petty production can go not only to expand production but also to expand consumption by the independent producers themselves on a scale that is only indirectly regulated by the law of value of labor power; similarly, the level of consumption can fall far below the level of the average wage of the workers.

Of course, even in an analysis of reproduction of concrete capitalism we cannot take a single step without drawing on Marx's analysis of reproduction under pure capitalism. But, on the other hand, without an analysis of equilibrium under concrete capital-

*We use the word "capital," referring to the means of production of the independent petty producers, in a conditional sense, only for the sake of simplicity; according to Marx's terminology this is not capital.

ism, that is, without an analysis of the equilibrium between capitalist production and independent petty commodity production, we shall find it very difficult to study the equilibrium in the economic system of the USSR, where there is an interweaving of three forms of reproduction under the conditions of commodity exchange: the simple commodity economy, capitalism, and the state economy of the proletariat. Concrete experience in studying the equilibrium in our economic system leads to the conviction that this problem will most easily be solved if we first investigate the simpler forms of equilibrium in a mixed capitalist economy. This approach is required not only by pedagogical considerations or for convenience in exposition but also by the essence of the problem itself.

In the theoretical section of the present discussion, we shall examine five fundamental problems: (1) simple reproduction in a mixed economy of capitalism and simple commodity production; (2) expanded reproduction under pure capitalism when the organic composition of capital is rising; (3) expanded reproduction under *concrete capitalism*, that is, when capitalist production is interwoven with petit bourgeois production; (4) declining reproduction under the same economic conditions; and (5) equilibrium during expanded reproduction in the economy of the USSR.

I intend to deal with the first four of these questions only in their broadest outlines, and I make no claims whatsoever to touching on all the interesting problems that arise in a study of this kind. For the ultimate aim of the investigation remains a purely concrete analysis of the living, growing Soviet economy, with all the concrete facts and figures that relate to it.

Simple Reproduction in a Mixed Economy of Capitalism and Simple Commodity Production

Before beginning our investigation of this problem, let us make a couple of methodological observations.

In his analysis of the problem of proportionality during simple reproduction under pure capitalism, Marx operates with two departments: department I for the production of means of production, and department II for the production of means of consumption. Does an analysis of proportionality in a mixed economy require us to introduce new departments, that is, departments for the sector of simple commodity production?

The answer to this question must be "yes," for the following reason: if it were possible simply to add the production of means of production in the petit bourgeois economy to department I of the capitalist sector and add the production of means of consumption to department II of that sector, then this would presume in advance that the entire mixed form, from the standpoint of the conditions of equilibrium, represents nothing new in comparison with the conditions of equilibrium already analyzed by Marx. We would then have a simple arithmetical increase in both departments, with the equilibrium conditions necessary for simple capitalist reproduction being preserved. But this is an incorrect assumption.

First of all, in simple capitalist reproduction the gross annual product is broken down into $c + v + s$, that is, used-up constant capital, wages, and surplus value, whereas in the petit bourgeois sector in simple reproduction the annual product consists merely of constant capital and the income consumed by the petty producers. This income can be designated as v only in a conditional sense, because it is not completely regulated by the law of value of labor power. Thus, the surplus value consumed by the capitalists has no precise equivalent in the schemes for petty production, whereas the correspondence between v of the capitalist sector and the income consumed by the petty producers is also equally inexact. This circumstance, together with the abovementioned peculiarities of the petty producers' consumption fund, exerts considerable influence on the aggregate of equilibrium conditions in the mixed form of economy as a whole. This is not to mention the changes caused by the circumstance that, as a rule, petty production is not entirely commodity production; in its concrete form it has often not yet severed its umbilical cord to the natural economy. This fact is of tremendous importance for concrete investigations, although here, at the present stage of this study, we shall proceed from the assumption that we are dealing with such petty production as functions exclusively for the market and whose production and exchange process, insofar as it is tied to the market, is subject to the law of value.

We must also bear in mind the sharp distinction between the organic composition of capital in the capitalist sector and the ratio of constant to variable capital (using both these terms in the conditional sense) in simple commodity production; given the dominant role of large-scale production in competitive branches, this inevitably leads to nonequivalent exchange from the standpoint of expenditure of labor in petty production.[3]

Further, only by setting up parallel schemes for capitalist production and simple commodity production can we clearly see all the processes involved in the expanded reproduction of a mixed system and follow the dynamics of the ousting of petty production by large-scale production with maintenance of a flexible equilibrium in the economy as a whole. Moreover, setting up such schemes will also make it easier for us to approach the fundamental regularities of declining reproduction.

The whole investigation could, it seems, be simplifed by analyzing only the part of petty commodity production that participates in the exchange of values with the capitalist sector of the economy; consumption in natural form and internal exchange within the petty production sector could be disregarded. But this abstraction, inconvenient as it may be when analyzing a mixed system in which petty production is predominant, would in every other aspect mean a refusal to investigate the immediate causes of a strengthening or weakening of the link between petty and capitalist production; it would mean a refusal to investigate more deeply the conditions of proportionality within the economic system as a whole and, in particular, the preconditions for any disproportion that in an actual economy are brought to the surface only by a series of new phenomena, not only in the capitalist but in the petit bourgeois sector of the economy as well.

Finally, there is one more essential circumstance to bear in mind in an analysis of equilibrium under concrete capitalism during both simple and expanded reproduction. Marx, in his analysis of this process, proceeds on the assumption that "the fact that prices diverge from values cannot . . . exert any influence on the movements of the social capital. On the whole there is the same exchange of the same quantities of products, although the individual capitalists are involved in value-relations no longer proportional to their respective advances and to the quantities of surplus value produced singly by every one of them."* This assumption of Marx's is perfectly correct insofar as one is dealing with the self-contained system of pure capitalism; however, when one examines the exchange of goods between the capitalist and petit bourgeois sectors of the

---

**Capital*, vol. II, p. 368, Stepanov's translation (Progress Publishers English edition, p. 397).

economy, the problem of a divergence of prices from values—especially the problem of a systematic lag of the prices of goods produced in petty production behind the actual labor expended on them, as well as the problem of market-determined changes in that sphere—takes on a completely different meaning. Here it is a question not of redistribution within a single sector but of redistribution between two sectors that historically and economically represent two different types of organization of human labor. Here it is impossible to carry out a concrete analysis without investigating the divergence of prices from values. Herein lies yet another difference in the methods one must use to analyze equilibrium under concrete capitalism on the one hand and abstract capitalism on the other.

Let us first take Marx's scheme for simple reproduction under pure capitalism and then turn it into a scheme for reproduction under concrete capitalism.

In the second volume of *Capital*, Marx writes:

"The total product, and therefore the total production, of society may be divided into two major departments:

I. *Means of Production*, commodities having a form in which they must, or at least may, pass into productive consumption.

II. *Articles of Consumption*, commodities having a form in which they pass into the individual consumption of the capitalist and the working class.

All the various branches of production pertaining to each of these two departments form one single great branch of production, that of the means of production in the one case, and that of articles of consumption in the other. The aggregate capital employed in each of these two branches of production constitutes a separate large department of the social capital."*

As a numerical example, Marx takes the following volumes of employed capital and annual reproduction:

I. $4{,}000c + 1{,}000v + 1{,}000s = 6{,}000$ means of production
II. $2{,}000c + 500v + 500s = 3{,}000$ means of consumption

Consequently, in this scheme the capital used in department I is equal to $4{,}000c$ (that is, constant capital) plus $1{,}000v$, (that is, vari-

Capital, vol. II, pp. 369-70, Stepanov's translation (Progress Publishers English edition, p. 399).

able capital), which goes for wages. The applied capital in department II is equal to 2,000*c* + 500*v*.

From the standpoint of the capitalist class, the new product is equal to the entire surplus value, or 1,000 + 500.

From the standpoint of society, the new product is equal to 3,000, of which 1,500 constitutes the capitalists' consumption fund and 1,500 that of the workers.

The fundamental law-governed regularity that Marx discovered in his analysis of simple reproduction, and that constitutes his greatest theoretical achievement, is that equilibrium under simple reproduction (that is, when the entire new product is completely consumed and there is no accumulation) requires that $v + s$ of department I be equal to *c* of department II. This means that the part of the annual product of department I that in value terms is equal to $v + s$ of that department and that in its material form consists of various types of means of production (machines, raw materials, fuel, and so on, intended for productive consumption) must necessarily be equal to *c* of department II, that is, to the value of the means of consumption that department II sells to department I, thereby enabling department I to sell to department II, for the same sum, means of production to replace II*c*.

Let us now assume that we are dealing not with pure capitalism but with concrete capitalism, that is, that part of the commodities in society which are produced under conditions of the simple commodity economy. Let us further assume that the gross product of the petty production sector is equal to the gross product of the capitalist sector, but, of course, with a different value relation between the reproduced means of production and the consumed part of the gross product because, owing to the low level of technology in this sector, what we have termed—in a conditional sense—"constant capital" must be relatively (and with the figures we have taken, absolutely as well) less than in the capitalist sector. Finally, of course, we have to assume that the sector of simple commodity production carries on an uninterrupted exchange of goods with the capitalist sector in the form of exchange of means of consumption—an assumption that generally corresponds to the typical relations existing within the economy under actual capitalism in the case where petty production is totally subordinate to market relations.

Given these conditions, Marx's numerical scheme, reduced to an annual production of 8,250, will look something like the following:

(To save space we shall label the departments of the capitalist sector by the letter K and those of the precapitalist sector by the letter P; similarly, we shall let p represent the values obtained by sector K from sector P through exchange, and let k represent those obtained by P from K.)[4]

$$\left.\begin{array}{r} \text{KI. } 4{,}000c(3{,}750k + 250p) + 1{,}000v + 1{,}000s = 6{,}000 \\ {[1{,}000p + 1{,}000k = \text{KI}v + s]} \\ \text{KII. } 1{,}500c(1{,}000k + 500p) + 375v = 375s = 2{,}250 \end{array}\right\} 8{,}250$$

$$\left.\begin{array}{r} \text{PI. } 750c(500p + 250k) + 1{,}500(1{,}000p + 500k) = 2{,}250^{*} \\ \text{PII. } 2{,}000c(1{,}000p + 1{,}000k) + 4{,}000 \text{ consumption} \\ \text{fund} = 6{,}000 \end{array}\right\} 8{,}250$$

Here we have a scheme of economic equilibrium during simple reproduction under conditions of concrete capitalism, that is, when simple commodity production and capitalist production exist side by side. We disregard the inequality of actual labor expenditure in the exchange of equal exchange values. For the sake of simplicity we shall also ignore intradepartmental exchange of commodities that are consumed within both departments II.

What conclusions can be drawn from an analysis of the scheme we have just presented?

The most obvious conclusion of all is that under conditions of simple reproduction in concrete capitalism the equilibrium of the whole system by no means requires that $\text{I}(v + s)$ be equal to $\text{II}c$ in the capitalist sector; on the contrary, the two magnitudes are, as a rule, never equal.

The second conclusion is that, *in the economy as a whole*, $(v + s)$ of department I of the capitalist sector together with the consumed income of department I of the petit bourgeois sector (in our example, $1{,}000v + 1{,}000s$ from KI plus 1,500 from sector P) is equal to the constant capital c of department II of the capitalist sector (1,500) plus the value of the reproduced means of production of the petit bourgeois sector (2,000).[5] Thus, although Marx's equality of the proportions of exchange between departments I and II for pure capitalism ($\text{I}(v + s) = \text{II}c$) is not obligatory for the capitalist sector in our case, *it does take on the form of an analogous equal-*

*In this example, in contrast to the following ones, we take the same ratio of consumption fund to constant capital (that is, 1:2) in both departments of the precapitalist sector.

ity for the economy as a whole if we take the production of the means of production of both sectors as one department and the aggregate production of means of consumption as the other.[6]

Let us now examine why we obtain both of these results.

In the capitalist sector KI($v + s$) can be equal to KIIc only under one condition, namely, if exchange between the petit bourgeois and capitalist sectors takes place on the basis of an equality of the proportions of mutual exchange within the production of means of production on the one hand and within the production of means of consumption of both sectors on the other. In other words, KIc sells to PIc for 100 or, let us say, 200 and receives in return means of production of the second type for exactly the same sum. The same must be the case with internal exchange between the departments II of both sectors. It is perfectly obvious that in this case in order for I($v + s$) to be equal to IIc the value of consumed income of department I of the petit bourgeois sector must equal the value of the means of production of that sector's department II. But such an equality of proportions could only be purely coincidental and is completely uncharacteristic for the economy of actual capitalism. And, conversely, it is by no means coincidental that as soon as we have to set up proportions for actual capitalism, that is, for a mixed capitalist and petit bourgeois economy, we find that if we keep Marx's figures for department I, we are forced to change the ones he used for department II. And if we keep his figures for department II, we have to change the scale of production in department I, a change that of course, as we shall see below, corresponds to a new technological structure for the whole of society's economy.

But if in KI the quantity ($v + s$), which in its material form represents means of production, cannot be exchanged completely for KIIc, that is, for articles of consumption produced in department II of the capitalist sector that go to replace constant capital in KII, then equilibrium can be established only by drawing PII into exchange. In other words, department I of the capitalist sector sells means of production not only to department II of its own sector but to PII as well, that is, in our own case, for example, to the peasant economy, which produces means of consumption. This process in turn gives the peasant economy the means of production (for example, agricultural machinery, artificial fertilizers, and so on) that are not furnished in sufficient quantity by the petit bourgeois department of means of production.

As we shall see below, the situation will be exactly the same, as far as establishing equilibrium is concerned, if things are reversed, that is, if KII*c* cannot be completely exchanged for KI($v + s$), and so covers its deficit in means of production out of the realized income of PI—which has the natural form of means of production of petit bourgeois origin (peasant raw materials such as flax, cotton, or hides, petty artisan repairs, and so on)—offering factory-produced means of consumption (for example, textiles or sugar) in exchange.

As regards the inevitability of an equality, *for the economy as a whole*, of the proportions of exchange between the means of production of both sectors that are exchanged for means of consumption from both departments II on the one hand and the value of replaced constant capital of both departments II on the other, then under the conditions of simple reproduction this equality is obligatory for any economy with a market system of exchange, be it a petit bourgeois–capitalist economy or a mixed commodity-socialist economic system like our own. If this equality is upset during the exchange of the indicated values, it will inevitably mean either underconsumption or incomplete reproduction of constant capital, that is, a violation of the fundamental premise of simple reproduction.

In a mixed economy, however, particular significance attaches to that part of the petit bourgeois sector that is least trapped in the iron vice of proportionality of the entire social economy: we are speaking of the consumption fund in department II of the petit bourgeois sector. The peculiarity of this part of the product, from the standpoint of its weaker dependence on exchange of goods within the entire economy, is already evident from Marx's scheme for simple reproduction, but it is only in department II of the petit bourgeois sector that this peculiarity is most noticeable.

Indeed, in Marx's department II, 500v + 500s is the part of the means of consumption that is both created and consumed within that same department. If we assume that, given the same volume of II*c* (that is, 2,000), the total annual production of means of consumption drops from 3,000 to 2,800 as a result of a poor harvest in capitalist agriculture, then this would have to lead either to a decrease in s from 500 to 300 or to a reduction of both s and v in one or another proportion. In this case the proportionality between departments I and II would not be upset, since the value of commodities from department II will be determined by the value of production in a typical, average year, and not by the expenditure of labor per unit product in this particular, exceptional year. However, it is quite difficult to reduce *v* from 500 to 400, because in capitalist production the wage fund has a tendency to fluctuate around the value of labor power in the whole economy, and a reduction of *v*, all other conditions being equal, must severely cut into *s*. Conversely, if (*v* + *s*) in department I were to be reduced while I*c* was kept at the same level, we would have not only a reduction of consumption in department I but also the impossibility of fully reproducing II*c*, that is, the constant capital of department II, which can be exchanged only for *v* and for the surplus value of department I that is consumed by the capitalists.

Now, if we take the consumption fund of PII, that is, department II of the petit bourgeois sector, then in the case of underproduction throughout PII, but maintaining the old scale of reproduction of the means of production, the consumption fund can be contracted without upsetting the equilibrium of the system as a whole, just as it can be increased if production is expanded—for example, as a result of a good harvest in the peasant sector. In both cases the divergence can under certain conditions, be either fully overcome or attenuated by a redistribution between personal and productive consumption within department II itself.

An entirely different situation arises when there is underproduction in department I of *both the capitalist and petit bourgeois sectors*, if, as in the first case, we assume that constant capital in KI and PI is reproduced at the same rate as before. Then, if instead of 1,000*v* + 1,000*s* we have, let us say 900*v* + 900*s*, or 1,000*v* + 800*s*, the deficit of 200—which in material terms is a deficit in means of production—makes it impossible to reproduce 200 in constant capital of department II.

The same thing will happen if the consumption fund of department I of the petit bourgeois sector is reduced. Here, the disproportion cannot be overcome within this same department but will inevitably be shifted onto II*c* of both sectors and must thereby upset the entire economic system; we shall then have not only underconsumption during that one year in department I but also automatically underproduction in the departments II of both sectors as a result of the reduction in their constant capital. In practice this may easily be avoided as regards the part of II_c that consists of fixed capital, since the latter can often be fully used up without provision for depreciation costs in *that particular year* by making up for the deficit in the years following (thus taking the form of a loan from one's own fixed capital fund). However, the same thing cannot be done with respect to the part of *c* that makes up the circulating capital, such as fuel and raw materials. In fact, even if the disproportion is attenuated by carrying depreciation costs over to subsequent years, the conditions of simple reproduction will, strictly speaking, still be violated.

From the preceding discussion the reader will see, among other things, why economic disproportion is much more easily overcome when there is a rapid rate of expanded reproduction and, conversely, why it is such an extremely slow and painful process to reestablish proportionality when a country's economy approaches the level of simple reproduction (for example, contemporary Great Britain). But we shall return to this very important question when we analyze expanded and declining reproduction under concrete capitalism.

The unevenness that we have demonstrated in department I's relation to the whole as compared to that relationship for department II, as well as the fact that the pivotal point of proportionality in the economy is located in the sphere of exchange of means of production for articles of consumption rather than in the area of internal exchange within each department, explains why Marx began his analysis of capitalist reproduction by dividing both the aggregate social capital used in production and the total annual product itself into the two departments described above. Of course, the method that Marx used to analyze equilibrium does not exhaust the whole problem. But it is the only method that can serve as a *foundation* for further, more detailed study of the problem of equilibrium in a commodity economy. Such a detailed analysis, which would combine an investigation of equilibrium in the exchange of values with a study of the material aspect of commodity exchange, is especially necessary when one is studying economic equilibrium in a specific country or the world economy at a particular stage of its development.

The reader will see from our scheme that exchange both within department I of both sectors and within department II of both sectors has no effect on proportionality of the whole economic complex, if it is a question of exchange of equal values, consisting in their material form in the one case of means of production and in the other of means of consumption. If department I of the capitalist sector exchanges, let us say, 250 in its machines for 250 in raw materials from department I of the petit bourgeois sector, then the proportionality of exchange in value terms within the entire complex will not be upset, just as if 300 is exchanged for 300, or 350 for 350. The same is true if means of consumption of equal value are exchanged between the departments II of the capitalist and petit bourgeois sectors. Here we have approximately the same situation as that analyzed in passing by Marx when he dealt with the problem of distribution of means of consumption between the capitalists and workers of departments I and II from the standpoint of dividing the total consumption fund into necessary means of consumption and luxury articles.[7] That analysis showed that different proportions of exchange within the general consumption fund have no influence on proportionality within the economy as a whole, from the standpoint of the exchange of values between departments I and II. The situation is altered only if the exchange is unequal and the difference in the balance of exchange causes a shift of proportions in the exchange of values between the two different departments.[8]

But this is the way matters stand in an analysis of proportionality *in value terms*. As soon as we begin analyzing the natural composition of commodities that enter into the exchange, then we have even in the first case a different type of proportionality, namely, proportionality of the *material* composition of exchange. Although this is bound to complicate the study of the concrete economy of a given country or of the world economy as a whole, it is impossible to do without such a detailed analysis at a certain stage in the study of these phenomena.

Finally, one of the most obvious regularities of exchange between the capitalist and petit bourgeois sectors under conditions of simple reproduction is that the total sum of values passing from the first sector to the second must be equal to the sum of values passing from the second to the first. In the present case, 1,750 is equal to 1,750. An unequal balance of exchange in this case would inevitably mean that all the elements subject to exchange could not in fact be exchanged for one another; this situation would then lead to underproduction and underconsumption, and thereby to a violation of the very principle of simple reproduction.

Above, in our scheme of concrete capitalism, there was a shortage of 750 in the production of means of consumption in the capitalist sector. Given the existence of a petit bourgeois sector, this meant that proportionality could be attained by exchanging the excess means of production of department I of the capitalist sector for a corresponding sum in means of consumption from department II of the petit bourgeois sector, with the result that this department II would swell beyond the limits of what was necessary for the petit bourgeois sector itself. We would get exactly the opposite situation if instead of an overproduction of means of production and a shortage of means of consumption in the capitalist sector we were to have underproduction of means of production and overproduction of means of consumption. In this case the constant capital of department II of the capitalist sector could not be completely replaced out of ($v + s$) of department I, and the deficit would have to be covered out of department I of the petit bourgeois sector. This would then lead to a redistribution of productive forces within the petit bourgeois sector as well: production in department I would have to expand, whereas production in department II would have to contract.

To illustrate this process we shall present a scheme in which production in KI is lower than in Marx's scheme, whereas production in KII remains the same. This scheme appears below, along with our first one (but without internal exchanges between the corresponding departments of both sectors):

New Scheme

KI.	3,500c + 875v + 875s = 5,250	8,250
KII.	2,000c + 500v + 500s = 3,000	
PI.	1,000c + 2,000 consumption fund = 3,000	8,250
PII.	1,750c + 3,500 consumption fund = 5,250	

Earlier Scheme

KI.	4,000c + 1,000v + 1,000s = 6,000	8,250
KII.	1,500c + 375v + 375s = 2,250	
PI.	750c + 1,500 consumption fund = 2,250	8,250
PII.	2,000c + 4,000 consumption fund = 6,000	

By comparing our new scheme with the earlier one we see that, all other conditions being equal, a rise in the production of the means of production and a decrease in the production of means of consumption in the capitalist sector leads to a decrease in the production of means of production in the petit bourgeois sector and a growth of that sector's department II.[9]

Historically, as we shall see below, capitalism developed along a different path: department I of the capitalist sector, that is, capitalist production of machines, fuel, raw materials, and so on, grew *along with* increasing capitalist production of means of consumption. However, owing to a rise in the organic composition of capital, department I grew more rapidly than department II, at the same time that department II tended to accumulate more quickly. Meanwhile, the role of petit bourgeois production in the economy of society steadily diminished—in some cases absolutely, and to a much greater degree, relatively.

In fact, if we take our new scheme for the capitalist sector and compare it with the corresponding scheme for pure capitalism, in which department II remains the same but the production of means of production grows, that is, if we compare it with the scheme:

$$\begin{aligned} &\text{I. } 4{,}000c + 1{,}000v + 1{,}000s \\ &\text{II. } 2{,}000c + \phantom{1{,}}500v + \phantom{1{,}}500s, \end{aligned}$$

we see that in this case department II's deficit of 500*c* is covered by the development of capitalist production of the means of production, that is, capitalism manages without having to exchange means of consumption from its own department II for constant capital produced in department I of the petit bourgeois sector. This means that the capitalist sector itself covers its own deficit of means of production, freeing itself from economic dependence on the petit bourgeois sector.*

On the other hand, if we compare our earlier scheme, which shows a deficit in means of consumption, with that of Marx, we see that in Marx's scheme capitalism attains equilibrium within its own self-contained sphere by developing capitalist production of the means of consumption to such an extent that it will guarantee department I both an adequate supply of means of consumption and a market for the sale of means of production within capitalism itself.

Historically, of course, these two tendencies developed simultaneously. The takeover by capitalist production of the entire manu-

*We shall not at this point examine proportionality in the *material composition* of exchange.

facture of means of consumption increased the capitalist supply of these articles; and the development of II*c* that inevitably accompanied this process in turn created a market for department I, especially for capitalist heavy industry.

Expanded Reproduction Under Pure Capitalism

Let us now turn our attention to a more complex but, at the same time, more interesting topic—the problem of proportionality in expanded reproduction. Before moving directly to an analysis of proportionality under actual capitalism, we must undertake an investigation of expanded reproduction under pure capitalism, since Marx's analysis of this problem abruptly breaks off right at the point where its continuation is absolutely necessary in order to understand equilibrium in the economy of actual capitalism.

Marx analyzed the basic elements of expanded reproduction under pure capitalism without, however, actually completing that analysis, since all his schemes of expanded reproduction assume the invariability of the organic composition of capital in departments I and II (that is, they assume a fixed and given level of technology). Yet even a highly abstract analysis of pure capitalism requires that a rise in the level of technology be reflected in the schemes of equilibrium. Such a rise implies a constant change in the organic composition of capital in both department I and department II, that is, a relative reduction of variable capital as compared to constant capital, along with the absolute increase of both.

To show why we cannot begin an analysis of equilibrium in developing concrete capitalism using only the two departments of the capitalist sector, we presented above a scheme for mixed petit bourgeois–capitalist production. We now must show why it is also necessary to lay new foundations for the schemes that relate to the problem of equilibrium of pure capitalism during expanded reproduction, but under conditions of constant change in the organic composition of capital.

Below is the five-year scheme of expanded reproduction that Marx elaborated in greatest detail.[10]

The initial scheme of accumulation is characterized by the following figures:

$$\left.\begin{array}{l} \text{I. } 4{,}000c + 1{,}000v + 1{,}000s = 6{,}000 \\ \text{II. } 1{,}500c + 750v + 750s = 3{,}000 \end{array}\right\} = 9{,}000$$

By making the rearrangements required by the tasks of expanded reproduction, Marx sets up the following scheme for the beginning of the first operational year:

Beginning of Year I

I. 4,400*c* + 1,100*v* + 500 consumption fund = 6,000
II. 1,600*c* + 800*v* + 600 consumption fund = 3,000 } 9,000

End of Year I

I. 4,400*c* + 1,100*v* + 1,100*s* = 6,600
II. 1,600*c* + 800*v* + 800*s* = 3,200 } 9,800

End of Year II

I. 4,840*c* + 1,210*v* + 1,210*s* = 7,260
II. 1,760*c* + 880*v* + 880*s* = 3,520 } 10,780

End of Year III

I. 5,324*c* + 1,331*v* + 1,331*s* = 7,986
II. 1,936*c* + 968*v* + 968*s* = 3,872 } 11,858

End of Year IV[11]

I. 5,856*c* + 1,464*v* + 1,464*s* = 8,784
II. 2,129*c* + 1,065*v* + 1,065*s* = 4,259 } 13,043

End of Year V

I. 6,442*c* + 1,610*v* + 1,610*s* = 9,662
II. 2,342*c* + 1,172*v* + 1,172*s* + 4,686 } 14,348

Even a cursory glance at this scheme shows the reader that in Marx's schemes equilibrium is attained in the following manner. For both departments, Marx assumes a given ratio of variable to constant capital; that is, he assumes a constant organic composition of capital. He furthermore assumes a constant rate of accumulation in department I, namely, half the total surplus value of that department. On the other hand, to achieve equilibrium in the exchange of Iv and the half of Is that is consumed by the capitalist class—which are both growing under these conditions—he is forced to adjust the accumulation of IIc to these values. He is therefore forced to manipulate the surplus value of II, always leaving for the consumption of the capitalists of that department an amount such that the other part of s, the part that is accumulated, will ensure (a) proportional exchange of the growing IIc for the growing $v + (s/2)$ and (b) the annual increment of v in department II. It is quite obvious that when the magnitudes are arranged in this way, Marx's numerical scheme reveals not only the fundamental regularities of expanded reproduction under pure capitalism (given a constant organic composition of capital) but also—if we may use this expression—the arithmetical regularities of the numerical example itself.

As a matter of fact, it is possible to begin with the same volume of total capital used in production and the same organic composition of capital and attain equilibrium by exactly the opposite approach. We can take department II, rather than department I, as the stationary axis. We can always set aside for accumulation a constant percentage (in the present case, half) of the surplus value of department II, and have the surplus value of department I as a maneuvering fund. We can see how this works by using Marx's same initial scheme: at the start of the new operating year we rearrange the capital on the basis of an accumulation rate of half the surplus value of department II rather than of department I. At the beginning of the operating year, the capital will then be distributed as follows:

$$\begin{aligned} &\text{I. } 4{,}250c + 1{,}062v + 688 \text{ consumption fund*} \\ &\text{II. } 1{,}750c + \phantom{1{,}}875v + 375 \text{ consumption fund} \end{aligned}$$

At the end of the year, we shall obtain

$$\begin{aligned} &\text{I. } 4{,}250c + 1{,}062v + 1{,}062s \\ &\text{II. } 1{,}750c + \phantom{1{,}}875v + \phantom{1{,}}875s \end{aligned}$$

and so on.

*Here, as in all the following cases that involve the capitalist sector, this term refers to the consumption fund of the capitalist class.

We see from this example that equilibrium on the basis of a constant accumulation rate of half the surplus value in II is attained by the capitalists of department I being compelled to consume more and accumulate less, so that department II will have a market for the sale of its articles of consumption and will be able to accumulate II*c* on the scale required by its rate of accumulation. The situation arising here is the opposite of the one we have in Marx's system. In the latter the capitalists of department II accumulate less than they consume and thereby make it possible to accumulate half of *s* in department I. In our scheme, on the other hand, the capitalists of department I consume more in order to ensure the accumulation of half of II*s*.

It is quite obvious why Marx chose department I rather than department II as the stationary axis in his numerical examples. If the scheme that we have presented here were to be extended for several more years, the systematic underaccumulation in department I and the more rapid accumulation in II, as a result of the lower composition of capital in II, would soon bar the way for further accumulation in department II, whereas in Marx's schemes, equilibrium can continue for a longer period. But in order to maintain the equilibrium, Marx also has to accept a different rate of consumption in department I than in department II, with the result that, over five years, the consumed surplus value in department I grows by 46.4 percent, whereas in department II it grows by 79 percent. In either case both department I and department II will consume and accumulate in different proportions—something that, generally speaking, does not occur under capitalism, with its equalizing tendencies.

But neither of these two schemes serves to illustrate capitalist reproduction when the organic composition of capital is rising, that is, when workers are being systematically replaced by machines and when, despite an absolute growth of *v* in both I and II, the constant capital of both departments grows steadily at an even faster rate.

In fact, if we take Marx's scheme for the first year and assume that owing to a rise in the organic composition of capital I*c* = 4,450 and I*v* = 1,050 (that is, that machines replace some of the workers who would have been employed had the organic composition of capital remained constant), then this would quickly upset the equilibrium, in the sense that, relatively speaking, department I's demand for articles of consumption falls off by an amount equal to the part of the additional capital that would have gone to increase v by 100 had the organic composition of capital remained the same but now goes to increase IIc by only 50.[12] The result of this is, first, that department II's market in I shrinks and, second, that it cannot obtain from department I an adequate amount of the additional means of production for its needs: if department I uses 50 of its surplus value to increase its constant capital, then department II receives that much less in means of production to increase IIc.

If, however, the organic composition of capital remains constant in department I and changes in department II, that is, if the ratio of c to v in department II grows, that will mean, all other conditions being equal, that IIc will outgrow the limits of possible proportionality of exchange of IIc for I$(v + s/2)$. Consequently, department I will not be able to satisfy fully department II's demand for means of production, and this in turn means that department I's market for articles of consumption will not be able to expand enough to absorb the goods sold by department II in I.

Finally, if the organic composition of capital rises in both departments at once, that is, if the demand for means of production increases in both, that will mean that the equilibrium will be upset at both ends at the same time. Although I$(v + s/2)$ will grow, it will grow more slowly than in Marx's schemes, which assumed a constant organic composition of capital, whereas IIc will increase more rapidly, owing to the systematic growth of the rate of increase of c as compared to the rate of increase of v (provided the capitalists in both departments consume at the same rate). In other words, the channel of proportionality, the passageway between Scylla and Charybdis through which IIc must pass to come into department I, will become increasingly narrower as I$(v + s/2)$ diminishes in relative terms (though it may grow in absolute figures), whereas the load on IIc will grow both relatively and absolutely along with a simultaneous relative and absolute growth of Ic.

Marx never completed his investigation of expanded reproduction under pure capitalism. By establishing the law of proportionality for simple reproduction, he made it possible to analyze expanded reproduction. But he examined expanded reproduction only under the conditions of a constant organic composition of capital and without any transfer of capital from one department to the other. Had he continued his work he inevitably would have had to introduce this new complicating condition, without which a scientific analysis of the problem remains incomplete, even though everything needed for solving it is present.*

Thus, we see that the numerical example with which Marx began his analysis of expanded reproduction does not serve to illustrate this process when the organic composition of capital is rising. But from our previous discussion we can see the type of changes that must be made in the arrangement of the individual parts of capital, as well as in the other conditions of the task.

If we begin by assuming that the organic composition of capital is rising in both departments, this will mean (1) a relative and absolute growth of IIc, that is, that department II's demand for means of production manufactured in department I will be greater than if the organic composition of capital were to remain constant; and (2) a relative decrease of I(v + s/x) ($s/2$ in Marx's scheme). Consequently, the growth of IIc, which increases both as a result of accumulation and as a result of the additional sum that comes from technological progress and the growth of c in relation to v, must be ensured by a corresponding increase of I(v + s/x). That is, there must be a growth of the consumption fund of department I, which prior to its exchange for IIc existed in the natural form of means of production (machines, fuel, raw materials) and is then exchanged for a growing IIc, which prior to exchange existed in the natural form of means of consumption produced in department II. When there is a general growth of production in both departments, when there is a general increase in the recruitment of new labor power, this may be accomplished only if I(v + s/x), which is decreasing in relative terms, grows in absolute figures—and in exact proportion to the absolute growth of IIc. It is possible to construct a numerical example from the other end as well, namely so that the growth of IIc would be adjusted to I(v + s/x). Translating this into the language of real economic relations, we shall in the first case be assuming that the growth of department I is determined by the growth of IIc, as its market base, and that the production of machines by more efficient machines is ultimately

*It is possible that among the photographs that Comrade Riazanov has taken of all the manuscripts of *Capital* we shall find something on this topic, too, since neither vol. II nor vol. III of *Capital*, in the form in which they were published by Engels, reproduces *the entirety* of Marx's legacy in the area under examination.

aimed at increasing and technologically rationalizing II*c*, that is, at cutting down on the expenditure of labor power involved in producing articles of consumption. In the second case, the other side of the problem is emphasized, namely, that department II adjusts to department I, or more specifically, to the volume of accumulation in department I: II*c* cannot grow any faster than the growth of I*c* will allow at any given moment. In other words, rationalization of II*c* has as its premise the rationalization of I*c*, which necessarily entails a certain relative reduction of *v*.

But from whatever direction we approach the problem, II*c* cannot—except during temporary fluctuations and crises—be reduced, because such a reduction would contradict the central premise of the problem: after all, II*c* must grow both as a result of the expansion of reproduction and as a result of the rise in the organic compositon of capital. We are left with the absolute increase in I($v + s/x$), which, given the relative decrease of *v* as compared to the rate of growth of I*c*, can occur only on the basis of an annual growth of the aggregate social capital invested in means of production, an annual growth that, moreover, proceeds at a faster pace than the growth of the social capital as a whole, not to mention the capital invested in the production of means of consumption.

We can easily satisfy ourselves that this is so by analyzing all the possible variations of the quantity I($v + s/x$). First of all, it must be made clear that transposing values between *v* and s/x has no effect for that particular year,* since the sum remains the same, and it is precisely the increase of the entire sum—as a whole—that is important. If we assume that, given the same volume of capital invested in department I, the amount accumulated can vary (and hence, of course, that the amount consumed also varies), then it is quite obvious that an increase in accumulation not only fails to solve the problem but, on the contrary, upsets the equilibrium even more, for a much larger share of the sum subtracted from s/x in one particular year goes to I*c* than to I*v*.

In such a case, the solution, as it were, consists in increasing s/x at the expense of accumulation. In other words, each year the capitalists of department I consume relatively more and more as com-

*We say "for that particular year" because in general an increase of *v* at the expense of the share consumed by the capitalists must in subsequent years lead to an increase in expanded reproduction of the means of production.

pared to the capitalists of department II, and each year the accumulated portion of I*s* is cut back. But it is quite obvious that equilibrium on this basis, though it may last for a year, or two, or three, is bound eventually to lead to a situation in which the retarded growth—and, later, the complete cessation of growth—of I*v* must result in a retardation and ultimately a halt in the growth of the entire sum of surplus value of department I—that is, to a drying-up of the spring from which the capitalists draw both their consumption fund and the reserves for raising the organic composition of capital in department I. Consequently, this method does not provide a long-term solution to the problem, because it violates the very precondition for solving the problem as a whole.

Thus, there remains only one way out, namely, for the entire capital of I to grow absolutely and at a faster rate than the capital of II, provided that the ratio of accumulation to capitalist consumption remains constant. But with fixed and given initial volumes of capital in departments I and II, the only way this can occur is if that capital is rearranged at the expense of department II. Hence, we arrive at the conclusion that, given a constant ratio of the consumed to the accumulated parts of surplus value and given a lower organic composition of capital in department II than in department I, there is no way to rearrange the capital between I and II so that proportionality would then automatically reestablish itself year after year. The problem cannot be solved on this basis. Consequently, the central premise of the problem requires a systematic transfer of capital from department II to department I.

But are we perhaps slaves of our own arithmetical examples? Might there not be an initial arrangement of capital between departments I and II such that the numerical superiority of the capital in I over the volume of capital in II would be so great that equilibrium would be attained by transferring capital from department I to department II, rather than from II to I? In view of this possibility, we can look with special interest at one of the simple arithmetical examples that Marx uses to illustrate his theses on expanded production under pure capitalism, namely, the last example in the chapter on accumulation and expanded reproduction in vol. II of *Capital.*[13] This example differs from his earlier schemes in that the organic composition of capital in department II is *just as high* as in department I. At the end of the third year, Marx obtains the following numerical scheme:

$$\begin{array}{l} \text{I. } 5{,}869c + 1{,}173v + 1{,}173s \\ \text{II. } 1{,}715c + 342v + 342s \end{array}$$

The reader can see from this scheme that $v + s/2$ is equal to 1,760, that is, it is 45 more than II*c*. Here, equilibrium may be attained only by transferring means of production from department I to department II. But if we add to this scheme a new condition—the rise in the organic composition of capital in both departments—then this excess of 45 may be disposed of both by the increase in II*c* and by the relative reduction of I*v* associated with the increase in I*c* as compared with Marx's scheme. Even in this example we will after a certain period probably encounter the same situation as in our analysis of Marx's first scheme, that is, we would once again be forced to transfer part of the excess capital from department II into department I. This is especially true since it is very difficult to imagine how the capital would be distributed when, with expanded reproduction there is at the outset a much more marked increase in reproduction in department I than in department II.*[14]

Consequently, we are obliged to try to solve the problem by establishing for each new year new proportions that will ensure equilibrium. For if we take one department as a base and adjust the distribution of capital within the other department to it, as the pivotal point, that could not give us any long-term solution to the problem. Therefore, at the end of each year we have first of all to set aside from the surplus value of both departments an amount necessary to maintain the level of production of the preceding year, and then to distribute the remaining surplus value of both departments, taken together, on the basis of the conditions of proportionality of the new year. Under the actual conditions of capitalist development, excluding, of course, periods of crisis, things proceed something like this: Allowing for "normal" bankruptcies in both departments, the general outlines of the preceding period's distribution of capital are retained; new capital accumulated in the preceding year through currency issues and new stock and bond issues is then distributed randomly, spontaneously, among the vari-

*Of course, if the organic composition of capital is higher in II than in I, the growth of the organic composition of capital cannot outstrip the growth of overproduction in I. But such a scheme does not correspond to the actual conditions of capitalist production.

ous branches by taking into account the interplay of market forces in each given case between departments I and II; and this new distribution of capital is adjusted again in the future through the market mechanism that regulates the whole system.

One may object to this thesis and say that capital cannot be transferred from one department to the other, because this capital already exists in definite forms of commodities *in natura*, and it is impossible, for example, to transfer means of consumption from department II to department I if department I needs means of production and not means of consumption.

This objection is undoubtedly of weight when it comes to forms of fixed capital that are already functioning in production. To take capital already invested in a railroad that has been rendered superfluous and transfer it to the production of gasoline engines or looms is a near impossibility unless one simply transfers the scrap metal, the bricks of dismantled buildings, and so on. But this difficulty also arises in transferring capital *within* each department. For example, it is even more difficult to convert an excess amount of soap into textiles, butter, and so on, or to convert coal into wool. The capitalist economy, however, is quite elastic, and, with a certain loss of value, it manages to solve all these problems—not by converting soap into butter, but first and foremost by redistributing labor power, and also by using the commodity stocks and fixed capital reserves—which are incompletely used under normal circumstances—without which no social economy can function normally. From this standpoint, the problem of transferring new capital from department II to department I is no more complex, since the economy as a whole usually functions with alternately expanding and contracting commodity reserves and the alternately expanding and contracting use of existing fixed capital. After all, it is simply a question here of the technique of shifting capitals—which are embodied in particular commodities—through the mechanism of monetary circulation. The investigator is here not at all bound by the fixed time intervals (for example, the yearly periods) that he himself has established for his schemes. These schemes are merely to illustrate the whole process and are not supposed to make the investigator a prisoner of his own arithmetical examples. As long as the proportions are analyzed in value terms, it simply comes down to the loss of a certain quantity of these values as a result of the transfer of capital from one branch to another.

To take a practical example, let us examine how it might be technically possible to transfer excess new capital from department II to department I for the purpose of establishing new proportions for the next working period, the next six months or new operating year. Let us assume that at the end of a given year the new capital which is to go for expanded reproduction and which is subject to redistribution on the basis of the new proportions between I and II is equal to 800 in department I and 350 in department II. Let us assume that with a rise in the organic composition of capital and with the old proportions of growth of consumption the absorption of the entire new capital in I ensures the absorption of 200 II*c*. II*v* thereby grows by 90. That leaves 60 yet to be placed. Not all 60 are transferred into department I, but rather 60 minus a certain quantity determined by the corresponding rise in production—and also, of course, in consumption—in department II. If the amount subtracted is equal to 10, then the whole problem comes down to department I absorbing a capital of 50 that is excess capital for department II and has the natural form of means of consumption. If we assume the existence of alternately expanding and contracting stocks under normal conditions of capitalist development, that is, during a period of noncrisis contraction of circulation and production, we can assume that means of consumption to the value of 50 are sold to replenish stocks for society's consumption fund; the money received for these goods is not returned to department II, but will, in the form of emissions, increase the money capital of department I. These stockpiled means of consumption together with the means of production drawn from department I's reserves will, on the basis of a more intensive use of fixed capital, make it possible to initiate additional expansion of production of the means of production in department I. This additional production creates a new additional fund of means of production, from which one part will go to replenish department I's depleted stocks and to augment the means of production already at work in department I as a result of previous expansion. For department II, on the other hand, this entire process amounts to a relative diminution of the expansion of the production of means of consumption and a lower rate of replacement of II*c* as compared with the previous year's pace. On the whole we shall have a relative reduction both of capital used and means of consumption produced in department II and a relative increase of capital applied and labor power exploited in department I, with an absolute and relative increase in the production of the means of production.

Of course, not all consumer goods can be stockpiled: means of consumption that perish quickly will either go to waste or be sold below their value. Such a loss of a certain portion of newly created values takes place continuously under unorganized production even during noncrisis periods, just as means of production continuously become obsolete as technology advances.

Similarly, capital may be transferred from department I to department II, although in this case the difficulties are considerably less, and the entire process demands from capitalism the loss of a smaller quantity of value.

More precisely, overproduction of the means of production means that I($v + s/x$) is greater than IIc. In terms of the material composition of capital, a transfer of capital from I to II means a transfer of means of production. But a transfer of means of production is precisely what II requires, because any increase of production in II means above all an increase in IIc. Thus, department II obtains the means of production it lacks from department I and pays for them with the money capital that, in the last analysis, flows from I into II. The problem of expanding production in II then comes down to increasing v from its own resources, that is, at the expense of the surplus value consumed by the capitalists of II. Since under developed capitalism IIc is always greater than IIv, a transfer of capital from I in the material form of means of production in itself solves a major part of the problem of expanding production in II. Additional workers, setting in motion additional means of production, create an additional fund of means of consumption to be used both for replenishing commodity reserves that were depleted in the beginning of the production process and for building stocks for the future, and also for increasing the fund of means of consumption to be used in exchange for additional means of production from department I so that IIc may be brought to its normal level. The expansion of production on precisely this scale solves the problem of proportionality in the case under examination.

We have examined the problem of transferring capital in what is technically the most difficult and economically the most unfavorable case possible. Under capitalism, however (except during periods of acute crisis), this problem is resolved much more simply. The equipment of enterprises in departments I and II is rarely kept running at full capacity. This is particularly true of heavy industry (one has only to take a ten-year average of idle blast furnaces in Europe and America, for example). Assuming a constant reserve of fixed capital in department I, the problem of transferring capital from II to I essentially comes down to transferring circulating capital, specifically, capital advanced for v, that is, for means of consumption for the additional workers in I. In general it should be noted that incomplete use of fixed capital is a very important instrument for achieving proportionality under capitalism, no less important than, for example, the industrial reserve army.

In investigating concrete capitalism, and especially in studying capitalist crises, we continually encounter not only overproduction in II but also, and much more frequently, overproduction of the means of production. Crises often begin right here, with overproduction in department I. This means that in the present case, if we disregard the factor of the distribution of effective consumer demand, the distribution of social capital spontaneously tends toward overdevelopment of I. But even if eight of every ten actual capitalist crises were to begin with overproduction in I, that would in no way contradict the general tendency in the distribution of productive forces that accompanies a rise in the organic composition of capital in a capitalist economy. If we were to plot the average growth curve of applied capital in both departments, along with the average growth of the aggregate social capital, then all three curves would rise, with II on the bottom, I on top, and the aggregate social capital somewhere between the two. Here the general line of development, the general tendency for the applied social capital to move from II to I, must never be confused with the external forms in which this whole process takes place. Certain tendencies in capitalist society often bear the external form of exactly the opposite processes. Our present case seems to be just such a situation. Since it is technically difficult to transfer capital from II to I and easier and less painful to shift it from I to II, the constant tendency of department I to grow not only absolutely but relatively as well is always bound to lead to expanded reproduction in department I outstripping that in II and to a subsequent equalization of proportions by a partial flow of capital from I into II. In view of the spontaneous expansion of the capitalist mode of production, it would seem mechanically easier to begin by sharply increasing department I and then later to correct the system by transferring part of the capital into II than to be compelled every six months, year, or whatever to grapple with the technical difficulties and loss of value involved in transferring capital from II to I. This is all the more true as the overwhelming majority of means of production—for example, all machine equipment, construction materials, and most fuels and raw materials—can be stored for long periods, whereas on the other hand a quite considerable category of means of consumption, food products, will not tolerate long storage. For this reason it would not be contradictory to state that the difficulties in transferring capital from II to I, given the continuously growing economic necessity of such a transfer, may lead to more frequent overproduction in I. It remains only to add in this connection that this fact throws light on just one, not all, of the conditions under which the equalization of proportions actually occurs in a capitalist economy.

In addition, there is one other circumstance that must be mentioned. Throughout our analysis we have assumed that all commodities are sold at their value. In view of the lengthy process of development during which fluctuations are evened out, and since our concern here is simply to explain the movement of an average curve, this approach is methodologically entirely correct. However, to analyze the whole process in greater detail we would also have to examine the action of the mechanism of the divergence of prices from values, that is, the mechanism that regulates the entire system of distribution of productive forces. In this case, a more or less prolonged deficit in means of production can lead to the transfer of a certain share of money capital from department II to department I, owing to a rise in prices of the means of production, with a more or less prolonged disruption in price-value relations. We shall not go into this process at this point, to avoid complicating our analysis of the general conditions of equilibrium when the organic composition of capital is rising. Such an analysis would be necessary only if we were to study the concrete economy of some particular country or to examine the separate sectors of world economy at a particular point in time.[15]

Thus, with a rise in the organic composition of capital and a broader capital structure in department II, the transfer of part of the excess capital from department II to department I is a general law of development of the productive forces. It operates quite independently of the fact that crises may more often be resolved precisely by temporary overproduction in department I—either for reasons we have already pointed out or for other reasons that have been brought out by research on capitalist crises.

It now remains for us to illustrate this entire process with a numerical example. In order to highlight most effectively how our present scheme differs from those of Marx in respect of the distribution of social capital—that is, to show what happens when this new condition, namely the rise in the organic composition of capital is added—we shall analyze Marx's own initial scheme of accumulation. We thus take an annual product distributed as follows:

$$\text{I. } 4{,}000c + 1{,}000v + 1{,}000s = 6{,}000$$
$$\text{II. } 1{,}500c + 750v + 750s = 3{,}000$$

As we have already stated, Marx attains equilibrium by assuming that half the surplus value of department I is accumulated and then adjusting the scale of accumulation and consumption in department II to fit I. As a result, the capitalists of department II have to consume relatively much more and accumulate less than the capitalists of I—a situation that, strictly speaking, could never occur in the long run under either actual or pure capitalism.

After rearranging the figures, Marx obtains the following scheme for the start of a new operating year:

$$\text{I. } 4{,}400c + 1{,}100v + 500 \text{ consumption fund}$$
$$\text{II. } 1{,}600c + 800v + 600 \text{ consumption fund}$$

In other words, in this case department II, in contrast to I, does not accumulate half its surplus value—it does not accumulate half of 750, but rather only 150—whereas the capitalists of II consume considerably more than the capitalists of I. Moreover, the organic composition of capital remains constant.

Our scheme, therefore, must introduce changes at these two points. First, the rate of consumption should be the same in both departments, and the entire accumulated social capital that remains should go to expand production. Secondly, the scheme should reflect the rise in the organic composition of capital. Our previous discussion should have made it quite clear that, all other conditions being equal, these two requirements cannot be met without transferring excess capital from department II to department I, which must then always develop more rapidly than II. Otherwise technical progress would not find its economic expression in a value analysis.

To construct a scheme that will satisfy these two conditions and reproduce not only the growth in the productively employed working population but also the growth of technology, we shall proceed as follows with Marx's initial scheme. First of all, like Marx, we shall use all the accumulated capital of I to expand production within that same department. This is by no means an arbitrary approach. As the level of technology rises, department I cannot develop on the basis of its own resources alone; thus it is all the more necessary that department I use all its own accumulated resources. In this case, all 500 must be distributed between I*c* and I*v*. As a first approximation to the desired scheme, let us then take the same distribution of capital for department I as does Marx, that is, 4,400*c* + 1,100*v* + 500 consumption fund.

Let us now turn to department II.

As was the case in department I, one-half the total surplus value created each year in II should be accumulated; in our example, this figure would be 375. This new capital must be used to (1) expand department II enough to bring it into equilibrium with the amount of capital that I has accumulated through its own resources (this means that II*c* must be equal to 1,100 + 500, that is, it must be equal to I*v* plus the consumption fund of the capitalists of I); (2) raise the organic composition of capital in I and II, which means additional development of all of I; and (3) increase production even more at the expense of the remaining surplus value of II.

These three conditions require that 100 of the 375 in new capital of department II be used to increase II*c* to meet the growth of I*v* + the consumption fund of the capitalists of I. As a result of this operation, another 50 will go to increase variable capital in II, which now, in this new approximation to the desired scheme, must be 750 + 50 = 800. We are left with 225 of the surplus value of II to be distributed. Assuming that the organic composition of capital is growing at a rate of 1 percent of the preceding year's constant capital, we obtain an increase of II*c* by 15 and an increase of I*c* by 40. Moreover, the increase of II*c* by 15 will, on the basis of the prevailing distribution of productive forces, call for an increase of I*v* by 15 and, finally, of the constant capital of I by 15 × 4 = 60. That is, the increase of the constant capital of department II by 15 must be ensured by developing the entire production apparatus of I in the appropriate proportions. A total of 130 of the 225 II*s* has now been absorbed in this manner. The remaining 95 are then distributed over the entire production apparatus as follows: 7.3 to increase variable capital in department II; 14.6 to increase constant capital in the same department; 14.6 to increase variable capital in department I; and 58.4 to increase constant capital in department I. Summing up, we see that the total excess capital to be transferred from II to I is 188. The whole scheme will look like this:[16]

$$\begin{aligned} &\text{I. } 4{,}558.4c + 1{,}129.6v + 500 \text{ consumption fund} = 6{,}188 \\ &\text{II. } 1{,}629.6c + 807.3v + 375 \text{ consumption fund} = \underline{2{,}811.9} \\ &\qquad\qquad\text{or, after rounding off: } 9{,}000 \end{aligned}$$

Our scheme will differ from that of Marx, which we presented above, in the following respect. As a result of the transfer to I of part of the capital of II, both the functioning capital and the level of total production in department I will be greater than in Marx's scheme. They will be greater in department II as well, but only because in Marx's scheme the capitalists of II consume considerably more than those in I, insofar as such an arrangement of figures in his scheme ensured the arithmetical equilibrium of expanded reproduction. In our scheme the capitalists in department II, like those in department I, consume half their surplus value; that is, the rate of consumption is the same in I and II. This leads to an increase of both II*c* and II*v* as compared to Marx's scheme in addition to the growth of II*c* resulting from the rise in the organic composition of capital.

But department II grows more slowly than department I, and this reflects the rise in the level of technology in both departments.

Thus, at the end of the first operating year, our rearrangement of capital yields the following result:

$$\begin{aligned} &\text{I. } 4{,}558.4c + 1{,}129.6v + 1{,}129.6s = 6{,}817.6 \\ &\text{II. } 1{,}629.6c + 807.3v + 807.3s = 3{,}244.2 \end{aligned}$$

We see from these figures that department I is 217.6 more than Marx's 6,600, and department II 44.2 more[17] than his 3,200.

Similarly, successive years will necessarily result in a steady increase of accumulation in II, over and above what it actually requires, along with a necessary and systematic deficit of capital in department I.[18] There is nothing mysterious in this whole phenomenon, because in our scheme (as in Marx's) the organic composition of capital in department II is lower than in department I. Here *v* is greater in comparison to *c* than in department I, and that is why, all other conditions being equal, accumulation is faster in II. If, on the other hand, the organic composition of capital in department I had been lower than in department II, then, with the same original volumes of total social capital, we would have had at the end of the first year, as well as thereafter, *systematic overaccumulation in department I and underaccumulation in department II.* It would not be difficult to show this with a concrete numerical example. Similarly, if we were to increase the organic composition of capital in department II so that it was only slightly lower than in department I, then the amount of surplus value that would be subject to transfer from II to I would be considerably less than the 188 in our example. Here it might have been possible to find a numerical example in which the whole process of transferring capital from department II to department I would have served only to increase the organic composition of capital in society.

Obviously, however, it was by no means accidental that in most of his schemes Marx used a higher organic composition of capital in department I than in department II. *Such is the actual developmental tendency of capitalism itself,* a tendency that will also be carried over to the socialist economy, provided that in the future the exhaustion of the earth's fertile lands does not lead to a situation in which further development of social production changes things in this area. However, a more detailed investigation of this problem is not part of our task.

Using the same initial base as in our scheme, we might have portrayed the process of further development of production differently: from the very outset we might have transferred a greater volume of capital from II to I than we actually did, and then introduced correctives by retransferring part of the capital from I to II. This happens quite often under actual capitalism. But, as we have already mentioned above, such a path of development of social production in no way alters the general tendency that we have established: if the organic composition of capital in society grows, and if in the initial schemes the organic composition of capital is higher in department I than in department II, there will be not only an absolute but also a relative growth in the volume of applied capital in department I.

Expanded Reproduction Under Concrete Capitalism

Our analysis of expanded reproduction under pure capitalism, as well as the analysis of simple reproduction under concrete capitalism, has already provided us with all the prerequisites for an abstract theoretical study of the conditions of equilibrium under concrete capitalism, that is, under a mixed economy of capitalism and petty commodity production. As in our investigation of simple reproduction under concrete capitalism, we shall be dealing here with two sectors in the economy with two departments in each sector, and we shall be using the same arbitrary terminology as before. Hence, we shall have the following algebraic scheme:

KI. $c + v + s$
KII. $c + v + s$
PI. c + consumption fund
PII. c + consumption fund*

In our investigation of the process of expanded reproduction in such a system we have quite a large number of theoretically and practically conceivable cases that should be subjected to analysis. We shall, however, take up only three of the most typical of these cases, those that best characterize the development of concrete capitalism and are most important for the further study of equilibrium in the Soviet system of economy.

The first case occurs when the capitalist sector is developing whereas, on the one hand, the volume of production in the petit bourgeois sector is decreasing both relatively and absolutely, and, on the other hand, social production as a whole is on the rise. The second case is when the capitalist sector develops but the volume of production in the petit bourgeois sector remains stable. Finally, the third case occurs when there is simultaneous growth of production in both sectors. In all three cases we assume that the organic composition of capital in the capitalist sector is rising.

We do not have to spend much time on the second case at this point. If the volume of production in the petit bourgois sector is stable and only the capitalist sector is developing, then all the important changes in the system of proportionality will originate in the capitalist sector. If there is not only a stable volume of production throughout the petit bourgeois sector taken as a whole but also constant proportions in the distribution of the productive forces

---

*If there is expanded reproduction in the petit bourgeois sector, we must have c + consumption fund + accumulation fund.

between its two departments, then this case can offer nothing new for our study: the entire analysis is then shifted to the capitalist sector, from which all changes in the equilibrium of the system must originate. The only situation that might prove interesting is when the volume of production in the petit bourgeois sector remains stable in terms of total value, but the distribution of productive forces between its two departments changes. In other words, if department I grows by a certain amount, then department II shrinks by the same amount, and vice versa. In the first case, growth in the production of means of production in the petit bourgeois sector at the expense of the production of means of consumption inevitably leads to the growth of the consumption fund of PI. This latter fund has the material form of means of production and is subject to exchange for means of consumption. Hence, a decrease of PII*c* must lead to an increased demand by PI for means of consumption produced in the capitalist sector. But this in turn requires that additional means of production from department I of the petit bourgeois sector find an additional market in the capitalist sector. In practical terms this means, for example, that an additional quantity of flax, cotton, hides, or wool of peasant production must find an additional market in the capitalist sector and that department II of the capitalist sector must supply additional means of consumption to department I of the petit bourgeois sector.

In the converse case, that is, when PII grows at the expense of PI, department II of the petit bourgeois sector must increase its constant capital by a certain additional amount. Failing to find this constant capital in department I of the petit bourgeois sector, PII must buy these means of production in department I of the capitalist sector and find there an additional market for its own additional means of consumption.

Let us now turn to another case of paramount interest for understanding the process of expanded reproduction under actual capitalism—what we labeled the "first case." Here the capitalist sector is in a state of more or less rapid development and is ousting petit bourgeois production from the spheres of production of both means of production and means of consumption. In reality this would mean, for example, that large-scale capitalist farming is replacing petty production in agriculture, whereas large-scale capitalist factories are ousting craft and artisan production in industry.

As an initial scheme, let us take an economic year that closed with the total annual product distributed as follows:

Capitalist Sector

$$\left.\begin{array}{l}\text{KI. } 2{,}000c + 500v + 500s = 3{,}000 \\ \text{KII. } 1{,}200c + 400v + 400s = 2{,}000\end{array}\right\} 5{,}000$$

Petit Bourgeois Sector

$$\left.\begin{array}{l}\text{PI. } 1{,}500c + 1{,}500 \text{ consumption fund} = 3{,}000 \\ \text{PII. } 1{,}050c + 2{,}100 \text{ consumption fund} = 3{,}150\end{array}\right\} 6{,}150$$

In this scheme the overall volume of production in the capitalist sector is less than in the petit bourgeois sector. The organic composition of capital in department I of the capitalist sector is higher than in department II.

The volume of production in department I of the precapitalist sector is almost equal to that in department II, but the ratio of constant capital to the consumption fund in the two departments differs. This is because petty craft and petty peasant production of means of production usually require the application of a greater volume of constant capital than does petit bourgeois production of means of consumption, mainly in the form of raw materials. In the present example, this ratio has, of course, been arbitrarily set, using proportions in PII that would approximate those prevailing in nonintensive petty peasant production.

For the sake of simplicity, our scheme does not include mutual exchange of values between the corresponding departments of both sectors—that is, exchange, let us say, between peasant-produced raw materials on the one hand and machines from the capitalist sector on the other. Or, to take another example, exchange of peasant grain and butter for capitalist-produced cloth and footwear. In its present form, therefore, the scheme characterizes only the proportionality of exchange between *the different departments of the two sectors.* As we have already demonstrated above in the scheme for simple reproduction, internal exchange between corresponding departments of both sectors—provided it is mutual exchange of equal values—does not affect proportionality within the system as a whole, *since we are abstracting from an analysis of the natural composition of the commodities subject to exchange and are analyzing them exclusively in value terms.*

Even a cursory glance at the scheme tells the reader that the capitalist sector has a deficit in means of production. Department I has at its disposal a total of only 750 with which to replace 1,200 II*c*. The deficit is covered from department I of the petit bourgeois sector, which exchanges 1,500 in means of production for a corresponding amount of means of consumption. Of this, 1,050 goes to replace the constant capital of department II of the petit bourgeois sector, and the other 450 to make up the deficit in means of production in KII. On the other hand, PI receives 1,050 in means of consumption from its own sector and 450 from department II of the capitalist sector.

In examining this scheme one must always bear in mind that reducing the entire proportionality of exchange between the capitalist and petit bourgeois sectors to the simple exchange of 450 in means of consumption of capitalist production for 450 in means of production from the petit bourgeois sector is merely an abstraction fcr the purposes of a value analysis, and that for the moment we cannot overstep the bounds of this analysis. In actual fact, of course, KI buys both means of consumption and means of production in P, that is, not only cotton and hides of peasant production, for example, but grain as well. KII, on the other hand, buys not only means of production in P but also exchanges means of consumption in definite proportions with PII. PI and PII likewise buy in both capitalist departments. However when we strike out the mutually offsetting exchanges of values between the same departments of the different sectors of the economy, the problems of proportionality will come down to what is expressed in the scheme: the exchange of 450 in means of consumption from KII for 450 in means of production from PI.

Let us now look at the whole scheme in motion. We shall be assuming throughout that: (1) half the surplus value is accumulated annually in the capitalist sector; (2) the organic composition of capital grows in both departments of the capitalist sector at the rate of 1 percent of the previous year's constant capital; and (3) in the petit bourgeois sector, on the other hand, reproduction declines at the rate of 2 percent per year.

Under these initial conditions the aggregate social capital used in production will be rearranged as follows to begin a new operating year.[19]

Capitalist Sector

KI. 2,204c + 546v + 250 consumption fund
KII. 1,353c + 447v + 200 consumption fund

If, as a result of a general decline of production in the petit bourgeois sector the volume of its applied capital drops by 2 percent in both departments (if, in other words, capitalist competition forces a number of enterprises to cut back or totally halt production), then we will obtain the following figures:

Precapitalist Sector

PI. 1,470c + 1,470 consumption fund = 2,940
PII. 1,029c + 2,058 consumption fund = 3,087[20]
} 6,027

Now if we compare these two schemes from the standpoint of proportionality, we see that in order for department II of the capitalist sector to replace its constant capital it has to exchange 557 in its means of consumption within the petit bourgeois sector; however, the petit bourgeois sector has only 1,470 – 1,029 = 441 to offer.

The result is (1) a deficit of 116 in the means of production needed to replace KII and (2) the lack of markets for the sale of an equal amount in capitalist-produced means of consumption.

There are two possible ways out of this dilemma: (1) a transfer of capital from KII to KI, that is, the most difficult and unprofitable path for capitalism, and one that in this case would not even be fully effective, since KI requires considerably more than KII has to offer in order to reestablish proportionality; (2) an adjustment of the petit bourgeois sector to the needs of capitalist development through internal redistribution between PI and PII; or (3) use of both methods at the same time. Given the dominant role of capitalist economy and the subordinate status of the petit bourgeois sector, it is in general easier to adjust the petit bourgeois sector to the capitalist one. Provided that we retain our basic premise—that the petit bourgeois sector is cutting back its total annual reproduction—this adjustment can generally be accomplished in two ways; either the entire reduction falls on PII, whereas PI maintains the same volume of production, or PII is not only cut back by the entire 2 percent drop in production of the petit bourgeois sector, but in addition there is a rearrangement within P so that PI increases at the expense of PII, which is already declining in any case.

In our example the first method cannot achieve our goal, because the disproportion is too great: it cannot be overcome simply by stopping the drop in production in PI and shifting the entire decline in production within the petit bourgeois sector onto PII.

Let us assume that production in the capitalist sector continues to develop at its old rate, despite the previous year's disproportion. We shall assume that the disproportion has somehow been temporarily eliminated. As long as we are not dealing with the world economy as a whole, but—let us say—with the economy of a particular country, this can be achieved in the present case by exporting the excess means of consumption and importing means of production for the same sum.

At the end of the year the capitalist sector will look like this:[21]

$$\left.\begin{array}{l}\text{KI. } 2{,}204c + 546v + 546s = 3{,}296 \\ \text{KII. } 1{,}353c + 447v + 447s = 2.247\end{array}\right\} 5{,}543$$

Arranging the capital for the new year (that is, the third year after the initial scheme) yields the following:

$$\begin{array}{l}\text{KI. } 2{,}426c + \quad 596v + \quad 273 \text{ consumption fund*} \\ \text{KII. } 1{,}524c + 499.5v + 223.5 \text{ consumption fund}\end{array}$$

If we now cut down the overall volume of production in the petit bourgeois sector by 2 percent such that the entire reduction falls on department II, we obtain

$$\left.\begin{array}{l}\text{PI. } 1{,}470c + 1{,}470 \text{ consumption fund} = 2{,}940^{22} \\ \text{PII. } \quad 989c + 1{,}978 \text{ consumption fund} = 2{,}967\end{array}\right\} 5{,}907$$

As things now stand, KII's deficit in means of production is equal to 655 − 481 = 174.[23]

Granted, this deficit will be smaller than the one that would have resulted had both departments of P cut back production in the same proportions; nevertheless the deficit is still very large. To reestablish equilibrium, capital will have to be rearranged within P. If to attain that end capital is rearranged so that total production in PI is increased by 210 and production in PII de-

*The difference of 1 from the preceding scheme results from rounding-off fractions.

creased by the same amount, then with the same ratio of constant capital to consumption fund in P we will obtain the following scheme for petit bourgeois production:

$$\left.\begin{array}{l}\text{PI. } 1{,}575c + 1{,}575 \text{ consumption fund} = 3{,}150 \\ \text{PII. } 919c + 1{,}838 \text{ consumption fund} = 2{,}757\end{array}\right\} 5{,}907$$

As we see, the volume of production in the P sector in this second version remains the same as in the first; that is, it has declined 2 percent from the previous year. On the other hand, however, the internal rearrangement of productive forces within the petit bourgeois sector leads to a diminution of the production of means of consumption and to an increase in the production of means of production to the extent that the remaining means of production available for exchange with KII already amount to 656, whereas KII needs to buy means of production and sell its own products for 655.

Thus, we have reestablished the equilibrium that was upset by the too-rapid growth of KII given both a relatively slower growth of KI from the standpoint of proportionality within the capitalist sector and a reduction of PI from the previous year.

What might this whole process mean in practical terms?

(1) The absolute decrease of PII by 2 percent would mean the ousting of peasant production of means of consumption by capitalist production of the same articles, that is, a drop in the peasantry's acreage under grain crops intended for individual consumption and a decrease in the production of eggs, butter, and so on.

(2) The rearrangement of productive forces between PI and PII would mean an increase in flax, hemp, and cotton acreage at the expense of cereal grains; increased expenditures on feed for livestock supplying KII with hides, wool, and so on; and expanded cultivation of potatoes for further processing. During the development of capitalism, this process has been evident in cases where the expansion of urban industry heightens the demand for peasant raw materials but peasant production of grain diminishes, giving way to capitalist grain factories or large-scale capitalist farms.

It is quite obvious that for capitalism a rearrangement within the petit bourgeois sector is a very important means of attaining proportionality within the system as a whole, if this rearrangement simultaneously satisfies the requirements of proportionality in the material elements of commodity exchange as well. If we had been dealing with overproduction in KII under pure capitalism, that is, with the equilibrium of a self-contained unit, the only possible way for the society's economy to attain proportionality would have been at worst an industrial crisis or at best a transfer of capital from KII to KI, an alternative that often entails a loss of value and a temporary retardation of the whole process of expanded reproduction.

In addition, however, our example is a striking demonstration of the incorrectness of Rosa Luxemburg's theory on the role of the petit bourgeois milieu in the development of capitalism. In our scheme the petit bourgeois sector is drawn into capitalist circulation; but not only does it not expand, it contracts. And yet this in no way hinders the growth of total social production. In fact, the initial scheme sets total annual production at 5,000 for the capitalist sector and 6,150 for the petit bourgeois sector, or 11,150 in all. At the end of the first year—although the petit bourgeois sector has cut back its production by 2 percent—the pace of accumulation in the capitalist sector more than offsets this process, resulting in a total annual production of 11,570.[24] In the last scheme, if we take the result at the end of the year, the capitalist sector has already overtaken the petit bourgeois sector in terms of the total value of its production: 6,141 versus 5,907 for the petit bourgeois sector, bringing total social production to 12,048.[25]

Thus, it is entirely possible for capitalist reproduction to expand while precapitalist economic forms are declining. It is entirely possible for this to occur without any transfer of capital from one department of the capitalist sector to the other, provided that the necessary rearrangement of productive forces takes place within the petit bourgeois sector. Nor would it be much trouble to construct a scheme in which the petit bourgeois sector was reduced to such an extent that the capitalist sector could expand its own departments without requiring major rearrangements within the petit bourgeois sector. To do this, the capitalist sector's exchange deficit against the petit bourgeois sector would have to be offset by an appropriate additional expansion of production within the capitalist sector itself.

It must also be noted that it is in general easier, and involves the loss of fewer values, to rearrange within P than within the capitalist sector. For example, the peasant economy can increase its production of industrial crops at the expense of cereal grains without having to change its working livestock or, in most cases, its implements. It simply changes the seed and increases expenditures on fertilizer, in addition to using more animal feed for intensifying livestock production.

The degree to which such a rearrangement of the productive forces is possible from the standpoint of the material composition of the commodities whose production is to be increased is another question entirely. In the present case, if the deficit of KII*c* extends not only to cotton, flax, hemp, hides, seeds for the oil-extraction industry, sugar beets, potatoes for processing into alcohol and syrup, etc., but also to machines, coal, and oil, then the problem of proportionality cannot be fully solved by a rearrangement within the petit bourgeois sector alone. Thus, the deficit of 174[26] in means of production that was discussed above would have to be overcome when capital is distributed for the next year's production, partly by rearranging capital within P and partly by transferring capital from KII to KI. However, this is already another question, one that does not concern a value analysis of proportionality and takes the investigation on to the problem of a combined value-*in natura* analysis of the problems of equilibrium or, in other words, to a study of concrete economy.

Let us now look at our same numerical examples, but this time using a 2 percent annual rise, rather than fall, in production in P. We shall then have the following arrangement for the first year:

Capitalist Sector

KI. 2,204c + 546v + 250 consumption fund

KII. 1,353c + 447v + 200 consumption fund

Petit Bourgeois Sector

PI. 1,530c + 1,530 consumption fund

PII. 1,071c + 2,142 consumption fund

In the present case KII's deficit in means of production and the shortage of demand for means of consumption of capitalist production is 98. This means that from the standpoint of the market the disproportion is somewhat less, because as a result of the general increase of PI, its demand for means of consumption grows faster than their supply. Since PI's demand is not met, it buys more from KII, that is, the growth of craft production and the growth of peasant production of industrial crops is accompanied by an increased demand for textiles, footwear, sugar, and other items of capitalist production.

From the standpoint of satisfying the KII's need for means of production, all this means an increased supply of these goods from PI; in other words, KII receives more cotton, hides, flax, and so on from the petit bourgeois sector.

Proportionality is attained here in the same way as we explained in the case above: by transferring capital from KII to KI, by rearranging production between PI and PII so as to increase PI, or by a combination of the two methods. The difference between this example and our first scheme is that if the entire burden of rearranging production is shifted onto the petit bourgeois sector, it takes a less extensive—and hence considerably easier—transfer of productive forces from PII to PI to attain proportionality.

Let us now examine the scheme for the equilibrium of actual capitalism where, instead of overproduction of means of consumption and deficit in constant capital, the capitalist sector has an overproduction of means of production and a deficit in means of consumption—a situation that, as we shall see below, once again leads us automatically to a deficit in means of production.

To obtain a suitable numerical example and yet introduce as few changes as possible in the figures we have already presented, we can take the same volume of social production and either (1) reduce the volume of capital used in department II of the capitalist sector while increasing production in department I by the same amount or (2) sharply raise the organic composition of capital in KII without altering the total volume of capital used in the capitalist sector as a whole. Although in the latter case the disproportion will be *even greater in the beginning* because of the sharp increase in II*c*, it will quickly disappear owing to the sharp relative drop in accumulation in KII. Let us take an example. If we set the ratio of variable to constant capital in department II of the capitalist sector at 1:6, we shall have 1,500*c* + 250*v* + 250*s*.[27] This means that as accumulation continues, it will not only have a smaller II_v to draw on in the very beginning–that is, 250 instead of 400–but also, for this very reason, the annual deductions from the accumulated surplus value to increase II*c* will yield a relatively much slower growth of *v*. This slower growth of II*v* will eventually slow down the tempo of II*c*'s growth as well. This will mean that KII*c* will in the future grow more slowly than KI(v + s/x) or, in other words, that each year there will be a heavier influx of KI's excess means of production onto the petit bourgeois market. Equilibrium will then be attained either by a transfer of capital into KII, or by the reduction of PI and the growth of PII. We shall not examine this case in greater detail at this point. Though it is theoretically conceivable, it is of little relevance for illustrating the development of actual capitalism, where the organic composition of capital in department II is usually lower, not higher, than in I.

Let us therefore turn our attention to the first method: that is, we keep the same total annual production in the capitalist sector, round off the figure for annual production in the petit bourgeois sector, leave the organic composition of capital in KII lower than in KI, and merely increase the volume of capital employed in KI at the expense of KII. If we reduce the annual production in KII by 600 and increase KI by an equal amount, we obtain the following initial scheme:

$$\left.\begin{array}{ll}\text{KI.} & 2{,}400c + 600v + 600s = 3{,}600 \\ \text{KII.} & 840c + 280v + 280s = 1{,}400\end{array}\right\} 5{,}000$$

Correspondingly, in the petit bourgeois sector we shall have a considerable rearrangement between departments I and II, with PII increased at the expense of PI. Given a total annual production of 6,100 and leaving the other conditions unchanged, the equalization of proportionality of exchange with the capitalist sector requires the following new arrangement in P:

$$\left.\begin{array}{l}\text{PI. } 1{,}184c + 1{,}184 \text{ consumption fund} = 2{,}368 \\ \text{PII. } 1{,}244c + 2{,}488 \text{ consumption fund} = 3{,}732\end{array}\right\} 6{,}100$$

[28]

Thus we now have in the capitalist sector an overproduction of means of production by 60. These excess 60 in means of production in the capitalist sector go to make up the deficit of PII_c, which cannot be covered in the petit bourgeois sector. PII thereby serves as an additional market for the placement of the 60. KI, in its turn, uses this sum to buy the 60 worth of means of consumption from PII that it could not obtain from depart-partment II of its own sector.

Let us now look at the way in which the conditions of proportionality will change if at the outset of the new operating year in the capitalist sector the surplus value is rearranged as usual, half of it being set aside for accumulation, whereas the petit bourgeois sector begins the operating year with a 2 percent expansion of production in each of its departments.

If we capitalize half of the surplus value in both departments (that is, 300 in I and 140 in II), deduct an amount equal to 1 percent of the previous year's constant capital to increase the organic composition of capital (that is, 24 for department I and 8.4 for department II), and then divide the remainder of the surplus value of the two departments in proportion to their organic compositions of capital, we obtain an increase of Iv by 55.2 and an increase of IIv by 32.9. The scheme as a whole will then be as follows:[29]

KI. 2,644.8c + 655.2v + 300 consumption fund
KII. 947c + 312.9v + 140 consumption fund

We thus have an excess of means of production in the capitalist sector in the amount of 655.2 + 300 − 947, or 8.2.

With a 2 percent rise in production, the figures for the petit bourgeois sector will be as follows:*

PI. 1,207c + 1,207 consumption fund
PII. 1,269c + 2,538 consumption fund

In the petit bourgeois sector we shall have a deficit of 62 in means of production. This deficit is somewhat higher than the deficit shown by the initial scheme for sector P, because PIIc, being larger than the consumption fund of PI to begin with, grows slightly faster than the latter.[30] However, whereas in the earlier case the entire deficit in means of production in PII could be made good from the capitalist sector, that is, from what remained after the exchange of KI($v + s/2$) for KIIc, this remainder now amounts to only 8.2. Thus, we end up with a situation in which the expansion of department II of the capitalist sector replaces department II of the petit bourgeois sector both as a market for the sale of KI's production and as a supplier to KI of articles of consumption. As a result, PII cannot replace 62 − 8.2, or 53.8, of its con-

*For the sake of brevity, we shall not in any of our examples repeat the schemes for the petit bourgeois sector at the end of the year, that is, with the addition of the accumulation fund to c + consumption fund. As in Marx's schemes for expanded reproduction, we shall establish proportionality only between the constant capital replaced for that year and the consumption fund ($c + v + s/x$), and at the beginning of the operating year we shall distribute the accumulation fund as we draw up the scheme for reproduction for this new year. In general, the petit bourgeois sector in the present case will be as follows at the end of the year:

PI. 1,184c + 1,184 consumption fund + 47 accumulation fund
PII. 1,244c + 2,488 consumption fund + 74 accumulation fund

stant capital. On the one hand, it lacks a market for that amount of its own goods, and on the other hand, it suffers a corresponding shortage of means of production in their material form.

Equilibrium can be restored either by cutting back production throughout PII or by transferring productive forces from PII to PI in the following year.

We can see all the conditions of proportionality of the case under consideration even more clearly if we ignore the disproportion and continue on to the next year, that is, if we let the disproportion develop further.

Thus, constructing the next year's scheme on the basis of the production results of the previous year, we obtain the following figures for the distribution of productive forces:

Annual Product in the Capitalist Sector

KI. $2{,}644.8c + 655.2v + 655.2s$
KII. $947c + 312.9v + 312.9s$

The rearrangement for the next year's production on this basis will be the following: [31]

KI. $2{,}912.2c + 715v$ + 327.6 consumption fund
KII. $1{,}066.7c + 349.5v$ + 156.4 consumption fund

Petit Bourgeois Sector

PI. $1{,}231c$ + 1,231 consumption fund
PII. $1{,}294c$ + 2,588 consumption fund

An analysis of this result shows that in this year the capitalist sector not only has no excess means of production to sell in the petit bourgeois sector, but itself has a deficit of means of production equal to 24.1. Nor can KII obtain these means of production needed to replace its constant capital, from PI, because the petit bourgeois sector in its turn shows a deficit in means of production, and an overproduction of means of consumption. Here department II of this sector fails, on the one hand, to find a market for 63 worth of its means of consumption, which have to reproduce the part of constant capital that it lacks, and, on the other hand, to find means of production for an equal amount. We thus have throughout the whole of social production a goods famine in means of production to the amount of 63 + 24.1 = 87.1.

This situation (not counting the slight discrepancy between the growth rates of PII*c* and the consumption fund of PI) is due to two factors: first, to the rise in the organic composition of capital in both departments of the capitalist sector, and second, to the more rapid rate of accumulation in KII, which resulted from the lower organic composition of capital as compared to KI. Here, then, as the process of expanded reproduction develops mechanically, the tendency of a capitalist economy that we pointed out above—the tendency toward systematic overaccumulation in branches with a low organic composition of capital, that is, in the present case in the sphere of capitalist production of means of consumption—forces its way to the fore. This in turn compels society, whether more or less elastically or through a crisis, to redistribute its productive forces by increasing the capital invested in the sphere of production of means of production.

This last example, which is characteristic of capitalist economy during its period of development, is of special interest to us for the additional reason that it also reproduces in part (although in an overly general and abstract form) the processes that we, *mutatis mutandis*, can currently observe in the economy of the USSR, insofar as we study that economy from the standpoint of economic equilibrium in the system as a whole.

Before concluding this part of our investigation of accumulation and expanded reproduction under concrete capitalism, we would like to say a few words about one other problem. Now that we have examined the question of the transfer of capital from KII to KI, we might look briefly at the transfer of elements of production from the petit bourgeois to the capitalist sector. Disregarding all forms of noneconomic pressure that large-scale capital and its state might exercise on petit bourgeois production (for example, the tax system) and restricting ourselves to the sphere of purely economic relations and processes, we find the most interesting and most important form of the transfer of capital from the petit bourgeois sector to the capitalist sector to be the latter's use of petit bourgeois money accumulation.

From the standpoint of the exchange of values, this accumulation of money is a series of sales without corresponding purchases; and the money from this operation will later be put at the disposal of capitalist production. Let us assume that the total volume of capital used in petit bourgeois sector does not grow, but that consumption systematically exceeds the consumption fund. Or let us assume that production does expand, but not enough to absorb the entire surplus product, with the result that, let us say, 2 percent annually of the entire consumption fund (in the original scheme of our last example, 2% of [1,184 + 2,488], or 73.4)[32] represents partly the sale of means of production of petit bourgeois origin and partly the sale of means of consumption, without corresponding purchases. If the money from these sales is placed in banks and savings banks or used to purchase industrial bonds, then all these resources in money form will accrue, either through the banking system or directly, through subscriptions to industrial shares, to the capitalist sector of the economy and will serve as a source of further purchases from the petit bourgeois sector without any sales in return. If we disregard the partial return of values in the form of interest, the whole process, seen from an economic point of view, comes down to a one-way flow of values from the petit bourgeois sector into the capitalist sector—all under the cover of mutual financial and money relations. If PI sells means of production—for example, cotton and hides—to the capitalist sector without making purchases from the latter; if PII sells grain, meat, and butter without making purchases in return; and if the money obtained from these sales serves for the capitalist sector as a source of new purchases without sales, then the capitalist sector receives as a result of this whole process additional resources for its own expansion: in the present case, it increases its constant and variable capital without having to draw on its own accumulated resources. Both departments of K receive additional means of consumption for increasing their variable capital, as well as additional means of production for increasing their constant capital. This reinforcement of the resources of capitalist accumulation from without, that is, from sources outside the capitalist sector, plays a very important role in overcoming disproportions both in the case where the capitalists lack the resources for increasing their variable capital and where the expansion of production, required by the whole course of accumulation of the previous year, encounters a shortage of new capital in the material form of means of production—means of production that, moreover, can be produced in petty production.

Thus, if the rearrangement of productive forces within the petit bourgeois sector—a rearrangement dictated to that sector by the mechanism of the capitalist market—serves within certain limits as an essential element for attaining equilibrium in the capitalist sector of the economy, then on the other hand, petit bourgeois accumulation, although a very important factor facilitating capitalist expanded reproduction, also increases the elasticity of the entire mechanism for attaining economic equilibrium.

* * *

After this brief investigation into the conditions of economic equilibrium under concrete capitalism, we are equipped to pass on to a value analysis of equilibrium when the economy has stopped developing, and further, when the productive forces of society suffer a decline, and finally, when there is a turn back toward reconstruction—in short, we can now begin a general examination of the process of declining reproduction. Several countries of postwar Western Europe provide a striking contemporary example of an economy of this type. But the very nature of our topic compels us at this point to examine what happens when we change certain of the conditions that in our foregoing investigation were kept constant: we have to examine the influence of changes in the area of productivity of labor, the rate of exploitation, changes in the ratio of consumed to accumulated surplus value, and several other aspects of the problem.

EDITOR'S NOTES

[1] By "simple commodity economy," Preobrazhensky means an economy of petty producers who own and work their capital themselves. Although market exchange exists, it is not fully developed as under modern capitalism. Rather a significant portion of the product of each producer is produced not for exchange but is consumed *in natura*, either productively (as means of production) or individually (as means of consumption).

[2] Methodologically this follows from Preobrazhensky's theoretical approach to the Soviet economy, which held that it was governed by two regulators of economic activity, the law of value and the law of primitive socialist accumulation. In the case of "concrete capitalism," Preobrazhensky is making a similar point both here and in the ensuing discussion. The economic activity of the petty producers is organized differently than under capitalism, obeying different constraints and exhibiting different regularities. These differences must necessarily be reflected in any analysis using reproduction schemes, since even from a quantitative point of view changes in the magnitudes of production in the capitalist and precapitalist sectors will have different causes and must therefore be examined separately. The object of Preobrazhensky's

investigation, then, is to study how these sectors interrelate with one another as distinct, historically defined formations.

[3] The concept of nonequivalent exchange is central to Preobrazhensky's writings of the 1920's. Briefly, it refers to the fact that one hour's labor expended in the capitalist sector will yield a greater mass of the same types of use values than one hour's labor in precapitalist production. In terms of values (or exchange value), where we must take into account the labor that is socially necessary, the precapitalist sector will be expending more labor on its production than is socially required, so that in exchange between the two sectors the product of one hour's labor in the petty commodity sector would exchange, for example, for the product of 15 minutes' labor expended within capitalist industry. Conversely, if—as Preobrazhensky assumes here for convenience of exposition—they each exchanged the product of one hour's labor in each case, the petty commodity sector would in reality be acquiring more values from the capitalist sector than it was giving in return. In short, exchange would be nonequivalent. In reality, however, it is petty production, whose productivity of labor is lower than that of capitalism, that is subordinated to the exchange relations established by capitalism, so that one hour of its labor would be "undervalued" in terms of the internal exchange relations that prevail within the petit bourgeois sector. Thus, equivalence takes on the appearance of nonequivalence to the detriment of the precapitalist economy, precisely because their conditions of labor are unequal.

[4] There is a misprint in the Russian text, which gives KI*c* as 4,000*c* (3,725*k* + 250*p*), so that the figures in parentheses do not add up to 4,000.

[5] Taken literally, "the reproduced means of production of the petit bourgeois sector" must include the means of production used up and replaced in that sector's department I. What Preobrazhensky is actually referring to here is PII*c*, that is, the means of production of the petit bourgeois sector's department II, which can be reproduced only through exchange with the two departments I.

[6] If we follow the movements of exchange between the various departments indicated by *k* and *p*, we see that the above account is too simplistic. First of all, KI does not exchange with PII merely the part of its ($v + s$) that KII does not purchase. It actually buys *more* from PII (1,000) than its deficit with KII (which is only 500). It buys the rest of its needed means of consumption (1,000) from KII, well enough, but this comes to only 1,000, whereas KII must replace 1,500 in constant capital. It now turns out that KII, and not KI, has the unsold commodities. Clearly something more is needed, as KII must sell this 500 in means of consumption somewhere. It sells them to PI, which has an overall need of 1,500 to replenish its consumption fund. So far so good. KI has sold all of its exchangeable means of production (half to KII and half to PII) and has obtained all of the means of consumption it requires. KII has disposed of all its exchangeable means of consumption—1,000 to KI and 500 to PI—and in return has acquired all its necessary means of production, two-thirds of which are of capitalist origin, one-third from peasant agriculture. What remains of the total social product to be exchanged is 1,000 in peasant means of production in PI for 1,000 in peasant means of consumption in PII. This is a simple transaction within the peasant sector. Thus we see that for the combined KI($v + s$) plus PI's consumption fund to exchange for the combined KII*c* plus PII*c*, a fairly complicated circuit is called for. This complexity is dictated by the technical structure of production in each of the two departments that produce means of consumption: They need means of pro-

duction from both the industrial-capitalist and agricultural-peasant sectors, which are of a qualitatively different type.

As Preobrazhensky noted, this still does not exhaust all the exchanges that take place. There is also a direct exchange between the departments I of both sectors, necessitated by the fact that they, too, need both peasant-produced and industrially produced means of production. In Preobrazhensky's scheme this internal exchange between the two departments I is in balance. Yet if it were not—if, for example, department I of the capitalist sector needed more from PI than vice versa—PI could only satisfy KI's demand for raw materials and other means of production coming from petty production if it dipped into the stocks it had set aside for exchange with either KII or PII. In that case, even though exchange between KI and PI would be in balance, all other pects of equilibrium would then be disrupted. Therefore, we see that the inequality of this internal exchange between KI and PI is every bit as much a condition of equilibrium for the system as a whole as is that between the aggregate II*c*'s and the aggregate consumption funds of the combined departments I.

Preobrazhensky does not deal with the problem of how the individual components of each department's product exchange against each other (in both material and value terms) until the second and third articles in this series ("Economic Equilibrium Under Concrete Capitalism and In the System of the USSR" and "Economic Equilibrium in the System of the USSR"). Even here, however, his discussion remains descriptive, with only occasional attempts to develop the quantitative relationships involved. Despite this limitation, this still marks one of the major developments he made in the use of the schemes of reproduction, and it proved central to his theories of crisis in the Soviet economy and crises under advanced capitalism.

Finally, it might seem that the equilibrium relations Preobrazhensky has established are an artifact of his figures, since he has set $\text{KI}(v + s)$ equal to PII*c* and PI's consumption fund equal to KII*c*. Obviously the system as a whole will then balance. This latter set of equalities, however, is itself an artifact of the symmetry he has established between production in the two sectors. Total output in K equals that in P, output in KI equals that in PII, and that in PI equals that in KII. We could easily set up a different scheme where the volume of production differs between K and P and where the above accidental relations do not occur:

$$\left.\begin{array}{l}\text{KI. } 6{,}000c + 1{,}500v + 1{,}500s = 9{,}000 \\ \text{KII. } 1{,}500c + 375v + 375s = 2{,}250\end{array}\right\} 11{,}250$$

$$\left.\begin{array}{l}\text{PI. } 2{,}000c + 4{,}000 \text{ consumption fund} = 6{,}000 \\ \text{PII. } 5{,}500c + 11{,}000 \text{ consumption fund} = 16{,}500\end{array}\right\} 22{,}500$$

Here we have simple reproduction for the system taken as a whole, but equilibrium does not exist within any one sector on its own.

[7] The reference is to *Capital*, vol. II, English edition, pp. 406-15. Marx divided department II into the part producing necessities consumed by both workers and capitalists (subdivision IIa) and the part producing only luxuries (consumed by the capitalists alone—subdivision IIb). The subdivision of department II producing luxuries (IIb) must exchange part of its product with the subdivision producing necessities (IIa) in order to meet both the consumption needs of its workers (who can consume only necessities, and not the luxuries produced within IIb), and the demand for necessities on the part

of its own capitalists. Thus the total demand for necessities by IIb must equal the demand for luxuries on the part of IIa. In addition, this internal relationship dictates the relative sizes of the two subdivisions, since the branch of department II producing necessities must be of such a size that its capitalists demand a quantity of luxuries equal in value to the necessities required by IIb. All these relationships, then, become necessary conditions of simple reproduction, independently of the basic exchange between department I's consumption fund $(v + s)$ and department II's constant capital. It was through this discussion of exchange *within* department II that Marx was able to demonstrate that proportionality in the economy depended not only on the equal exchange of values between the various branches of production, but upon the production and exchange of *the right kinds* of commodities that each branch requires.

[8] That is, the exchanges between IIa and IIb do not balance, with one subdivision demanding more of the other's product than vice versa. By "unequal" exchange Preobrazhensky is not referring to a nonequivalent exchange of values between the two subdivisions.

[9] The Russian text (*VKA* 17, p. 46) actually reads as follows: "By comparing our new scheme with the earlier one, we see that, all other conditions being equal, a rise in the production of the means of production and a decrease in the production of means of consumption in the capitalist sector leads to a decrease in the production of articles of consumption in the petit bourgeois sector and a growth of that sector's department I." In other words, KI and PI move together, as do KII and PII. However, both the argument on the preceding pages and the reproduction schemes make it perfectly clear that these are inverse relationships—that is, production in PI falls as KI rises, and PII rises as KII falls. The point that Preobrazhensky is, after all, trying to emphasize here is how imbalances arising within capitalist production are alleviated by adjustments in the petty commodity sector.

[10] Marx's schemes for expanded reproduction appear in *Capital*, vol. II, English edition, pp. 515-17.

[11] There are two misprints in the Russian text for the end of Year IV: II's product is given as 4,249 and the total product as 13,033.

[12] In other words, the relative reduction of the additional Iv to only 50 means that (a) I's demand for means of consumption is lower than it would have been had Iv increased by the 100 in Marx's scheme (thus leaving department II with 50 unsold units of IIc); and (b) there is an equal reduction in the supply of I's product (which consists of means of production) available for exchange with department II, which would have gone to increase II's constant capital.

[13] *Capital*, vol. II, English edition, p. 523.

[14] Throughout this discussion of the effects of a rise in the organic composition of capital, Preobrazhensky makes passing reference to the fact that the organic composition of capital is different in the two departments. Yet this itself gives rise to a tendency for department II to grow faster than department I and for IIc to continually outstrip I$(v + s/x)$, a fact that Preobrazhensky discusses at the close of this section of the article. If we take Marx's initial scheme for expanded reproduction, with which Preobrazhensky opened this section, and allow each department to accumulate half its surplus value (rather than adjusting accumulation in department II to that in department I), we will have, after redistributing the capital between constant and variable capital:

$$\left.\begin{array}{l} \text{I. } 4{,}400c + 1{,}100v + 1{,}100s = 6{,}600 \\ \text{II. } 1{,}750c + 875v + 875s = 3{,}500 \end{array}\right\} \text{Total production} = 10{,}100$$

IIc is greater than I($v + s/2$) by 100. If we were to carry out accumulation in this way for a number of years, this disparity would grow. In real terms, it would mean that department II would be unable to convert an increasing portion of its exchangeable product into new constant capital; it would be unable to sell that fraction of its commodities and it would be unable to purchase an equal amount of means of production from department I, which simply would not have produced them. This tendency will exist wherever one department has a lower organic composition of capital than the other: The department with the lower c/v will accumulate more quickly than the department with a higher organic composition. The reason is not hard to see. Although department II is devoting less of its accumulated surplus value to c than is department I, it is, on the other hand, adding a greater percentage of it to v—that is, to the portion of productive capital that gives rise to *new* surplus value. Thus the surplus value of department II will grow at a faster rate than the surplus value of department I. Algebraically it can be shown that c, v, and s all grow in direct proportion to the rate of accumulation (that is, the fraction of s that is accumulated) and in inverse proportion to the organic composition of capital. In the example we are using here the rate of accumulation is 1/2 in each department. Out of this, department I devotes one-fifth to new variable capital, so that variable capital grows by 10 percent of the total surplus value. But since we are assuming that the rate of exploitation equals 1 and that as a result $v = s$, this is the same as saying that v grows by 10 percent of its old value. Similarly, this 10 percent rise in v means a new surplus value that is also 10 percent greater than its previous value; thus the consumed part of s, s/x, grows by 10 percent as well. In sum, I($v + s/x$) as a whole grows by 10 percent. In department II the rate of accumulation is 1/2, but the organic composition of capital is only 2:1, so that one-third rather than one-fifth of the accumulated s goes to augment v. Variable capital grows by one-sixth, or 16.7 percent. It therefore follows that surplus value in II also grows by one-sixth. However, the equation for production is linear: IIc is a constant multiple of IIv and IIs, being twice as large. Therefore, IIc also grows by one-sixth. From this we can conclude that if we start from a position of equilibrium, where IIc = I($v + s/x$), but where IIc/v is lower than Ic/v, IIc will grow more rapidly than I($v + s/x$). In the example here, IIc will grow by 16.7 percent, and I($v + s/x$) by only 10 percent.

However, this raises the question of whether or not Preobrazhensky's argument about the rise in the organic composition of capital is not an artifact of the static way he has illustrated it. In other words, would we still get the same result if the organic compositions of capital were identical in the two departments? Then a uniform rise in c/v in both I and II would keep their organic compositions equal, and we would expect IIc and I($v + s/x$) to grow in step with one another.

To see why this is not the case, take the following scheme for expanded reproduction, where the organic compositions of capital in departments I and II are equal:

$$\left.\begin{array}{l} \text{I. } 4{,}000c + 1{,}000v + 1{,}000s = 6{,}000 \\ \text{II. } 1{,}500c + 375v + 375s = 2{,}250 \end{array}\right\} \text{Total production} = 8{,}250$$

Here the organic composition is 4:1 in both departments. Assume, however, that there is a uniform 1 percent rise in the organic composition of capital in both I and II, from 4:1 to 4.04:1. If we rearranged the productive capital accordingly we would have

$$\begin{aligned} &\text{I. } 4{,}008c + 992v + 992s \\ &\text{II. } 1{,}503c + 372v + 372s \end{aligned}$$

There is already a disequilibrium of 15 between IIc and I($v + s/x$), before any accumulation takes place. If we carried out accumulation and production for one year, we would get

$$\begin{aligned} &\text{I. } 4{,}405.6c + 1{,}090.4v + 1{,}090.4s \\ &\text{II. } 1{,}652.1c + 408.9v + 408.9s \end{aligned}$$

IIc is greater than I($v + s/x$) by 16.5. The discrepancy here is due strictly to the fact that by raising the organic composition of capital we disrupted the initial equilibrium between the two departments. Even though they would now have equal organic compositions of capital and equal rates of accumulation and exploitation, this disproportion would persist. It could only be rectified if we altered the overall volume of capital in department I such that, with a now larger c/v, I($v + s/x$) were equal to IIc. Such an arrangement would be

$$\begin{aligned} &\text{I. } 4{,}048.1c + 1{,}002v + 1{,}002s \\ &\text{II. } 1{,}503c + 372v + 372s \end{aligned}$$

Now I($v + s/x$) equals 1,503, the same as IIc. If there were no further changes in the organic composition of capital in either department, accumulation would maintain the equilibrium that now exists. It is Preobrazhensky's argument, however, that the rise in the organic composition of capital is ongoing by the very nature of capitalist production. Thus, rearrangement of society's capital will be necessary with each new production year.

15 If we were to apply prices of production to the reproduction schemes, whereby the total surplus value of both departments taken together is apportioned in relation to the size of their total capitals, we would obtain precisely the result Preobrazhensky has described: overproduction in department I rather than in department II. This would indicate that the systematic deviation of prices from values discussed by Marx in vol. III of *Capital* (English edition, chaps. VIII–XII) is in fact one mechanism through which capitalism at least partially overcomes the natural disproportion uncovered here by Preobrazhensky.

16 Although it may appear that Preobrazhensky has arrived at this solution in a somewhat hit-or-miss fashion, it actually lends itself to a rather neat algebraic solution. If we take the scheme after the initial accumulation in department I and after department II has added enough to its constant and variable capital to both bring IIc into line with I($v + s/x$) and maintain the existing proportions between IIc and IIv, we have

$$\begin{aligned} &\text{I. } 4{,}400c + 1{,}100v + 500 \text{ consumption fund} \\ &\text{II. } 1{,}600c + 800v + 375 \text{ consumption fund} \end{aligned}$$

In addition, there is still 225 of department II's accumulated surplus value to be apportioned between the two departments. First, we know that the organic composition of capital is to rise by 1 percent in each department, that is, to 4.04:1 in department I and to 2.02:1 in department II. This means that in department I a certain amount must be added to I*c* and another amount to I*v*, such that the *total* constant capital stands to the *total* variable capital in a ratio of 4.04:1. That means that the ratio of the amount *added* to I*c* to that *added* to I*v* will actually be considerably greater than 4.04:1. We would expect something very similar to take place in an actual economy. There new machinery would be introduced that would require significantly less labor power to set it in motion than the existing stock of means of production to which it has been added. However, the old stock does not disappear but rather is kept in operation alongside of the new machinery. The effect is that the new machinery has brought the *average* organic composition of capital for the old and new machinery together up to 4.04:1. The same process is at work in department II, except that there the new machinery raises the organic composition to 2.02:1 (that is, by 1 percent, the same as in department I). In the example with which Preobrazhensky is working, this would give us the following equations for the rise in the organic composition of capital:

$$\text{I. } 4{,}400 + x = 4.04(1{,}100 + y)$$

An amount x is added to the 4,400 I*c* such that the new value for I*c* is 4.04 times the new I*v*, which equals $1{,}100 + y$:

$$\text{II. } 1{,}600 + y = 2.02(800 + z)$$

The amount y to be added to II*c*, which will bring the new value of II*c* to 2.02 times the new value of II*v* (the old 800 II*v* plus a new amount, z), is the same y as is to be added to I*v*. This is because the condition to be satisfied is that what is added to $\text{I}(v + s/x)$ is also added to II*c*, so that the equality between them is maintained. However, we have had to add a third variable, z, to the equations to represent the amount of new variable capital added to II*v*. This means that we have three unknowns, and in order to solve them we will need a third equation. We can derive this from the fact that the sum total of what we add to I*c*, I*v*, II*c*, and II*v* must equal 225. However, because what is added to I*v* equals what is added to II*c*, we have

$$x + 2y + z = 225$$

Solving these three equations we have $x = 160.6$; $y = 28.86$; and $z = 6.4$. Therefore, the final arrangement is

$$\text{I. } 4{,}560.6c + 1{,}128.9v + 500 \text{ consumption fund}$$
$$\text{II. } 1{,}628.9c + 806.4v + 375 \text{ consumption fund}$$

The conditions of equilibrium, where $\text{I}(v + s/x) = \text{II}c$, are satisfied. The slight discrepancies between this scheme and that of Preobrazhensky are due to the fact that, after making an initial boost in the organic composition of capital by 1 percent, Preobrazhensky did not maintain that ratio when adding subsequent increments to II*v*, II*c*, I*v*, and I*c*. As a result, his figure for I*c* is somewhat understated, whereas his figures for I*v*, II*c*, and II*v* are slightly too high.

We should also note that there is an error in the Russian text, which gives II*v* in the final reproduction scheme as 806.3, whereas his figures add up to 807.3.

[17] The Russian text mistakenly gives the rise in II*v* as 42.2.

[18] Although $\text{I}(v + s/x)$ exceeds II*c* by 64.8, if we carried out accumulation and

production for a further year we would have (assuming I$c/v = 4.04$ and II$c/v = 2.02$)

$$\text{I. } 5{,}010.6c + 1{,}241.7v + 1{,}241.7s$$
$$\text{II. } 1{,}899.4c + 940.9v + 940.9s$$

IIc is now greater than I$(v + s/x)$ by about 36.8.

[19] The distribution of capital in each department, allowing for a 1 percent rise in the organic composition of capital, can be calculated by solving the following simultaneous equations:

$$\text{I. } (2{,}000 + x)/(500 + y) = 4.04$$
$$x + y = 250$$
$$x \text{ (the amount added to I}c) \approx 204.4$$
$$y \text{(the amount added to I}v) \approx 45.6$$

$$\text{II. } (1{,}200 + x)/(400 + y) = 3.03$$
$$x + y = 200$$
$$x \text{(the amount added to II}c) \approx 153.3$$
$$y \text{(the amount added to II}v) \approx 46.7$$

[20] There is an error in the Russian text, which gives production in PII as 3,187.

[21] There is an error in the Russian text, giving KIv as 596.

[22] The Russian text mistakenly gives production in PI as 2,490.

[23] There is an error in the Russian text, which lists KII's deficit as 655 − 483 = 173.

[24] The Russian text gives this figure as 11,874. However, production in P after the first year equals 6,027, and production in K is 5,543, the sum of which is 11,570.

[25] This comment by Preobrazhensky is somewhat surprising, since his conclusion here does not seem to contradict Luxemburg's theory. In the course of capitalism's growing encroachment upon the precapitalist economy it requires the latter to increase the share of its production *that enters into exchange with capitalism*. This is certainly true in the current example, where P must make up the deficit in K (which is growing) by rearranging its production so as to increase the share available for exchange with the capitalist sector. For a fuller discussion by Preobrazhensky on Luxemburg, see *Zakat kapitalizma*, pp. 14-15, 77.

[26] The Russian text gives this figure as 173, repeating the error corrected in note 23.

[27] The Russian text gives the organic composition of capital in KII as 1:5, which is incorrect on the basis of the figures Preobrazhensky has provided here.

[28] There is an error in the Russian text, which gives production in PI equal to 2,378.

[29] Preobrazhensky has rounded off the figure for KIIc.

[30] This is not, strictly speaking, correct. The greater deficit comes from the fact that Preobrazhensky has rounded off the figures for PIIc and for PI's consumption fund. The real deficit, allowing for a 2 percent growth in each department of P, equals 61.2, which is an increase of 2 percent—exactly

what we would expect. PII*c* grows at the same rate as PI's consumption fund, not *more rapidly*. The increased deficit (in absolute terms) comes simply from the fact that PII*c* is larger.

[31] Preobrazhensky has calculated this scheme by deducting 1 percent of the previous year's I*c* (26.4) from the accumulated portion of surplus value and then dividing up the remainder (301.2) according to the organic composition of capital from the year before. Thus the new I*v* = 301.2/5.04, and the new I*c* = (301.4/5.04) × 4.04 + 26.4. This method tends to slightly underestimate the organic composition of capital, which now calculates out to 4.07:1 instead of the 4.08:1 that a rise of 1 percent over two successive years would have given. His calculations are also hard to follow. The problem can also be solved by the use of simultaneous equations, as we have shown in the example on p. 108 above and its accompanying note.

There is also an error in the Russian text, which gives KII's consumption fund as 154.4.

[32] The example Preobrazhensky is referring to is that on p. 120 above.

Economic Equilibrium Under Concrete Capitalism and in the System of the USSR
1926

Declining Reproduction

An investigation of the problem of proportionality under declining capitalist reproduction is of more than theoretical interest. Our reasons for undertaking this investigation have nothing to do with wanting pedantically to complete our analysis of simple and expanded capitalist reproduction by examining "all possible cases." Ever since capitalism entered the stage of collapse, ever since a number of capitalist countries experienced years of declining reproduction (after the outbreak of the imperialist war)—an economic situation in which some of them, such as Great Britain, still find themselves today—ever since it became possible that one or another sector of the world capitalist economy might at any given moment embark upon a rapid economic decline, an analysis of the conditions of declining reproduction and its consequences has taken on tremendous practical interest. Especially in view of the growing ties between our economy and the world economy, such an investigation is also necessary for an understanding of certain specific conditions of our existence, of our economic development. It is only unfortunate that I have to limit the investigation of this problem to the most essential aspects, so as not to stray too far from my basic topic.

The theoretically possible—and most characteristic—cases of declining reproduction are the following: (1) when, with a given and constant rate of nonproductive consumption by capitalist society, there is either (a) a steady reduction of the productively employed working population, (b) a drop in the productivity of labor of the same mass of labor power at the same level of wages, or (c) a simultaneous reduction of productively employed labor power and a drop in the productivity of labor; and (2) when, with a constant—or even temporarily growing—employed working population and a constant or rising level of the productivity of labor, the nonproductive expenditures of capitalist society grow so fast that they not only devour the part of the annual surplus value that is to be accumulated but also eat up each year part of the fixed and circulating capital of production. This will then necessarily lead to a year-to-year decrease in the volume of variable capital and hence to a year-to-year decrease in the surplus value created.

The difference between the first and second cases is that in the first case the surplus value diminishes as a result of the reduction of *v*, whereas the rate of exploitation remains constant. If nonproductive consumption continues at the same rate, there comes a point when this nonproductive consumption becomes greater than the entire quantity *s*, and erosion of the country's fixed capital begins. In the second case, nonproductive consumption grows faster than *v* and the newly created surplus value; the country passes through a period of a falling rate of accumulation, and it finally arrives at the same result as in the first case: that is, erosion of fixed capital begins, circulating capital is contracted, the level of variable capital is reduced, and the additional consumption increasingly exceeds accumulation.[1]

In both cases the point may be reached when the economy has collapsed so far that the "normal" volume of nonproductive consumption that prevailed at the onset of the collapse will exceed the amount of annual surplus value created under conditions of "normal" exploitation of the given number of workers, and the collapse will automatically continue. At that point it will be absolutely impossible to return to the conditions of expanded capitalist reproduction without a drastic cutback in nonproductive consumption and a drastic increase in the rate of exploitation.

The economies of the belligerent countries of Europe at the outbreak of the world war provide examples of a combination of both these cases: (1) labor power used in production was generally reduced as a result of repeated mobilizations; (2) the productivity of labor dropped, since some of the skilled workers who had been mobilized were replaced by untrained workers, women, and children; (3) the productivity of labor dropped as a result of inferior raw materials and the reduction of capital outlays for reequipping industry, that is, as a result of the deterioration of the instruments of production; and (4) first fixed and then circulating capital were used up without being replaced *in natura*, including a failure to maintain sufficient supplies of raw materials and the exhaustion of normal stocks.

In the interests of simplifying the investigation, we shall in our analysis examine the equilibrium, in value terms, of reproduction under conditions where nonproductive consumption grows so quickly that it eats up the entire surplus value of society and necessitates a systematic erosion of its fixed and circulating capital. We shall proceed from the following assumptions: ordinary nonproductive consumption remains the same, in absolute figures, as at the onset of the economic decline; the rate of exploitation and the productivity of labor are the same as before; and all the changes that take place in the economy are due to a sharp growth in nonproductive consumption beyond the normal limits of the society in question. This case is not entirely typical of the European economies during the war, since it simplifies the situation; however, it does provide the broad outlines for understanding the processes that occurred in the European economy during the war and created the postwar situation in the West. In Europe we had a reduction of variable capital, but owing not so much to a reduction of capital used in production as to the mobilizations. The results, however, were the same; the reduction of variable capital and surplus value caused by the drop in the quality of labor power and the reduced wages paid for it tended to have the same effect. Fixed and circulating capital was also eroded at an enormous rate as nonproductive expenditures sharply exceeded the amount of surplus value created each year. The characteristic feature of this erosion, however, was that the nonproductive consumption appeared not only as the squandering of created values but also as an increase in the production of values—as well as in the apparatus for their production—exclusively for nonproductive spending; we have in mind here the war industry. It would not be particularly difficult to introduce, in addition to the two standard departments used by Marx, a sector of war industry for the economy of belligerent Europe, that is, a sector for the specific form in which the productive forces of society were primarily used up. However, there is scarcely a need for this if we allow in advance for the fate of the fixed capital of the war industry when we speak of the conditions of postwar reconstruction of the European economy. Or, to put it more precisely, if in addition to the usual nonproductive consumption of society, we recognize that society must cover a new, extraordinary amount of nonproductive consumption resulting from the war, then we have to ask (1) where can this sum be taken from? and (2) in what form will it be spent? If society maintains its usual rate of nonproductive consumption and rate of exploitation, the first source for covering this extraordinary expense will be the part of the surplus value that previously was accumulated and used for expanded reproduction. The second source, if one disregards the depletion of stocks, is to consume the constant capital used in production without replacing it. Specifically, if for each 1 million in value of output in a certain branch of industry the depreciation charges on fixed capital are 300,000 and raw material costs 500,000, then failure to pay the depreciation charges on fixed capital will release all or most of this 300,000 and leave it prey to nonproductive consumption. If in a period of declining reproduction the circulating capital of industry is also reduced, then a certain part of this 500,000 will also be transferred into the fund of nonproductive consumption. Given an actual decline in reproduction, part of the capital that goes to advance the wages fund is also released. This is why, in constructing a scheme for declining reproduction, we can simply subtract the sums that exceed the accumulation fund from the value of the annual product and reduce the volume of constant and variable capital of both departments of the capitalist economy by this amount.

At this point we are left with only the extremely complex question of the interrelations between the total fixed capital of a country and the part of it that is worn out each year. If, for example, of 1,000*c* that is replaced annually under conditions of simple or expanded reproduction only 900*c* is replaced under declining reproduction, this does not always mean that a new cycle must begin with a 10 percent reduction in the total fixed capital (capital *C*) actually at work.[2] The matter is, in fact, much more complicated. If for a year or two no depreciation allowance (in the economic sense, rather than the bookkeeping sense) is made for a machine that has six working years left, that is, if the machine is not replaced by an appropriate level of machine-building in the country but serves instead for a couple of years past the time when it would normally have been replaced, this means that temporarily a somewhat greater volume of fixed capital can function in production that can be embodied in the numerical schemes for the actual restoration of fixed capital. What we will have is a unique type of loan from society's total stock of fixed capital. None of this, however, is significant in the long term, but only for periods shorter than the average length of service of the country's fixed capital. Hence, despite its practical importance, we can ignore this question altogether in our *theoretical* analysis of the conditions of declining reproduction and purposely simplify the problem by deducting the entire unrestored part of the functioning capital from the active capital of production. This will be the correct approach for understanding how the process we are studying tends to operate over the long term. But we shall return to this question below, since the whole problem will become clearer once we have set forth a numerical scheme to illustrate declining reproduction.

Now another question arises: What happens to the distribution of labor in society when a certain part of the total sum of previously functioning capital is not replaced each successive year?

If in our example 100*c* of the 1,000*c* is not replaced, and of this 100, fixed capital accounts for 70 and circulating capital in its material form (that is, raw materials, fuel, and so on) accounts for 30, this means that the number of workers that were required to restore 70*c* by producing machines, constructing buildings, and so on are no longer employed in department I. The same is true of the number of workers needed to replace the 30*c* of raw materials, fuel, and so on.* In other words, a rise in nonproductive consumption to the point that it erodes society's capital means, in the present case, a reduction in the number of productively employed workers and an increase in the nonproductive army of labor. In the case at hand, this can mean an increase in the number of unemployed, whereas during wartime it is expressed primarily in an increase in the number of workers called into active military service, and finally, in an increase in the number of workers engaged in war industry, producing weapons.

This last circumstance must be studied in somewhat greater detail. It might seem strange to put workers in war industry in the same category as the army of the unemployed or as those in active military service, since these workers are employed in production,

*If it is a question of the economy of an individual country, then things are more complex. Specifically, failure to replace 30 in circulating capital in its *in natura* form may in some cases mean a reduction of *imports*, or it may *give rise to* a reduction of imports because of a drop in exports.

even though it is, to use Comrade Bukharin's term, "negative expanded reproduction." This is nevertheless a correct procedure. Workers in war industry do produce values, but they are values that are destroyed. They produce neither articles of individual consumption, nor articles of productive consumption, nor the means of production of articles of consumption. Workers in war industry also produce surplus value, but that surplus value has the material form of those same instruments of war, that is, they are values that are directly destroyed. Before its realization, the capitalists' surplus value exists in the *in natura* form of cannons, machine guns, rifles, artillery shells, equipment for combat engineers, ammunition, and so on. And its realization consists in the exchange of all this for money or bonds of various types and time limits received from the government, that is, for money or titles to income. When means of production are purchased for war industry and consumer goods bought for its workers and capitalists, there is a one-way withdrawal of values from the country's resources: these values are not replaced in their *in natura* form either by means of production or by means of consumption for other branches of social reproduction and consumption. Under these conditions, the surplus value produced by the workers of war industry plays the following role: the machines, metal, fuel, and workers' means of consumption destined for war industry are not simply destroyed, but they are destroyed after they have been augmented by the value of the surplus labor of the workers. A record of this surplus value is very important for keeping account of military spending, but it is entirely unimportant for analyzing the conditions of proportionality of social reproduction as a whole, because the surplus value of war industry plays no part in that reproduction. All the expenditures for raw materials, for worn-out fixed capital, and for workers' consumption go into the column of society's nonproductive expenditures.

After what has been said, we still must mention what happens to the material values that are taken away from society's capital during declining reproduction, as well as what happens to the surplus value of branches other than war industry. The values that have the *in natura* form of means of consumption go to maintain armies of various types and into the consumption fund of the workers and capitalists of war industry. The values that have the *in natura* form of means of production, whether they be machines for the production of arms and ammunition or whether they be metal or fuel, act as constant capital in the reproduction of implements of war and military supplies and, once they have been processed through that stage, are subject to destruction. In those cases where the war industry itself produces means of production whose *in natura* form enables them to serve in production during normal periods, these means of production figure in the expenditures of society to the extent of their actual wear or consumption.

From the above discussion, the reader can see why, even in a case as familiar as the period of the world war, we do not feel it necessary to supplement the usual two Marxist schemes of social reproduction with a third, a scheme for war industry, in studying the equilibrium conditions of declining reproduction. This type of nonproductive consumption, which takes the form of nonproductive reproduction, may be studied within the schemes for reproduction of society as a whole simply as a direct squandering of means of production and consumption. A study of the war economy of a particular country would be a different matter: there an analysis in value terms would be quite inadequate, and we would have to study the proportionality of the material elements of exchange as well. Moreover, the decline in reproduction in departments I and II would never prove to be anywhere near uniform.

Let us now turn our attention to arithmetical schemes, which should most graphically illustrate the process of declining reproduction as expressed in terms of value.

As our initial scheme we shall take the production of a normal prewar year, distributed as follows:

$$\left.\begin{array}{l}\text{I. } 5{,}000c + 1{,}000v + 1{,}000s = 7{,}000 \\ \text{II. } 1{,}500c + \quad 375v + \quad 375s = 2{,}250\end{array}\right\} 9{,}250$$

Of this amount—that is, society's gross income—its net income (from the standpoint of society, not of the capitalist class) is equal to $v + s$ of both departments, or 2,750.[3] The organic composition of capital—which we assume remains constant throughout the entire period of declining reproduction—is higher in department I (5:1) than in department II (4:1). Likewise we assume that the absolute figure for the consumption of the capitalist class also remains constant throughout, that is, it remains equal to 500 for department I and 375/2, or 187.5, for department II. We make this assumption not only for the sake of simplicity but also because—as experience in Europe during and after the war has shown—the nonproductive expenditures of capitalist countries are only gradually amenable to reduction. Though they may be reduced by cutting the salaries of government employees, they are increased as a result of other factors directly or indirectly connected with the war, such as the growth of the state apparatus and the splitting up of territories formerly part of one large state. Furthermore, we assume a constant rate of exploitation of the working class, taking it equal to 100 percent, as in Marx's schemes. In economic terms this means that in the version of declining reproduction that we shall first examine, production does not decline as a result of a drop in the productivity of labor and a decrease in accumulation for each worker employed in production. The cause of the decline is different: in the present case, it results from the decrease in productively employed labor power (workers being called into active military service or recruited into war industry) and the simultaneous withdrawal from production each year of a certain part of the capital that had functioned in production before the war.

Let us now assume that in the first year 40 percent is withdrawn from the total national income of society—that is, 1,100 of the 2,750 in our initial prewar scheme. Let us assume that this amount is withdrawn proportional to the net income of each department; in other words, 800 is withdrawn from the income of department I and 300 from department II. But each of these sums is greater than the surplus value of the respective departments.[4] Therefore, withdrawal of the indicated sum from the national income entails the withdrawal of part of the functioning capital of both departments. Now, of the 1,000 in surplus value of department I, 500 goes to cover the usual expenses of the capitalist class and all the people whom the capitalists support with their consumption fund; and, as we have already stipulated, this figure remains constant for the entire period of declining reproduction. The remaining 500, which earlier (in the period of expanded reproduction) served as the accumulation fund, is now totally devoured by nonproductive consumption as well. This still leaves 800 – 500, or 300, to be covered. This 300 is taken from the capital of department I proportional to the distribution of constant and variable capital in that department. From the standpoint of the distribution of labor in society, the removal of part of the variable capital of I means a corresponding transfer of part of the workers into the army of the nonproductive. Thus, Iv, which was 1,000 in the initial scheme, has now shrunk by 50 to 950, whereas

Ic has dropped proportionally from 5,000 to 4,750.

Exactly the same thing occurs in department II except that 300, rather than 800, is withdrawn from its income. This then requires that 300 − 187.5 be withdrawn from the *capital* of II (that is, 300 minus the surplus value that previously was accumulated but now, during the war, passes into exceptional, nonproductive consumption). Hence, 112.5 is withdrawn from the capital: 22.5 from the variable capital (leaving 352.5 II*v*) and 90 from the constant capital (leaving 1,410 II*c*).

After all these withdrawals, the distribution of social capital for the first year of declining reproduction will be as follows:

I. 4,750*c* + 950*v* + 500 consumption fund of the capitalist class
II. 1,410*c* + 352.5*v* + 187.5 consumption fund of the capitalist class

If we compare the amount of variable capital plus the consumption fund of department I with the constant capital of department II, that is, the magnitudes that must be equal to maintain proportionality in the economy, we see that there is a disproportion here. Namely, 950 + 500 = 1,450, which exceeds 1,410 by 40. The cause of this disproportion under the given conditions of a decline in reproduction is quite obvious. Department II has a lower organic composition of capital than department I—hence its constant capital is relatively less than its variable capital, and its net income is relatively greater. Therefore, if a uniform "war tax" is imposed on the incomes of both departments, the withdrawal made from the *capital* of department II is a heavier burden for II and takes a larger bite out of its constant capital, whereas the "normal" consumption fund of the capitalist class of department I remains at a constant 500 throughout.[5] We shall see below that what we have here is not the fortuitous disproportion of a single year but rather a constant process, characteristic of a gradual transition to the proportions of simple reproduction. Consequently, under the conditions of declining reproduction that we have set for ourselves in this example, disproportion lies at the very foundation of the process. What we have here is the direct opposite of the law that we established for expanded reproduction when the organic composition of capital was rising and department II had a lower organic composition of capital (and hence faster accumulation) than department I. In that case, equilibrium was established by transferring capital from II to I, whereas in the present case it can be attained by the reverse operation: by a faster withdrawal of capital from I and a slower withdrawal from II (provided that the total amount to be withdrawn is a fixed quantity).

Let us now see what this whole process that we have just described means for the economy of society. A reduction of I*c* by 250 means, first of all, that this 250 in its material form of machines, metal, fuel, raw materials, and so on, is withdrawn from the functioning capital of department I and passes into nonproductive consumption; that is, it is buried in the ground as artillery shells, converted into the constant capital of war industry, consumed as fuel for troop transports, and so on. Second, it means that this 250 will not be reproduced in the economy of society even in the future—a fact that in turn entails the reduction of I*v* by 50, or 5 percent. This 5 percent, in the form of money capital advanced for a corresponding 5 percent of *v*, is now released; taken in its *in natura* form, on the other hand, it represents means of production that are cast away into the pit of war. Finally, 5 percent of the workers themselves are either called into active military service or recruited to work in war industry. Even if they do not directly produce instruments of war, but merely the means of production for war industry, they have still been cut off, as it were, from the production apparatus of society and cease to exist for it for a certain period.

It goes without saying that in the eyes of the accountant—looking at the depreciation of the fixed capital in the individual enterprises in I, for example—all this may appear quite different. Indeed, as we intimated above, withdrawing 250 from little *c* of department I does not have to mean reducing the actually functioning fixed capital by that full amount: the reduction may actually be less, because part may be offset from the reserves of C (capital C), that is, from the fixed capital of *society as a whole* (insofar as we are dealing with fixed capital). Hence, the failure to restore fixed capital can assume the form of a temporary loan from the country's fixed capital assets.

As regards department II, a withdrawal of 90 from II can have the following consequences in economic terms. This 90 has the *in natura* form of means of consumption (textiles, foodstuffs, and so on). Normally it would pass into department I and exchange for an equal quantity in value of the means of production that II requires—that is, machines, raw materials and fuel. Now, in the form of means of consumption, it falls to the disposal of a belligerent state and is nonproductively consumed at the front. On the other hand, it cannot be exchanged for means of production from I anyway: I has cut back its exchange fund by reducing the number of workers, and hence part of the fund Iv in its natural form of means of production is no longer being reproduced. But here, too, it is possible that functioning capital is not *actually* reduced by the full 90, even though the entire 90 has already been nonproductively consumed. What may in fact happen is that the part of IIc that consists of raw materials and fuel can no longer be replaced from I, whereas the *fixed* capital of IIc can still be used for a certain period without being replaced. The fixed capital crisis occurs all the more forcibly later on, that is, it occurs on a scale that far exceeds the amount of uncompensated wear and tear during that one particular year. A reduction of IIv means decreased production of new values in the form of means of consumption, a corresponding failure to replace part of the variable capital, and a corresponding transfer of part of the workers into the army of the nonproductive. However, if it is impossible to reduce production of means of consumption to the extent dictated by the withdrawal of capital from II, then that reduction can be postponed by rearranging capital within II: the total amount of capital withdrawn from II remains the same, but less is withdrawn from IIv. More capital can then be taken from fixed capital reserves to make up the difference. Thus, one can maintain a balanced exchange of I$(v + s/x)$ for IIc and still minimize the inevitable reduction of the gross production of means of consumption—a prime goal precisely in a war economy.

Contrary to expectations at the outbreak of the war, European capitalism proved to be highly flexible and elastic in overcoming the difficulties that the war presented—precisely because it drew so very heavily from its fixed capital reserves without replacing them. For example, it converted machines, buildings, and so on into means of production and means of consumption to a much greater extent than would have been possible under conditions of normal depreciation. It thereby also released a corresponding mass of labor power to be used at the front or in war industry.[6]

Let us now take another look at our scheme. At the end of the first year of declining reproduction, the contraction of production (with the same rate of exploitation) yields the following:

$$\left.\begin{array}{l} \text{KI. } 4{,}750c + 950v + 950s = 6{,}650 \\ \text{KII. } 1{,}410c + 352.5v + 352.5s = 2{,}115 \end{array}\right\} 8{,}765$$

The volume of gross production has dropped as compared to the initial scheme, but the drop is considerably less if we compare our 8,765 with the total we would have obtained had we taken the same initial scheme under conditions of expanded reproduction.

Let us now assume further that before the new year begins, an even greater amount than before is withdrawn from the national income, that is, 50 percent rather than 40 percent is removed from the net income of the initial prewar scheme. In other words, production resumes after 1,375 has been withdrawn (as is known, expenditures increased from year to year in the belligerent countries of Europe). We now make deductions similar to those we made above. However, in order not only to eliminate the disproportion of the first year but also to prevent a disproportion for the second year, we withdraw from department II 105 less than called for by the net income of II. Thus, we end up with the following distribution of capital for the second operating year of declining reproduction:

$$\begin{array}{l} \text{KI. } 4{,}200c + 840v + 500 \text{ consumption fund} \\ \text{KII. } 1{,}348c + 337v + 187.5 \text{ consumption fund} \end{array}$$

With this volume of social capital, we shall obtain at the end of the year:[7]

$$\left.\begin{array}{l} \text{KI. } 4{,}200c + 840v + 840s = 5{,}880 \\ \text{KII. } 1{,}348c + 337v + 337s = 2{,}022 \end{array}\right\} 7{,}902$$

If we were to continue in the following years to withdraw the same or a slightly larger quantity of value from the gross income, we would very quickly—within three or four years—find that the variable capital of both departments would be reduced so much that the mass of surplus value created by all the workers of the country, given the same rate of exploitation would drop down to and then below the normal consumption fund of the capitalist class (that is, below 500 in department I and below 187.5 in department II). In that case, even a complete cessation of the exceptional war expenditures and related outlays of social capital and of the reduction of the number of productively employed workers would not prevent the automatic collapse of capitalist society. Unless the nonproductive consumption of the capitalist class were stopped or the rate of exploitation raised, the productive forces would be destroyed without any war—merely on the basis of a discrepancy between "normal" nonproductive consumption and the amount of newly created surplus value. Capitalist society would automatically come to ruin.

The process of declining reproduction that we have outlined here has two important critical points that should be noted: the point of simple reproduction at the prewar level of productive forces and the point of simple reproduction at a considerably lower level. During the course of this whole process, the equilibrium conditions change as follows: (1) the initial scheme begins with the equilibrium of expanded reproduction; (2) nonproductive consumption then begins to grow, reaching a point where there is simple reproduction *on the level of the last year of expanded reproduction.* In our scheme we began directly with a rate of declining reproduction such that not only was the entire accumulation fund absorbed in the first year, but part of the capital of society was also used up without replacement. But we can return to our initial scheme and reconstruct this first critical point that changes the conditions of equilibrium.

We have in the beginning

$$\begin{aligned} \text{I. } & 5{,}000c + 1{,}000v + 1{,}000s \\ \text{II. } & 1{,}500c + 375v + 375s \end{aligned}$$

Let us assume that nonproductive consumption, which in a normal prewar year under conditions of expanded reproduction is equal to (1,000/2) + (375/2), or 687.5, now doubles, whether for reasons connected with war expenditures or for other reasons. The entire surplus value of society, 1,375 will then be absorbed by this nonproductive consumption, and accumulation will cease. But in this case not only will expanded reproduction cease, but the distribution of capital between departments I and II will have to change radically. Under simple reproduction $I(v + s)$ must equal IIc. But in our example $1{,}000v + 1{,}000s$ is greater than $1{,}500c$. For the economy of society to be held in check at or near the level of simple reproduction for a certain period of time, there must inevitably be a major rearrangement of the productive forces. Given the same volume of capital that we have in our scheme, the cessation of accumulation and a transition to simple reproduction must lead to a reduction of capital used in department I and an increase of capital in department II.

In fact, the entire capital of both departments (that is, 7,875) will now be distributed as follows:[8]

$$\text{I. } 4{,}632.6c + 926.4v$$
$$\text{II. } 1{,}852.8c + 463.2v$$

and at the end of the year, under simple reproduction, the product is

$$\text{I. } 4{,}632.6c + 926.4v + 926.4s$$
$$\text{II. } 1{,}852.8c + 463.2v + 463.2s$$

The surplus value, now completely consumed by capitalist society, will be 1,389.6 instead of 1,375 owing to the lower composition of capital and faster accumulation in II, because the increment in IIv and accumulation in II more than compensate for the drop in accumulation resulting from the reduction of Iv.

From this example we can draw two conclusions. First, if the growth of nonproductive consumption compels society to pass from expanded to simple reproduction, this changes the equilibrium conditions within the economy as a whole, inevitably reducing the relative share of the sector of the production of the means of production. Second, under expanded reproduction the problem of new markets is very acute. Sometimes this is due to an overaccumulation in the sphere of production of means of consumption, sometimes to the swelling of the production apparatus and overproduction in department I—which in turn result from the periodic changes of fixed capital that stem especially from widespread technological improvements. With the transition to simple reproduction the problem of the market loses its acuteness and assumes an entirely different meaning and significance. For an individual country the question of markets may, of course, appear differently, since reproduction within that country is dependent upon the worldwide division of labor. Or, more concretely, it may need certain imports which in turn requires corresponding exports to foreign markets.

Thus, the transition from expanded to simple reproduction—a transition that occurs because nonproductive consumption grows but the total volume of capital remains the same as in the last year of expanded reproduction—is the first critical point in the regression of capitalist reproduction that we are examining here. Beyond that point, nonproductive consumption grows to the point at which it begins devouring the capital of society. And at this stage, as we have shown, equilibrium conditions cause a faster devouring of capital in department I (assuming that proportionally equal amounts are subtracted from the net income of both departments), as long as the organic composition of capital in department II is lower than in department I and normal nonproductive consumption in I remains unchanged.

If despite its exceptional, temporary character the growth of nonproductive consumption continues long enough to upset the productive forces of society so severely that the newly created surplus value is only capable of making good society's normal nonproductive expenditures, then the economy will approach a new critical point. If this point is passed, not even a complete halt in the exceptional nonproductive consumption can save the productive forces from further ruin. The only salvation lies in a reduction of the normal nonproductive consumption of bourgeois society, or intensified exploitation of the working class, or both.

We have examined one possible version of declining reproduction, where nonproductive consumption grows because of enormous military expenditures, the capital of society is being devoured, and the productively employed labor power is being simultaneously cut back.

Let us now briefly examine how the same situation can result from other causes, taken separately or together.

Let us look at our initial scheme once again.

Since the total variable capital in both departments equals 1,375*v*, the surplus value produced annually is equal to 1,375*s*. If we assume that all the conditions that entail a cessation of accumulation and a decline of reproduction will be operating, we can obtain a situation of declining reproduction even without the acute and sudden growth of nonproductive, war-related consumption that figured in our previous example.

First, let ordinary nonproductive consumption grow, but no more than 10 percent, let us say, of the "normal." Such a growth may be due, as we see from the example of postwar Europe, to increased expenditures on the army, to a larger number of states and state apparatuses after the war, to increased numbers of disabled workers, to payments of war debts and reparations, and so on. This yields an increase in the consumption fund of the capitalist class from 687.5 to 824, or 136.5.[9]

Let us further assume that there is a drop in the productivity of labor caused by the irrational use of industry within the new national boundaries, by inferior raw materials and wear and tear on equipment, by inferior quality of labor power and a decline in the intensity of labor, and so on. As a result of this drop in the productivity of labor, annual output falls by 15 percent, or 412.5. If in addition there is a reduction in the productively employed population by 15 percent, that is, in proportions that are not too far from the actual chronic unemployment figures in Europe, then we shall have a situation where society stands on the verge of passing from expanded to simple reproduction or of plunging outright into the first stage of declining reproduction. Finally, we can add to all this the difficulties that individual countries have as a result of the world division of labor, when they require raw materials that cannot be supplied locally—that is, difficulties that arise in reproducing part of the circulating capital, especially in the case of an unfavorable balance of payments vis-à-vis raw-materials-producing countries. We shall then have in certain sectors of the world economy even more conditions that pave the way to simple or even declining reproduction.

This brief theoretical outline of the conditions of declining reproduction and of the new equilibrium conditions of the economic system under this type of reproduction may also be of practical value. It can be used to one degree or another in an analysis of the European economy during and after the war. Moreover, since world capitalism in general is in a state of collapse, certain of its sectors are bound to pass from a retarded process of expanded reproduction to simple and then declining reproduction for causes other than those directly connected with the consequences of the war. In all these cases, the theory of declining reproduction can serve as an auxiliary tool for studying the concrete economy of particular countries. It can also aid in gaining a deeper understanding of the situation when one sector of the world economy is experiencing expanded reproduction at the same time that others are either regressing or standing still in their economic development. In particular, it is only through a theoretical analysis of expanded reproduction with a steadily decelerating rate of accumulation and an analysis of declining reproduction in the different sectors of world capitalism and in particular periods that one can understand the nature of current industrial crises.

Let us now try to apply the results of our theoretical analysis to understand some of the basic processes that we have observed in the economy of Europe during and after the war.

First of all, there was a reduction in productively employed labor power in all the belligerent countries, owing to the mass mobilizations of the proletariat for the front and for service in war industry. This development was accompanied by a drop in the productivity of labor resulting from the use of women, youths, and insufficiently skilled workers to replace those who had been called up. This in turn led to a general reduction of variable capital and to a decrease in the total mass of surplus value created in the countries that were at war.

In all the belligerent countries an enormous proportion of the gross income was wasted—far in excess of the amount of surplus value. This inevitably led to the depletion of normal production reserves and to the consumption of fixed—and, to some extent, circulating—capital without replacement. Essentially, any one of these causes taken by itself would have been capable of causing declining reproduction. A reduction of productively employed labor power can at a certain point put part of the social capital out of operation and lead to the stage of declining reproduction. Conversely, a rapid erosion of fixed capital through its conversion into means of consumption for the army, into implements of war, or into the means of production for war industry can, at a certain point in this process, make part of the labor power idle (although generally speaking this result can be greatly delayed and restricted by using fixed capital reserves to the limit). During the war, both these processes occurred simultaneously. On the one hand, workers were routinely pulled from production even in cases where the existing volume of capital would have permitted their use in the production process. And simultaneously with the reduction in the number of productively employed, the fixed and circulating capital of the belligerent countries was also being eroded.

As regards the volume of production of coal, pig iron, and steel, one must at the same time bear in mind the rate of consumption of these means of production by war industry. Here, production was to a considerable degree merely the first stage of nonproductive consumption. The production of coal, pig iron, iron, etc.

directly for war needs might rightly be excluded from the overall production of a country as a form of nonproductive consumption, were it not for the fact that a number of other branches of production were to some extent in the same situation and that at the end of the war the entire production apparatus of these branches was automatically included in the production apparatus of the peacetime economy.

Our schemes of declining reproduction based on a sharp rise in nonproductive consumption give a general idea of the actual process of the destruction of productive forces that we saw in the belligerent countries of Europe. However, this picture is too general and does not capture a number of the specific features of the European war economy. Here we are faced with a problem that always arises in the transition from a general theoretical analysis of reproduction to a study of reproduction in a concrete country or group of countries during a particular historical period. A theoretical analysis of equilibrium in value terms only provides the groundwork for such a study, whereas now we must study equilibrium from the standpoint of the material composition of reproduction, the balance of payments with other countries, monetary relations, debts and credits, and so on.

In particular, our scheme—even if it accurately depicted the year-to-year movement of gross production—would require the study of a number of other important processes: (1) the rate at which fixed capital reserves were used; (2) changes in the conditions of the supply of raw materials to the belligerent countries, which included not only interruptions in their supply and sharp rises in their prices but also the total stoppage in the supply of certain types of raw materials and a transition to processing related or imitation products (a circumstance that, of course, inevitably altered the distribution of productive forces within the country as compared to the prewar situation); (3) a reduction of exports or an almost total cessation of exports for certain countries, which, when war loans and commercial loans were being contracted abroad, resulted in a one-way flow of values into the country from the outside, at the expense of the nation's future income. All these processes taken together strikingly altered the equilibrium conditions that had existed before the war. They created a special economic system that is almost completely unamenable to study on the basis of the law of value, insofar as the action of this economic regulator was itself so extremely distorted by the intensification of state capitalist tendencies and the profound disorganization of the world market.

But let us assume that we have the ideal investigation of the European economy during the world war, where a value analysis—within the limits of its applicability—is accompanied by an analysis of the material composition of exchange and by all the adjustments that arise from the existence of state-capitalist tendencies. Let us assume that the investigation provides us with an exhaustive description of the entire production apparatus of European capitalism as it emerged from the war; it establishes the link between European and world capitalism with respect to markets and the supply of raw materials and to new liabilities resulting from war debts, reparations, and so on. The question arises, Can we study the European economy from 1919 onward as an economy of expanded capitalist reproduction? Let us pose the question more concretely. If we take the total volume of European production in 1919 and compare it with the year in the past that most closely resembled 1919 in terms of gross production, will we find a process of reproduction that is at all similar to the expanded reproduction of, say, 1890 or 1900?

The answer to this question can only be negative. The European economy from 1919 onward, with its unstable equilibrium, its convulsions provoked by monetary breakdown, the lack of markets, and interruptions in the supply of raw materials, the gaping disproportion between heavy and light industry, the sharp rise in nonproductive consumption as compared to before the war, and so on, in no sense lends itself to study on the basis of the equilibrium conditions of capitalist expanded reproduction. Even the instances of reconstruction that we can see are by no means expanded reproduction of the normal type. In other cases, what we have is simple reproduction on the basis of decreased production of surplus value and a tremendous rise in nonproductive consumption, with intermittent dips toward declining reproduction. When the reconstruction process seems to prevail and the curve of gross production begins to attain its prewar level—even surpassing it in certain countries such as France, Italy and Belgium—the successes attained prove to be highly tenuous, caused as they are by the increased exploitation of labor power and the ruin of the petite bourgeoisie, and they are called into question if and when the currency is stabilized.

We shall look first of all at the reconstruction process. Equilibrium of the reconstruction process is quite different from equilibrium of expanded reproduction for the following reason. Owing to the enormous development of war industry, the production apparatus of heavy industry in Europe, mainly metallurgy and machine building, had swollen beyond proportion. When reconstruction began, heavy and light industry had to develop under different conditions, from the standpoint of the equilibrium of the economy as a whole. Let us illustrate this situation with an arbitrary scheme. Let us assume that, instead of the initial scheme we used above, production in the capitalist countries of Europe during the first stage of reconstruction is characterized by the following figures, leaving the capitalist consumption fund at its prewar level:

I. 3,000c + 600v + 500 consumption fund
II. 1,100c + 275v + 187.5 consumption fund

It is already apparent from this scheme that reducing v while keeping the consumed portion of s at its prewar levels brings the entire economy of the society down close to simple reproduction and that this in turn increases the relative weight of department II as a whole. Further, if reconstruction is initiated, department I, which now accumulates only 100 of its surplus value instead of the prewar total of 500, is nevertheless able to expand its reproduction to a much greater extent, because it has greater reserves of fixed capital. If we had here the usual process of expanded reproduction and if each department were to expand solely on the basis of its own accumulation fund, then given the fact that expansion required the creation of new constant capital, the 100 in new capital of department I would be distributed between c and v in the proportions of 5:1, and we would have a total of 3,083.6c + 616.4v for the new year—that is, a very small increase of v. But in our case, if most of the additional c is drawn from fixed capital reserves, that is, if inactive blast furnaces, the idle equipment of machine-building factories, and so on are set into motion, then the 100 in new capital now goes to increase the part of c that consists of circulating capital, and to a much greater degree to increase v. If 80 out of 100 goes to v, then we shall have a slight disproportion with IIc, even in this year, and an even greater disproportion the year after. In light industry, on the other hand, fixed capital reserves *shrank* during the war, and the part of the surplus value that previously went to increase IIv must now be siphoned off and used to plug up the leaks in IIc caused by the war, since no other capital is available in money form. But this is bound to widen the disproportion between departments I and II even further.[10]

The unfavorable position of light industry is further aggravated by the fact that it must buy part of its raw materials outside Europe (if we are speaking of capitalist Europe as a whole) or abroad (if we are speaking about one particular European capitalist country). As a result, even if the expansion of production in I fully absorbed that part of the additional product of department II that goes to cover the additional IIc, this would by no means solve the question of reproduction for department II. Department II does not merely have to sell; it has to sell so that it acquires the currency of countries that can supply light industry with raw materials. If heavy industry sells in the same countries, the problem is solved at both ends at the same time. Conversely, when light industry itself encounters difficulties in realizing its products abroad at the same time that heavy industry also fails to find sufficient foreign markets, then the internal exchange between departments I and II—guaranteed by definite proportions between IIc and I$(v + s/x)$—cannot fully take place either. Even if the magnitudes of exchange balance out in terms of value, *which is possible when the links between both departments and the world economy are normal*, the exchange of values will be hampered by a new factor: a lack of correspondence in the material elements of exchange. As a result of all this, the situation arises in which light industry cannot replace its c proportional to what it might do under the given conditions (with the given I$[v + s/x]$) of accumulation—that is, it cannot sell consumer goods in I and abroad for an amount equal to the increment of c. Department I then has overproduction for two reasons. First, since its reserve fixed capital has entered into the production process, it already has overproduction because the exchange fund I$(v + s/x)$ exceeds IIc. But in addition, it cannot sell enough means of production in department II even to ensure the necessary growth of IIc, since the replacement of IIc is associated with a definite material composition of means of production, part of which *under any conditions* must be purchased outside Europe (cotton, rubber, wool, and so on).[11]

Herein lies the origin of the chronic crisis of the reconstruction process in Europe that has characterized its economic life ever since the end of the war. This crisis of heavy industry—which also hindered the development of light industry, owing to the dynamic links between both departments of social production—was, among other things, expressed in value terms in the constant, higher price index on products of light industry. It is enough just to look at the prices of textiles: their relative growth cannot be explained solely by the rise in raw material prices. As a result, the European economy for seven years now has represented a whole tangle of glaring contradictions. Despite the enormous exhaustion of the fixed capital of light industry during the war, machine-building remains, with the temporary exception of France and Belgium, in a state of permanent crisis. Despite the drop in per capita consumption of the products of light industry, the latter continues a very slow and painful growth. Chronic unemployment has driven several million workers out of production. Exports are expanding only in countries with depreciating currencies, whereas in Great Britain, a country that has gone over to a provisional gold standard, foreign trade is falling from year to year. All this is occurring while the equipment of heavy industry is running at slightly more than half capacity.

It is interesting at the same time to observe the specific forms taken by the reconstruction process in countries that went through a period where their currency was depreciating. In general, the depreciation of currencies in Europe had its origin in the war. But once the currency has started to depreciate, the reconstruction process follows its own peculiar paths and itself becomes one of the conditions that perpetuates the state of monetary chaos. What distinguishes reproduction during inflation from reproduction when the currency is stable?

The principal difference lies in the fact that in the former case we do not have reproduction in the strict sense; rather, the country's labor power and the fixed capital of production are sold off below their value.[12] We can best see what happens here if we apply inflationary conditions to the scheme of the reconstruction process in Europe that we have just examined. If exchange takes place on the basis of value, then both departments together will have the following gross production to be realized:

$$4{,}100c + 875v + 875s = 5{,}850$$

Now, if we assume that the entire gross product is sold not at its value but at 10 percent below its value, then the total production will bring in only 5,265 instead of 5,850. If the deficit is distributed equally over *c*, *v*, and *s*, this will mean 410 of the constant capital will not be replaced, and the wages fund and surplus value will be cut by 87.5 each. If the surplus value does not suffer but 410 of the constant capital is not replaced, real wages will have to fall by 20 percent, rather than 10 percent, to produce the same result. On the other hand, if under inflationary conditions there is not a decline in reproduction but rather a process of reconstruction, the 410 of the constant capital that is eroded will affect only the fixed capital, and not the part consisting of circulating capital (fuel, raw materials, and so on). We can see from the example of Germany that during an inflation a country's labor power is sold off at bargain prices that are much lower than 20 percent below its value. In 1919 the real wages of skilled workers in Germany were 75.4 as compared to a prewar index of 100. By 1922–23 they had sunk to 62.2. In other words, in the years when inflation was at its peak, that is, in 1922 and 1923, the wages fund had dropped 37.8 percent from its prewar level. During that time, fixed capital was also being used up without replacement in a number of branches (at the same time that it was being accumulated in others).*[13] In Italy, on the other hand, wages fell only slightly more than 10 percent by 1925. In France, the drop by that same year was even less, but here one has to keep in mind the growth of relative surplus value brought about by the extensive reequipping of French industry, which in turn makes a comparison with the prewar level quite incorrect. This applies to some extent to Italy as well.

Now let us pose the question, What was and is the economic significance of selling labor power and fixed capital below their value in an inflationary period?

If we take the part of reproduction that is limited to the exchange of values within the country, then here the same branches that lose as sellers gain as buyers, and only the workers lose in all

---

*The following method may be used to calculate whether Germany was using up or accumulating fixed capital during the inflationary period as a whole. Take the gross product measured in world-market prices in gold. Subtract from that figure the gross product measured in domestic prices in gold. Take the share of the gross product that is spent on wages and calculate the amount of underpayment to the wages fund. Calculate the size of *personal* domestic consumption and export. If the underpayment of wages is higher, then this means that the constant capital grew by the difference between the two figures. If the underpayment of wages is lower, then an amount of constant capital equal to the difference was used up without replacement.

cases. The balance of losses and gains may vary widely from one particular branch of production to another, but from the standpoint of the national economy as a whole, an inflationary decline in prices[14] leads only to a general fall in the gold index of domestic, as compared to world, prices (at the same time, of course, that prices in paper money are rising). In the part of the economy that comes into contact with the world market, on the other hand, a leak is formed through which a mass of commodities flows out onto the world market below the value of its production (taking the cost of v in terms of the prewar index) and below world prices, and hence the products of national production are bargained away at a loss. However, after America had captured Europe's world markets and industrialization of the colonies had intensified, this selling off at bargain prices provided the only serious means (not counting commercial loans) for Europe to force its way back onto the markets it had lost. In particular, it was the only way Europe had to increase trade with America and to in general acquire the necessary foreign exchange reserves and begin expanded reproduction of the part of circulating capital consisting of foreign raw materials. As we have seen above, Europe's heavy industry has a hypertrophied production apparatus. When the expansion of production encounters difficulties, first of all in increasing circulating capital, and above all in increasing the part of it that consists *in natura* of foreign raw materials, the sale of excess fixed capital—materialized into commodities—at prices considerably lower than its cost (not to mention the bargaining away of labor power, which never grieves capital) represents a patently favorable operation *under the given conditions*, since this is the only way that circulating capital can be expanded. Such was the significance of inflation for the reconstruction process in Germany, France, Belgium, and Italy.

There is still another side to this whole process. Selling off fixed capital below cost is highly advantageous for capitalism wherever this capital is in any case becoming obsolete and where selling it, along with labor power, at bargain prices enables the capitalists to renew their fixed capital with minimal losses. Without a doubt, this was a partial cause of the inflationary bargain sale in Germany, where low wages permitted considerable work to be done in reconstructing the instruments of production and adapting them to modern technological requirements. This process played an even greater role in France, where the postwar inflation saw a rapid reequipping of French industry and selling off the old fixed capital accomplished two goals simultaneously: France could reenter the world economy and obtain resources for buying raw materials, and she could sell cheaply the equipment that would have had to be scrapped in any case.

From this brief excursion into the sphere of the European economy we see that not only during the war (which is quite obvious) but during the entire postwar period it is impossible to study the economic equilibrium of Europe from the angle of ordinary expanded reproduction and on the basis of the regularities of an economy of that type. The reconstruction process here has its own laws of unstable equilibrium, which are most clearly evident in the inflationary period and which continue to find their expression in the disproportion between heavy and light industry and in the impossibility of Europe once again finding a place on the world market commensurate with its level of industrialization.

One of the most characteristic features of the postwar European economy is chronic unemployment, which represents the result not of an ordinary protracted capitalist crisis but of a crisis of European capitalism as a whole. Great Britain, which was the first country to prove itself incapable of reassuming its prewar position in the world division of labor, has already experienced seven years in which about 1.5 million of its workers have been permanently cast into the ranks of the excess population. After the inflationary speculative boom in German industry, the same process began there as well. Now that the currency is stabilized and the limits of Germany's share of the world market established, unemployment hovers around 2 million. We shall see exactly the same process in France once the franc has stabilized, that is, after France has been allotted its "normal" share of the world market. The process of casting several million European workers—apparently permanently—into the army of the nonproductive is being intensified even more as a result of the rationalization of production that is currently taking place, primarily in Germany. This rationalization, in contrast to what happened under developing capitalism, rarely pushes a country beyond the limits of its fixed share of the world market and leads first and foremost to a rise in unemployment, as well as to a combination of American methods of exploiting workers with European wages. In contrast to the preceding period of capitalist history, when technological progress and the reduction in the cost of production and prices were accompanied by a growth in the number of workers being drawn into production, the present rationalization has meant a reduction in the number of employed workers, and without any drop in prices.[15] An increasingly large sector of the working class of Europe is permanently put out of the running. It is as though Marx foresaw the theoretical possibility of such a dead end for capitalism when he wrote in volume III of *Capital*:

> A development of productive forces which would diminish the absolute number of laborers, i.e., enable the entire nation to accomplish its total production in a shorter time span, would cause a revolution, because it would put the bulk of the population out of the running. This is another manifestation of the specific barrier of capitalist production, showing also that capitalist production is by no means an absolute form for the development of the productive forces and for the creation of wealth, but rather that at a certain point it comes into collision with this development.[16]

The European working population is clearly put out of the running, precisely because the European sector of the world economy has come up against "the specific barrier of capitalist production" in general.

The second problem facing European capitalism is to reconquer the markets it lost during the period of declining reproduction and which still elude the grasp of countries such as Great Britain, which have already set one foot firmly on the foundation of an economy experiencing declining reproduction. But this task is very difficult for old Europe to accomplish: its enormous nonproductive consumption and relatively modest resources for accumulation are insufficient for the expensive reconstruction of the entire economy that is needed to compete successfully on the world market.

In conclusion, it should be pointed out that for the era of declining reproduction or for an economy wavering around the level of simple reproduction, the fascist type of state is in many countries the most appropriate order for preventing further decline and trying to initiate expanded reproduction at the expense of the working class. In its socioeconomic base, fascism is a new discipline of labor in addition to the existing forces—*the scorpions of hunger and the buying and selling of labor power on the basis of the law of value*—that drive the working class to the capitalist factory and place it within the definite framework of bourgeois exploitation.

We cannot go into this topic at length in this connection. We are also compelled to forego an answer to the question of what must happen within the sphere of the capitalist economy in the period when the capitalist form has exhausted itself from the standpoint of the development of the productive forces but a historically higher form has not arrived to replace it. An investigation of this sort would already mean moving from economics to sociology and politics—fields that are not included in our present task.

EDITOR'S NOTES

[1] The way in which Preobrazhensky has used the term "circulating capital" here implies that it refers only to various types of means of production, a usage inconsistent both with Marx and with Preobrazhensky's other writings. For Marx what distinguishes fixed from circulating capital are not the physical characteristics of the commodities involved, but *the way in which their value is transferred to the value of the annual product*. Fixed capital is that part of the productive capital whose value remains to a greater or lesser degree embodied, or fixed, in particular means of production outside the value of the annual product. Its value is transferred to that of the product only gradually, over more than one production period. Circulating capital is capital whose value is transferred completely to that of the product in the course of a single production period, so that its entire value circulates as part of that of the commodity-product in whose production it participates. Marx's reason for defining fixed and circulating capital in this way is that they are fixed or circulating capital only insofar as they function in production *as capital, that is, as a value relation*. The distinction is not one of physical properties. On the basis of this definition Marx divided constant capital into two components: a fixed component, such as plant, machinery, some fertilizers or seed, and any means of production that retain part of their value by virtue of their ability to function beyond only one production period, and a circulating component, such as raw materials, fuels, and intermediary products, whose value is completely imparted within one production period to the commodities they go to produce. On the basis of this distinction Marx further divided circulating capital itself into two parts: a constant capital portion, consisting of means of production, which function as circulating capital, and the variable capital portion, since variable capital is a capital value advanced in the course of production whose value is transferred wholly to that of the commodities created by the workers. Thus, the differentiation between fixed and circulating capital is not between different kinds of means of production, nor is it between means of production and means of subsistence. It is also worth noting that the distinction between fixed and circulating capital is one *entirely within productive capital*, a point that Marx considered it especially necessary to stress given the frequently encountered confusion (in Adam Smith, for example) of *circulation* capital, or money capital and commodity capital (which are the functional forms that industrial capital assumes in its path of circulation), with *circulating* capital (capital that is distinguished by the manner in which it transfers its value to the value of the product, something that can only be done in production, where capital has the functional form of productive capital). In Preobrazhensky's other writings, especially in *Zakat kap-*

italizma, where the functional distinctions between fixed and circulating constant capital form a major topic of discussion, his use of terminology is more precise, and when talking of circulating capital he referred to either its constant or variable component, as appropriate. For Marx's treatment of fixed and circulating capital see *Capital*, vol. II, English edition, chaps. VIII, X, and XI.

[2] Preobrazhensky has here introduced the notation of capital C to designate the total stock of fixed capital in society, as opposed to little c, the symbol for the constant capital component of the value of the annual product. Little c represents only the value that passes into that of the product, rather than the total value of the means of production engaged in production. Thus, it includes the value of the entire circulating portion of constant capital plus the value equivalent of the fixed capital depreciation for that year. Using Preobrazhensky's symbols, C will most certainly be a good deal larger than c, since only a fraction of the value of the fixed capital used in production actually is lost in wear and tear in the course of a year, and it is only this fraction that shows up in c. We should not confuse Preobrazhensky's notation with that of Marx in vol. III of *Capital*, where Marx used C to represent the *total capital* used in production, that is, $C = c + v$.

[3] What Preobrazhensky here calls the net income of society is the newly created value of a given year. The aggregate value of society's commodity-product breaks down into c, v, and s. Of these, c, the constant capital component, is not value newly created in that year, but old value, created in some past production period and merely transferred to the value of current production. The newly created value is that which is added by the laborers, which itself breaks down into two parts: one covering the value of the means of subsistence needed to restore the laborer's ability to work in the next period (variable capital v), and the other over and above this magnitude, or surplus value. In other words, it is not just s that represents newly added value, or net income. Marx discusses this problem in some detail in *Capital*, vol. II, English edition, pp. 433-37.

[4] This is obviously not the case. The sums withdrawn from the income of each department are greater than $s/2$, that is, what is available out of s for accumulation after allowing for what Preobrazhensky calls here "normal" capitalist consumption.

[5] Actually there are two phenomena at work here. Department II must cut the level of IIc, leaving Is/x unchanged, giving rise to a *relative* overproduction in department I. This is responsible for the disproportion Preobrazhensky has just described. In addition to that, however, we have the fact that II's organic composition of capital is lower than that in department I. This in turn means that IIv will fall faster than Iv if the demands of this exceptional nonproductive consumption continue. But the faster fall of IIv means also a more rapid fall in IIs. Thus II's surplus value can sustain relatively less of the burden of nonproductive consumption, which can only mean that the rest must necessarily come out of II's capital, including IIc, which will decline faster than the consumption fund of department I and deepen the tendency to overproduction in I.

[6] We should be clear that when Preobrazhensky is talking about "loans" of fixed capital or taking from fixed capital reserves he is not talking about the actual physical transfer of machines from one department to another (although this may occasionally take place) or their physical conversion to other uses. In the example he gives above, dealing with department I, that department

will sell its annual product for a given monetary sum. Of this a certain portion would normally have gone to replace used-up fixed capital. If instead those machines that would have been scrapped are kept in operation, this money can be put to other uses. In the case of nonproductive expenditures, department I will sell an equivalent of this product—which exists physically as means of production—to war industries or to other branches of the economy whose output does not figure in the future reproduction of society but is squandered as nonproductive consumption. Even if it is able to retain the money received from these sales rather than losing it in various forms of taxes, department I could not apply these funds to the purchase of replacement fixed capital, since the machines, buildings, and so on that would have been devoted to this purpose have now been sold to the military and are no longer available for sale either within department I or to department II. Thus, this much fixed capital will not be restored, and production will fall proportionately. What Preobrazhensky is here arguing is that under normal circumstances the loss of this fixed capital will entail further reductions of production, since machines no longer functioning in production are not able to work up raw materials and do not require any workers for their operation. As a result, a corresponding amount of circulating constant capital will not be purchased and a corresponding number of workers will be laid off. They, too, will enter the production process of war industry, along with the "transferred" fixed capital. This is why in his previous numerical examples Preobrazhensky assumed that a cut in department I's capital owing to increased social expenditure on nonproductive consumption would be shared proportionally by fixed and circulation constant capital and by variable capital. However, as he explains here, this is not obligatory.

In his scheme on p. 142, department I cut its constant capital by 250 and its variable capital by 50. This left Ic at 4,750. Suppose that one-quarter of this amount (1,187.5) represents means of production intended to replace worn-out fixed capital, and three-quarters (3,562.5) is to restore used-up circulating constant capital. Suppose further that the cut in Ic breaks down into this same proportion of used-up fixed to used-up circulating constant capital, that is, 62.5 and 187.5, respectively. If out of the 1,187.5 in machines, buildings, and so on that were to be scrapped and replaced, department I keeps 237.5 of them in operation, it could, at least hypothetically, sell 50 of them to department II in exchange for means of subsistence and thereby make up the cut in its variable capital (assuming it could find replacement workers for those called into war industry or to the front). It could use the other 187.5 to restore the used-up circulating constant capital that would otherwise have gone unreplaced. The problem here is that these means of production would exist in the wrong physical form, as fixed capital, whereas department I would need raw materials, fuel, processed steel, and so on. Department I could perhaps escape from this bottleneck if it could export this 187.5 in machines (unlikely in time of war) to raw-materials-producing countries in exchange for means of production of the correct material form. In reality, as the experience of the major imperialist countries during both world wars shows (especially that of Germany prior to and during World War II), it would more likely be able to keep some of its expiring fixed capital functioning while relying on reserves or alternative sources of raw materials, on the one hand, and drawing into production members of the population previously excluded from it, on the other. But it would not be able to avoid a situation of declining reproduction altogether; and the erosion of its fixed capital in this way would strike the economy particularly hard later on, when masses of fixed capital would need renewal more or less simultaneously. This, of course, is precisely what occurred in the Soviet Union following World War I and the Civil War, and we can safely presume that Preobrazhensky's example here was chosen to highlight just this fact.

The situation with department II would be similar, but with fewer problems from the point of view of the physical makeup of II's product and its needs for means of production. Department II's product exists physically as means of consumption. If its capital is cut by 112.5, this means that this much in means of consumption that it would have sold either to department I in exchange for means of production (90) or to its own laborers as means of subsistence (22.5) is no longer available for these purposes. This leaves it with 1,410 in means of consumption that, if sold, will go to restore II's constant capital. Suppose that II's constant capital also divides up into one-quarter (or 352.5) replacement fixed capital and three-quarters (or 1,057.5) replacement circulating constant capital. If department II can keep 90 of this 352.5 expiring fixed capital in service, it either does not have to sell this equivalent in means of consumption, or it can use the money it receives from such sales for purposes other than buying fixed capital. It could, for example, take 22.5 of these means of production and use them within the department to restore the loss of means of subsistence that formed part of II*v* (as with department I, this presumes that II can either find new workers or increase the productivity of those still employed). This would leave it with 1,387.5 in means of consumption that it could sell to department I, out of which it could replace 262.5 fixed capital and 1,125 constant circulating capital—exactly what this portion of II*c* was before declining reproduction set in.

We should note one result of this that Preobrazhensky does not mention. If either department I or department II, or both of them together, relies on reserves of fixed capital to mitigate the effects of declining reproduction, this will worsen the disproportion that already exists between the two departments—that is, it will exacerbate the relative overproduction in department I. From department I's side, using its fixed capital reserves will allow it to increase its variable capital and hence its demand for means of subsistence from department II. If department II also uses its fixed capital reserves, it will lower its demand for means of production from I, at least to the extent that it shifts part of its product to maintaining II*v* at or near its old level.

[7] Preobrazhensky's calculations for department II in both of these schemes are incorrect. The relative shares of departments I and II in the total income of society are about 73 percent and 27 percent, respectively. Thus, of the 1,375 to be withdrawn from society's net income, 1,004 will come from I and 371 from II. However, we have the further condition that 105 of department II's burden is to be transferred to department I. Department I must, then, absorb a fall of 1,109. It can cover 450 of this out of the accumulated portion of its surplus value, since this is what is left after we deduct the 500 in capitalists' consumption from the 950 I*s*. This leaves 659 to come out of I's capital: 549.2 out of I*c* and 109.8 out of I*v*. Rounding off these figures to 550 for I*c* and 110 for I*v* (which is what Preobrazhensky did) we have

$$\text{I. } 4{,}200c + 840v + 500 \text{ consumption fund}$$

In working out the figures for department II, however, Preobrazhensky has made an error. II must lose 371 − 105, or 266. The accumulated part of II's surplus value is 352.5 − 187.5 capitalists' consumption fund = 165, and II can use this to cover 165 of its nonproductive consumption burden. This leaves 101 to come out of II's capital: 80.8 out of II*c* and 20.2 out of II*v*.

Rounding off these figures to 81 for II*c* and 20 for II*v*, we have

$$\text{II. } 1{,}329c + 332.5v + 187.5 \text{ consumption fund}$$

This still leaves an overproduction in department I of 11 (1,340 – 1,329). It seems that in working out his calculations for department II, Preobrazhensky mistakenly took the accumulated part of II*s* to be the same as the consumed portion, that is, as equal to 187.5 (in other words, he would have forgotten to subtract the capitalists' consumption from the lower value of II*s* obtained after one year of declining reproduction). If we do this and assume that II can cover 187.5 (as opposed to only 165) out of its accumulation fund, then only 78.5 has to come out of II's capital: 62.8 from II*c* and 15.7 from II*v*. This gives

$$\text{II. } 1{,}347.2c + 336.8v + 187.5 \text{ consumption fund}$$

which is very close to Preobrazhensky's figures in the Russian text.

To reestablish equilibrium between the two departments, 116 would have to be shifted from department II's "tax" to department I's. Then I loses 1,004 + 116 = 1,120, of which it can cover 450 from its accumulation fund. Then 670 must come out of its capital: 558.3 from I*c* and 111.6 from I*v*. Similarly, department II must withdraw 371 – 116 = 255 from its income. It can cover 165 of this from its accumulation fund, leaving 90 to come out of its capital: 72 from II*c* and 18 from II*v*. If we carry out these deductions and round off to whole digits we have for the two departments together

$$\begin{aligned}\text{I. } & 4{,}192c + 838v + 500 \text{ consumption fund}\\ \text{II. } & 1{,}338c + 334.5v + 187.5 \text{ consumption fund}\end{aligned}$$

There is also a misprint in the Russian text, which gives II*c* as 1,248 in the first reproduction scheme. Although the misprint was not repeated in the second scheme, it was obviously used to calculate both the total value of II's product (which is given as 1,922) and the value of the combined product of departments I and II (which reads 7,802).

[8] The distribution of capital between the two departments can be determined algebraically. If we let $\text{I}v = x$ and $\text{II}v = y$, we can express the production of the two departments as

$$\begin{aligned}\text{I. } & (5x)c + (x)v + (x)s = 7x\\ \text{II. } & (4y)c + (y)v + (y)s = 6y\end{aligned}$$

The basic condition we must satisfy under simple reproduction is that $\text{I}(v + s/x) = \text{II}c$; or, in this case, $2x = 4y$. We also know that total capital, that is, the combined $(c + v)$ in both departments, stays the same, at 7,875. Thus, $6x + 5y = 7{,}875$. Solving these two equations for x and y, we get $x = 926.46$ and $5x = 4{,}632.3$; $y = 463.23$ and $4y = 1{,}852.94$. If we round these off to one decimal place we get almost precisely the same figures as in Preobrazhensky's scheme.

[9] There is an error in the Russian text, which gives the increase in capitalist consumption as 135.5.

[10] It is unclear from this why a shift by department II of resources from variable capital to the restoration of fixed capital should exacerbate the disproportion in its exchange with department I. Under the conditions Preobra-

zhensky describes here and in the following paragraphs, this disproportion is one of relative overproduction in department I. The argument only makes sense if we consider that such a reduction in II*v* will have sharp negative effects on II's rate of growth and will lead to a relative underproduction in that department in the future. This would be equivalent to temporarily raising the organic composition in department II while lowering it in department I (which is in effect what Preobrazhensky is describing), such that it is department II, and not department I, with the higher *c*/*v*.

[11] We can illustrate this problem by referring back to Preobrazhensky's scheme on p. 153. Assume that, although department I's variable capital plus its consumption fund totals 1,100, it sells only 900 of these means of production to department II within its own country. This means, following the assumptions of Preobrazhensky's argument, that it must dispose of the other 200 abroad, in raw-materials-producing countries. Similarly, suppose that it purchases 200 in means of consumption from these same countries. In the case of department II, let us further suppose that its 1,100 II*c* is composed of 900 bought from its own department I and 200 that it must purchase from countries that produce raw materials. Under normal conditions its exchange with these countries would be in balance; it would sell these countries 200 in its own means of consumption and buy back 200 in raw materials. If we rearrange Preobrazhensky's scheme to reflect this, it will look as follows:

I. 3,000c + 600v + 500 consumption fund [300k + 200p]
II. 1,100c [900k + 200p] + 275v + 187.5 consumption fund

We have designated internal exchange with the letter *k* and exchange with raw materials producers with the letter *p*, to retain consistency with the schemes for concrete capitalism in the previous article. The raw materials need not, of course, come from petty production, though in this case we assume that they do.

In keeping with the situation detailed by Preobrazhensky, assume that department I cannot market its 200 means of production abroad. It will then have an unsold product of 200. It makes no difference in this case whether or not it is still able to buy means of consumption from these countries. Let us assume that department II is likewise unable to sell its 200 means of consumption to other countries. In this case it will not be able to purchase the 200 in raw materials it needs, since it cannot acquire the currency of these countries. If it cannot sell these means of consumption somewhere else for a currency that is convertible into the one it requires (as would have been a relevant constraint during the 1920's), it will not be able to reproduce this part of its constant capital. Under these circumstances department II will be able to purchase the 900 constant capital it needs from its own department I, but that is all. Even though department I will have unsold means of production equal in value to the shortage in department II, they have the wrong *in natura* form. Thus, there will be a simultaneous *overproduction* in department I and a *shortage* of means of production in department II. If, in addition to this, department I actually were still able to buy 200 in foreign made means of consumption, it would not even be capable of purchasing department II's unsold product for cash; and therefore all chance that department II could escape from its difficulties through a roundabout circuit of monetary and commodity exchanges would be eliminated.

[12] This topic, and the discussion of it that follows, are principal themes of Preobrazhensky's book *The Theory of Depreciating Currency.*

[13] Preobrazhensky's footnote, which at first glance must certainly appear almost incomprehensible, actually makes sense in terms of the argument presented in *The Theory of Depreciating Currency*. Domestic prices (in real terms) in Germany during the postwar period were considerably lower than those prevailing on the world market, precisely because the conditions of production were made more favorable by the depression of real wages and the accelerated amortization of fixed capital. The degree of "undervaluation" of Germany's production can be measured by subtracting its valuation in real domestic prices from its valuation in world market prices. This undervaluation in turn has two basic components: that attributable to the cheapness of labor power and that caused by the overly rapid writing off of fixed capital. If we take the share of the gross product spent on wages, evaluate that in both world and domestic real prices, and subtract the latter from the former, we will know how much the wages fund has been "underpaid." What is problematic, however is Preobrazhensky's reference to the level of personal domestic consumption and exports. This magnitude represents everything that is left over in the annual domestic product after deductions are made for fixed capital replacement and the costs of circulating constant capital (that is, it does not refer to average per capita consumption). In that case simply calculating the size of this component is not enough—we must then calculate the difference between this part of the national product evaluated in world market gold-based prices and its valuation in domestic gold-based prices. This will tell us the extent to which the *total* non-constant-capital share of production (that is, $v + s$) has been produced below "its value." If the undervaluation of wages is greater than this figure (that is, if wages have been depressed more than the value of domestic consumption as a whole), this means that there has been an actual subsidy of the constant capital fund from the wages fund. Put another way, if wages are depressed by 1,000 units but consumption has been depressed by only 900, then the other 100 values "taken" from the wages fund have necessarily been transferred to the constant-capital fund—probably to the fund for fixed capital replacement (as actually occurred in France and Germany during the 1920's). If, on the other hand, the underpayment of wages is less than the undervaluation of domestic consumption and exports, this means that the latter has come at least partially out of the constant capital fund by an amount equal, as Preobrazhensky says, to the difference between the two magnitudes—in other words, that much constant capital will have been used up without being replaced out of the revenues received from the sale of total domestic output (including exports). Finally, if the amount by which the domestic consumption/export part of the national product is sold below its value equals the level of underpayment of wages, then the subsidy has come entirely out of the wages fund, whereas the replacement of constant capital stays unaffected (abstracting from rises in foreign raw materials prices, which would necessitate a new balance between the portion of c going to replace fixed capital and the portion covering circulating constant capital, with some fixed capital not being replaced, in order to keep raw materials supplies from being cut back).

[14] By "an inflationary decline in prices" Preobrazhensky means a decline in real terms—for example, in terms of a gold index—brought about by inflation. This derives from the argument presented in his writings on monetary circulation, in particular *The Theory of Depreciating Currency*. There Preobrazhensky insisted that when assessing the extent of inflation it was incorrect to use as a basis of comparison the level of gold currency prevailing before the inflationary process got under way, for inflation itself has effects upon commodity

circulation and the amount of gold needed to sustain it. These changes take two forms: first, hyperinflation severely curtails the scope over which money performs its various economic functions (the volume of commodity circulation dropping owing to a reluctance to hold cash and a contraction of the mechanisms of credit, the population liquidating its money holdings, and so on), thus lowering the demand for even gold currency within the economy. Second, and as a parallel process, *the conditions of production will be altered* and will differ from those prevailing on the world market: Labor power will be sold below its value and fixed capital depreciation will be accelerated. As a result domestic prices in an economy suffering from hyperinflation will be lower in gold terms than corresponding (gold) prices on the world market. Preobrazhensky cites, for example, in several passages in *Teoriia padaiushchei valiuty* how over a number of years in the 1920's the domestic price index in gold terms in Germany and France was far lower than the gold price index of the United States or the world market as a whole. In effect production in these countries was being subsidized by the working class and through the rapid selling-off of fixed capital. In the end, however, it was the working class that paid, since the fixed capital that was so rapidly depleted was restored with more modern and up-to-date equipment, being for all intents and purposes bought at least partially out of workers' wages.

[15] Preobrazhensky developed this argument at some length in *The Decline of Capitalism*.

[16] *Capital*, English edition, vol. III, pp. 263–64. (Moscow: Progress Publishers, 1966).

Economic Equilibrium in the System of the USSR

1927

The Economy of War Communism

In the present article we will apply everything we said earlier about reproduction under concrete capitalism to an analysis of equilibrium in the present-day Soviet economy. But before we move directly to the situation today, let us say a few words about the period of "War Communism." We in the Soviet Union often underestimate the legacy that the New Economic Policy (NEP) received from War Communism in the sphere of interrelations between the state and private sectors of the economy. Thus, it would not be out of place to recall the true magnitude of the changes that were introduced into the interrelations between the private and state sectors by the transition to NEP.

The most characteristic feature of the period of War Communism in the sphere of interrelations between the state and private sectors of the economy was, if we may put it thus, the economically separate existence of petty production (primarily peasant production) on the one hand and the state economy on the other. No regular market exchange existed between these two sectors, although generally speaking an illegal and semilegal market did continue to exist throughout War Communism. The exchange that occurred in the form of requisitions on the one hand and deliveries of goods from urban production to the countryside through the People's Commissariat of Supply on the other was of a highly specific nature. The specific features of the interrelations between city and country, to the extent that they were regulated by the state, derived from the general political and economic conditions of War Communism. The principal goal of all production and distribution at that time (a goal that was imposed upon rural petty production from the outside) was not expanded reproduction within the state and private sectors. Rather, the aim was to produce the maximum amount of consumer goods for the army, the urban proletariat, and the rural poor and to produce arms for defense, without any concern for depreciation. Planned distribution of existing stocks played an equally important role in the economy. This distribution, too, was subordinate to the needs of defense rather than to the tasks of expanded reproduction. This was the economy of a beleaguered city that was pursuing the goal of holding out as long as possible to win a war, not the goal of normal reproduction in the economy. Disregarding the type of production relations, our economy under War Communism was one of declining reproduction: it thus resembled the declining capitalist production in Europe during and after the world war, which we discussed above. But in our case—speaking now of the state sector—this was declining reproduction in a *socialist* economy, and herein lies the uniqueness of this stage of our economic history.

Now, is it possible to illustrate the exchange within this economy—an economy marked by declining reproduction and a widening gap between its state and private sectors—by the same arithmetical schemes that we used in analyzing capitalist and petit bourgeois reproduction?

In principle, such an illustration is impossible. We must remember that what we want to illustrate here is by no means a process of reproduction of a commodity capitalist society where all operations are subject to the law of value. Rather, we are dealing with exchange based on *other law-governed regularities*, primarily the needs of defense, with total disregard for any sort of equivalency whatsoever, whether in the exchange of the total sum of articles of consumption of rural origin against urban products or in the internal distribution of the goods that the peasantry received according to the plans of the People's Commissariat of Supply. Marx's schemes are not suitable for illustrating reproduction in an economy of this type: Marx used his arithmetical examples to illustrate equilibrium conditions of exchange of values under pure capitalist reproduction. His schemes are no longer applicable once an economy has become "naturalized" and has largely ceased to be a money economy, when equilibrium in the exchange of values has been replaced by proportionality in the distribution of the material elements of production in kind, when measurements in terms of value are being replaced by measurements of labor time or by substitutes for that measurement, and when, finally, production is subordinate not to the needs of accumulation or even to those of simple reproduction but rather to the task of consuming constant capital with deliberate intent and converting it into articles of consumption and armaments. For this reason, the categories of value are not appropriate for a scientific analysis of the concrete economy of War Communism. However, we know at the same time that our economy under War Communism had been in existence for too short a time to have worked out the accounting methods that were organically inherent in it, that is, an accounting of the material elements of the economy and the means of consumption, elements that could in the final analysis be reduced to labor costs and thus be rationally measured by labor time—in other words, those that could be measured in a socialist manner. Under War Communism we used surrogate devices for socialist accounting, such as the prewar ruble, the commodity ruble, and grain and other rations (forms of accounting in kind). We used a *quantitative* accounting of industrial output, a quantitative accounting of what had been received from requisitions on peasant production, and so on. This measurement in kind had no value parallel, as it does now, but rather constituted the basis for all our calculations. If we could draw up even an approximate balance for the national economy of Soviet Russia for each year of War Communism, that is, in part for 1918 but primarily for 1919 and 1920, we would discover that these were not annual balances of reproduction. We would establish the following basic economic facts:

(1) The complete elimination of capitalist production and capitalist trade from the economy left us with only two sectors: the sector of the state economy and the sector of petty production, which to a considerable extent had lost the character of *commodity* production because of the "naturalization" of the peasant economy and the collapse of craft and artisan industry.

(2) Only a very minor portion of the fixed capital of the state sector that was used up during each year of War Communism was replaced. Consequently, it was systematically eroded. The fact that all production in the state sector was earmarked for consumption had its consequences: since the fixed capital of light industry,

which emerged from production in the material form of articles of consumption, was not replaced, the net result was an increase in the production of means of consumption at the expense of compensation for wear and tear on existing equipment. This situation radically upset the relation between the rate at which the fixed capital part of II*c* was being consumed in department II and the rate at which it was being reproduced in material form in department I. Not only did the resulting imbalance preclude expanded reproduction, it did not even meet the requirements of simple or even slowly declining reproduction. On the other hand, the part of the petty economy's means of production that previously had been produced in department I of the capitalist sector (or had been imported) was now also being consumed without replacement in department I of the state sector. Finally, the means of production of department I of the state sector that consisted of fixed capital were not replaced within that same sector, insofar as they were worn out in producing arms, including military transport vehicles. That is, they were swallowed up by nonproductive military consumption. All this meant the paralysis, above all, of the section of heavy industry whose function was to replace the fixed capital of II*c* of the state and private sectors.

(3) The part of constant capital of the state sector that consisted of fuel, imported raw materials, and raw materials of peasant origin could not be reproduced in sufficient proportions, since we had lost control of basic fuel-producing regions (the Donets Basin and Baku) for long periods during the war; we were subjected to blockades; and the peasants had cut back production of industrial crops at the same time as they began processing more of these same crops for their own use.

(4) As regards exchange between city and country, the single most important fact explaining the inevitability of the entire system of War Communism is the following: Even if normal market exchange had taken place between the city and the countryside, an overall reduction of peasant production to 50 percent of its prewar level would have prevented the peasant economy from supplying the city—*on the basis of exchange*—with the quantities of articles of consumption, industrial raw materials, and direct labor (freight transportation and so on) needed by the state during the Civil War. And, conversely, even if the countryside had been able to supply all these values through normal market exchange, then state production, considering that the volume of its output was at a

minimum whereas nonproductive consumption brought about by the war was enormous, would have been objectively unable to replace the goods that it received from the peasantry, even through grossly nonequivalent exchange and even with a high monetary tax on the countryside. This becomes quite obvious if we take the total production of means of consumption in state industry (in prewar rubles), subtract what was consumed by the city and the military, and then compare what might have been left over for exchange with the value (also in prewar rubles) of everything that was obtained through the requisitions on the peasantry. Although the discrepancy was not so great during the first year of War Communism —the Soviet government still had available old, prewar stocks—by 1920, the year that most typified War Communism, the peasantry was already delivering much more to the cities than it was getting in return. This demonstrates that market exchange relations between the state economy and petty production were completely impossible in that period.

The fact that the economy of that period was geared to military consumption was expressed in another way as well. When industrial products were supplied to the countryside in accordance with the state plan, the Committees of Poor Peasants distributed these goods among the rural inhabitants in a special way: it was not the strata that had supplied the greatest amounts to the state under the requisition that received the most in return. Rather, it was just the opposite. It was the poorest peasants who got the most, the peasants who had given nothing material to the state but who were lending it their political and military support in the Civil War. Hence, distribution of urban products was doubly nonequivalent, first in the sense that much less was returned to the countryside than had been obtained from it, and second in the sense that there was a principle of unequal distribution within the countryside itself. This class-based distribution, which ignored the exigencies of reproduction in the peasant economy, was countervailed to some extent by illegal exchange between the city and country, "bag trading," as it came to be called.[1] Here, the countryside took a measure of revenge, as it were, upon the distribution system that had been imposed upon it by the city. By exchanging grain, potatoes, and other foodstuffs, it bought for a mere trifle the cloth, footwear, furniture, and other items that had been stored in the cities for years.

The contradiction between city and country grew, and the peasant uprisings in late 1920 and early 1921 brought attention to bear on the urgent question of how the system of exchange in the Soviet economy could be adapted to the conditions of commodity production in agriculture. This adaptation took place with the transition to NEP. But the reasons for going over to NEP were rooted within the state economy itself, since it was entering into a peaceful period of existence. In our peasant country, the transition of the state economy from the declining reproduction of wartime to the expanded socialist reproduction of peacetime required changes in the relations between proletarian industry and the peasant sector. It demanded a market system of exchange and incentives for the production of peasant raw materials needed for state industry, the growth of exports, and so on. In examining these changes, however, we must be careful to distinguish between two different categories. First, certain changes were made in the methods of managing the state economy in order to squeeze everything of value from the usual capitalist techniques of accounting, calculation, and so on in the first stages of socialist construction; in other words, these were changes introduced in the interests of the state economy itself at a given level of socialist culture. These changes in the country's economy must not be confused with those that were imposed upon the state economy by the predominance of petty commodity production in the country. Had it been a question of the first years or the first decade of socialist construction in a country such as contemporary Germany, then the general conditions of development of a socialist economy might perhaps have required us, too, to maintain a market system of exchange until the methods of distribution appropriate to the socialist form of production had been discovered through experience. We, too, would perhaps have left not only petty trade but also medium-scale trade where the state sector still had dealings with the relatively insignificant private economy. But the conditions conducive to the *development* of commodity relations, i.e., the development of private capital in its various forms, would not have existed. However, in the USSR such a development, especially in agriculture, is an unavoidable fact, imposed upon the country's economy by the enormous preponderance of petty commodity production combined with the relative weakness of the state sector. This fact forces the state economy into an uninterrupted economic war with the tendencies of capitalist development, with the tendencies of capitalist restoration, which are reinforced by the outside pressure exerted on our economy by the world capitalist market. For this reason, our economic system cannot enjoy the internal stability that characterized the countries of youthful capitalism as it dissolved feudal relations and subordinated petty commodity production to itself. This solitary battle, waged by the socialist elements of the economy against the capitalist elements that are buttressed by the huge block of petty commodity production, leads as well to a dualism in the sphere of control or, in other words, to specific equilibrium conditions within the system as a whole.

Preliminary Observations

An analysis of equilibrium conditions in the present-day Soviet economy necessitates the division of the economy into three sectors: (a) the state sector, (b) the private capitalist sector, and (c) the sector of simple commodity production. The nature of the investigation, however, will frequently require us to counterpose the first sector to the other two taken together, since the two combined represent the private economy as a whole, and the lack of necessary data on the capitalist sector means that the only way to make a concrete study of reproduction is to divide the economy into two sectors.

The second feature—and this is what makes the investigation so difficult—is the fact that equilibrium of the system is not attained on the basis of the law of value of equivalent exchange, but rather on the basis of a clash between the law of value and the law of primitive socialist accumulation. For this reason we cannot, in analyzing equilibrium, start from Marx's assumption that commodities are usually sold at their value. In volume II of *Capital*, Marx, in posing the question of analyzing reproduction, makes the following reservation in connection with this point:

> It is furthermore assumed that products are exchanged at their values and also that there is no revolution in the values of the component parts of productive capital. The fact that prices diverge from values cannot, however, exert any influence on the movements of the social capital. On the whole, there is the same exchange of the same quantities of products, although the individual capitalists are involved in value-relations no longer proportional to their respective advances and to the quantities of surplus-value produced singly by every one of them.[2]

As we have already shown, this assumption by Marx is quite correct when one is analyzing equilibrium in a capitalist economy. However, when we analyze reproduction in our system, we start from the rule that prices diverge from values, as a rule, when we compare our domestic prices with world prices. From the standpoint of equilibrium, the distinguishing feature of our economy during the period of primitive socialist accumulation is precisely that it lacks the equivalent exchange toward which a capitalist economy naturally gravitates, and which it attains with greater or lesser deviations, primarily on the basis of free competition and by giving free rein to the law of value in the distribution of social labor. Under capitalism equivalent exchange may be considered the dominant tendency, no matter how numerous the variations in the general pattern and no matter how much these deviations accumulate historically as capitalism enters its monopoly stage. In the Soviet economy, on the other hand, during the period when the entire technological basis of the state sector is being replaced, the rule is *non*equivalent exchange. This nonequivalence underlies the whole existence of the state economy, and it constitutes one of the most important features of our system at the present stage of its development. War Communism meant, first, nonequivalence of exchange (*razmen*)*[3] of the products of state industry for the products of the countryside alienated from the peasantry through requisitions and second, absence of the market, commodity-money form of such exchange (*razmen*), that is, the absence of market exchange (*obmen*). Under War Communism the level of development of the productive forces in both the state and the peasant sectors was so low, and nonproductive military consumption so high, that the market form of exchange (*obmen*) would not have stood up under the pressure of the redistribution of national income necessitated by the Civil War. Conversely, if the market system of exchange (*obmen*) had held up, then the specific pattern of income distribution demanded by wartime conditions could not have been sustained, and with that the chances for victory might have been destroyed. As regards the period of NEP or, more precisely, the period of primitive socialist accumulation, the development of the productive forces in both sectors not only permits but even de-

* I use the word *razmen* instead of *obmen* in order to avoid using a term referring to commodity economy with an established meaning for an economy of quite a different type.

mands a market form of exchange (*obmen*) capable of guaranteeing the state economy the necessary conditions for its existence and development. But exchange (*razmen*) of the products of the state and private sectors, especially between state industry and the peasant economy, can still not be equivalent, either in terms of relating the labor actually expended on the products exchanged or in terms of their relation to the proportions of exchange (*obmen*) prevailing in world economy. Our system could not have sustained an equivalent exchange (*obmen*) controlled by the world market, and the whole process of reconstruction of the state economy would have necessarily come to a halt.

Thus, economic equilibrium in the Soviet system during the period of primitive socialist accumulation differs from the period of War Communism in two respects: we have now reestablished the link between the state and private sectors on a market basis and, additionally, the capitalist sector has reappeared on the scene. On the other hand, the present system resembles War Communism in the nonequivalence of exchange, which continues to exist, although in a much less extensive form as compared with 1919–20. This circumstance does not hinder all those investigators who build an unbridgeable gulf between War Communism and NEP and are incapable of scientifically establishing the historical continuity between the two forms of economic regulation. Apart from the fact that NEP did not in the slightest alter the system of ownership of large-scale industry and transportation, it retained a continuity with the era of War Communism and maintained an attenuated version of nonequivalence of exchange. To uncritically hold War Communism responsible for things that spring from the general economic backwardness of our country amounts to no more than childish stupidity and a failure to understand cause and effect in our economic history. To whom, indeed, is the complaint addressed that the level of development of the productive forces in our country was low and will continue to be so for a long time to come? One has to understand the consequences to which this leads at various stages of the existence of the Soviet system.

However, although during the period of primitive socialist accumulation we *hold to* nonequivalent exchange (*obmen*), using it for the reconstruction of our technological base, that does not mean that we will *hold out* for very long in such an extreme position if we do not overtake capitalism but continue to lag behind it or, while moving forward, nevertheless maintain the same relative distance from it in technology and in the development of our productive forces. Nonequivalent exchange (*obmen*), with all the apparatus for safeguarding it, such as the foreign trade monopoly, planned imports and rigid protectionism, may be an obligatory condition for the existence of the Soviet economy, with its state sector, but if our economy is to *continue* to exist, it is just as necessary that nonequivalence be gradually overcome and that our productive forces be brought to the level of the most advanced capitalist countries. These are the two equilibrium conditions of our system, insofar as they are connected with expanded reproduction of socialist relations, that is, with precisely that which distinguishes us from capitalist economy, and insofar as it is a question of the reproduction of capitalist relations in an economically backward country at a time when that backwardness is in the process of being overcome.

We must now make some preliminary observations on the capitalist sector of the Soviet economy. We have seen that as long as our economy lags behind capitalism both economically and technologically the existence of the state sector is the main source of nonequivalent exchange (which essentially comes down to a tax on the whole economy for the benefit of socialist reconstruction). But it is quite incorrect to infer from this that the capitalist sector of the Soviet economy, *taken as a whole*, is the domain of equivalent exchange or that it in general has inherent tendencies toward more equivalent exchange even within the bounds of the Soviet economic system. We must bear in mind that the commercial and industrial segment of the capitalist sector on the one hand and its agrarian segment on the other do not gravitate toward equivalent exchange to the same degree. The basic proportions of the domestic price structure are established by the interplay between state industry and transportation and the peasant economy. *Private industry is incapable of altering these proportions*, nor is it the least bit interested in doing so. It plays a passive, parasitic role here. Whereas nonequivalent exchange is for the state sector the material source of technological reconstruction and a prerequisite for the development of the productive forces in coming years, *private industry merely clings fast to the existing situation*. It finds its way into the pockets of nonequivalent exchange between large-scale Soviet industry and the countryside in order to accumulate, but without ever embarking upon productive industrial accumulation. Hence it can itself never help lower production costs, nor can it ever begin to compete with state industry in a positive manner. The only place where private industry successfully competes with state industry is in a few branches of light industry where expensive machinery does not yet play an important role or is inapplicable and where the role of personal initiative and energy, of personal involvement in the business, is relatively great. And even in these industries, the private entrepreneur's success rests chiefly on the extreme exploitation of labor power, often that of his own family. The bourgeoisie prefers to keep its accumulated resources in money form and feels that it is risky to convert them into the hard and fast form of new instruments of production. This is precisely the predicament in which private merchant capital finds itself. When a goods famine is compounded by poorly organized distribution in the state system of cooperatives (especially when that system has only existed for a few years), the private trade apparatus takes advantage of market trends to augment its normal profit and, in general, trades at higher prices than the state cooperative system. Here too, private capital plays chiefly a parasitic role in the sense that *it takes advantage of the favorable economic situation provided by nonequivalent exchange—a situation that it itself did not create—while doing nothing to help attain greater equivalence.*

The agrarian half of the capitalist sector, represented by the kulak and the well-to-do peasant, who is already halfway along the road toward systematic exploitation of the labor of others, finds itself in a different situation. Later on we will discuss the relative influence of this element of the capitalist sector and its growing importance in the country's economy. For now, let us merely note that the main weight of the capitalist sector, insofar as it will develop at all, will undoubtedly shift to its agrarian segment, where accumulation occurs in the form of means of production and of land leased from the poor peasants. It is the agrarian capitalism of the Soviet system that suffers first and suffers most from nonequivalent exchange, because the kulak buys more than the middle peasant and hence overpays more at our domestic prices as compared with world prices. The kulak sector sells more, and expanded reproduction within that sector can take place only through market exchange. Only through market exchange can the kulak sell the growing volume of his output, including the part that constitutes his surplus value. That is why the kulak is so pointedly and consciously hostile to the present economic order, although indeed to a certain extent the entire peasantry suffers from nonequivalent exchange insofar as it is dependent on the market and has not withdrawn into the shell of a natural economy. The kulak tries to offset the nonequivalence of exchange with the town, hoping that by not selling in months when the poor and middle peasant strata are marketing grain at the prices fixed by the state, he can thereby drive up grain prices in the spring. He experiments with replacing certain crops with other, more profitable ones. He tries to avoid the market and accumulate in kind by raising more livestock and poultry from his own production, by constructing new farm buildings, and so on. But the possibilities for such economic maneuvers are not very great, and in the end the kulak is forced into a confrontation with the entire Soviet system. And the longer it takes for this confrontation, the more the kulak will be inclined to seek a solution to the problem not by economic means within the Soviet system, not in a partial adjustment of the equilibrium in his favor, but by attempting to force his way through to the world market by counterrevolutionary means. Here, the problem of economic equilibrium rests squarely on the problem of social equilibrium, that is, the relation of class forces for and against the Soviet system. Two systems of equilibrium are struggling for supremacy: on the one hand, equilibrium on a capitalist basis—which means participation in the world economy regulated by the law of value—by abolishing the Soviet system and suppressing the proletariat, and on the other hand, equilibrium on the basis of temporarily nonequivalent exchange serving as the source of socialist reconstruction and *inevitably signifying the suppression of capitalist tendencies of development, particularly in agriculture.*

Marx's analysis of proportional distribution of labor under pure capitalist reproduction began with equivalent exchange as a necessary premise. In our own earlier analysis of equilibrium under concrete capitalism, we also began with this same premise. But from what we have just said above it is clear that the investigation of reproduction in the economy of the USSR that we are about to begin must start with nonequivalent exchange, even though the latter is to be gradually and systematically eliminated. *But this means that we always have to assume that the entire process is based upon the existence of two different systems of ownership of the means of production, and two different regulators of economic life, that is, the law of value and the law of primitive socialist accumulation.*

An Algebraic Scheme of Reproduction in the USSR

If we take the terminology Marx used to describe the capitalist economy and apply it in a conditional sense to the state economy and to the petit bourgeois sector, we will obtain the following algebraic scheme for the three sectors of the economy:

State Sector

Department I. $c + v$ + surplus product + (surplus product
Department II. $c + v$ + surplus product from other sectors)

Capitalist Sector

Department I. $c + v + s$
Department II. $c + v + s$

Petit Bourgeois Sector

Department I. c + consumption fund + surplus product
Department II. c + consumption fund + surplus product

However, the above scheme is inadequate for our purposes, because it fails to give an idea of how the individual magnitudes are broken down from the standpoint of their exchange with different departments of different sectors. A more detailed scheme, which we will use in the rest of this discussion (although we will often be taking the two private sectors together), would need to have the following form: [see pp. 182-83].

Let us say a few words to clarify this scheme, which even in the form presented far from exhausts all the various directions along which exchange proceeds in expanded reproduction in our system.

From the standpoint of exchange, the constant capital of department I of the state sector can be broken down into three parts: the first part is reproduced within the department itself; the second is reproduced by exchange with department I of the capitalist and petit bourgeois sectors; the third is reproduced by imports of means of production from abroad.

Wages of department I of the state sector are divided into two parts: one part is exchanged for means of consumption produced in department II of the state sector; the second part is reproduced by exchange with departments II of both the capitalist and petit bourgeois sectors.

The surplus product of that same department can be broken down into (1) an accumulation fund that is distributed proportionally between *c* and *v*, with the appropriate exchange of the additional *v* for means of consumption, and (2) a nonproductive consumption fund. The latter fund is consumed *in natura* in the same department only in the form of means of production for war industry, whereas the remaining part is exchanged with departments II of all sectors.

The constant capital of department II of the state sector is reproduced in the following ways: by exchange of means of consumption against one part of the wages fund of department I of the state sector, by exchange with the consumption fund[4] of the capitalist and petit bourgeois sectors (chiefly for peasant raw materials), or by imports of means of production (in the form of both machinery and raw materials such as cotton, wool, rubber, and hides).

The wages of department II of the state sector are reproduced in part within the department itself, in part by exchange with the consumption fund of the petit bourgeois sector, and in part by mutual exchange for II*v* of the capitalist sector.

The surplus product of department II of the state sector can be broken down in the same way as the surplus product of department I, that is, it consists of an accumulation fund and a nonproductive consumption fund. The latter is consumed *in natura*; the former can be broken down into two parts: one consists of additional *v* and is reproduced on the lines of the entire II*v* of the state sector; the other, which is earmarked for the purchase of means of production, is reproduced on the lines of II*c* of the state sector.

We will not make a detailed examination of exchange between the capitalist sector and the other sectors, since this process is clear from the above analysis of the departments of the state sector. The difference lies in the apportionment of the surplus value. Here we have two additional elements: the consumption of the capitalist class, which modifies the exchange of means of production for the means of consumption produced in the individual

STATE SECTOR

<table>
<tr><td rowspan="2">All of the fixed capital
c

Department I</td><td>The part of the constant capital annually reproduced on an expanding scale:</td><td>Wage fund:</td><td>Surplus product:</td><td rowspan="4">Surplus fund of socialist accumulation*</td></tr>
<tr><td>(a) via reproduction within the department

(b) by means of exchange with other departments I

(c) via imports</td><td>(a) the part that is replaced by means of exchange with IIc of the state sector

(b) by means of exchange with IIc of other departments</td><td>(a) accumulation fund
(1) For expanding existing enterprises
(2) For constructing new factories

(b) the fund of nonproductive consumption of the Soviet system, which passes into IIc of all sectors and into c of military industry</td></tr>
<tr><td rowspan="2">c

Department II</td><td>The part of the constant capital annually reproduced on an expanding scale:</td><td>Wage fund:</td><td>Surplus product:</td></tr>
<tr><td>(a) by means of exchange with department I of the state sector

(b) by means of exchange with the consumption funds of the departments I of other sectors

(c) by means of exchange with part of fund of nonproductive consumption of department I

(d) via imports</td><td>(a) the part replaced within the department itself

(b) the part replaced by means of exchange with the consumption funds of other departments II</td><td>(a) accumulation fund in the department itself (additional v, additional increase to its own c)

(b) the fund of nonproductive consumption of the Soviet system</td></tr>
</table>

* The movement of the material composition of the fund of socialist accumulation is clear from the entire scheme of reproduction. More detail about this will be given in the numerical analysis of the Control Figures of Gosplan.

CAPITALIST SECTOR

c	*c*	*+v*	*+s*
Department I	Same as in the state sector, except for imports	Same as in the state sector	(a) accumulation fund (b) fund of capitalist consumption (c) fund of nonproductive consumption of the Soviet system (d) expropriation for the fund of socialist accumulation
Dept II	Same as in the state sector	Same as in the state sector	Same as in department *I* of the capitalist sector

PETIT BOURGEOIS SECTOR

c	*Means of production for the production of means of production, which are annually reproduced on an expanding scale*	*Consumption fund*	*Surplus product*
Department I	(a) reproduced within the department	(a) reproduced by means of exchange with *IIc* of the state sector	(a) accumulation fund: (1) the part that remains within the department; (2) the part exchanged for addition to the consumption fund; (3) for additional means of production from other sectors
	(b) by means of exchange with *Ic* of the state and capitalist sectors	(b) by means of exchange with *IIc* of the capitalist sector	(b) fund of nonproductive consumption of the Soviet system
	(c) via imports	(c) by means of exchange with *IIc* of its own sector	(c) expropriation into the fund of socialist accumulation
c	*Means of production for the production of means of consumption annually reproduced on an expanding scale*	*Consumption fund*	*Surplus product*
Department II	(a) created within the department	(a) produced internally (predominant part)	(a) accumulation fund: (1) fund of additional comsumption produced internally; (2) exchange for additional means of production from other departments of other sectors; (3) own additional means of production
	(b) reproduced by means of exchange with the consumption fund and a part of the fund of nonproductive consumption of its own sector	(b) by means of exchange with a part of *IIv* of the state sector, and *IIv* of the capitalist sector	(b) fund of nonproductive consumption of Soviet society, in natural form
	(c) by means of exchange with *v* and a part of the fund of nonproductive consumption of department *I* of the state sector		(c) expropriation into the fund of socialist accumulation
	(d) by means of exchange with a part of *v* and *s* of department *I* of the capitalist sector		

sectors; and the deduction from *s* for the socialist accumulation fund, which also complicates the analysis of reproduction.*

The means of production for department I of the petit bourgeois sector, which consist of machinery, cattle, seed, fertilizer, and so on of peasant farms engaged in producing technical crops, as well as of the equipment and raw materials of a certain part of handicraft industry, are divided into two parts. One part is reproduced within the department itself; the other may be obtained by internal exchange for I*c* of the state sector or (at least in part) by imports.

The consumption fund of department I of the petit bourgeois sector, which has the material form of means of production, is exchanged in two directions: for II*c* of the state sector and the capitalist sector on the one hand and for a part of the means of production fund of department II of the petit bourgeois sector itself on the other.

The surplus product of department I of the petit bourgeois sector is divided into three main parts: (a) an accumulation fund; (b) a nonproductive consumption fund,[5] whose size is determined by the extent to which the department in question is compelled to help cover it; and (c) a socialist accumulation fund, which goes into the state sector.

The accumulation fund, in turn, consists of (a) additional means of production produced within the department itself, which go to increase its own *c in natura*, by way of internal redistribution, that is, without engaging in exchange with other sectors; (b) means of production that are exchanged for means of production produced in department I of the state and capitalist sectors; (c) means of production *in natura*, which serve as an extra consumption fund for new workers and which therefore, in order to be consumed, must be exchanged for means of consumption from the departments II of all three sectors in the same proportions as the overall consumption fund of this particular department.

The nonproductive consumption fund, which is similar to the nonproductive consumption fund of department I of the state sector (excluding means of production for war industry), must

*For the time being we will disregard the question of how to calculate reproduction which is complicated by the alienation of the surplus value of the capitalist sector and the surplus product of the petit bourgeois sector into the socialist accumulation fund. This is a methodological problem of major importance. Its solution brings up the question of the relationship between domestic prices and those on the world market.

be transformed into articles of consumption by exchange in the correct proportions with *departments II* of all three sectors, replacing their constant capital.

The portion of the surplus product that goes into the fund of socialist accumulation consists, first of all, of the part of taxes levied on petty production that is destined not for the nonproductive consumption of the employees of the state and the trade network but rather for increasing the capital funds of the state sector, including state funds for agricultural credit. Secondly, it includes the part of the fund of primitive socialist accumulation formed by exchanging the export fund of petty (chiefly peasant) production, which is valued in terms of domestic prices (which are lower than world prices), for the import fund of means of production for the state sector, also valued in terms of domestic prices (which are much higher than world prices).[6] If we consider the entire process of reproduction in the USSR in terms of the value relationships of the world market, we have to include in this fund the entire balance resulting from the exchange[7] of state output for private output, taking the output of both the state sector and the private sectors in terms of world market prices and deducting from the total the part that is absorbed by nonproductive comsumption.

The means of production of department II of the petit bourgeois sector consist of four parts. The first and largest part is reproduced in department II itself, since we are concerned primarily with peasant agriculture. Included here are seeds set aside from the harvest, the peasant's production of his own work stock, his own production of feed for his livestock, his own fertilizer, his own buildings, and so on. The second part is reproduced by exchange for the consumption fund of department I of the petit bourgeois sector or for part of Iv of the capitalist sector. The third part is exchanged for part of the wages fund of department I of the state sector. The fourth part is reproduced through imports.

The consumption fund of department II of the petit bourgeois sector consists of two parts: the first and by far the greater part is reproduced within the department itself; the second, considerably smaller part is exchanged for part of the wages fund of department II of the state and capitalist sectors.

As regards the fund of surplus product of department II of the petit bourgeois sector, it can be broken down into the same four parts as the surplus product of department I of that sector; the difference consists in all the changes in the system of exchange *that are associated with another material form of the aggregate product.* More precisely, the accumulation fund is divided, above all, proportionally between the extra consumption fund and a fund of additional means of production, where the extra consumption fund has the same composition as the basic consumption fund. The distinction between the process of reproduction of this fund and the reproduction of the same fund in department I of the petit bourgeois sector consists in the fact that in department I, before exchange occurs, this fund has the material form of means of production, all of which must be exchanged for means of consumption, whereas here—that is, in department II—this fund has, from the very beginning, the natural form of means of consumption, and the bulk of it is also consumed here. Only its minor part is exchanged for means of consumption of the other two departments II. The fund of extra means of production, in turn, has the same composition as the means of production of that department in general. This means that part of the fund of extra means of production is created in the petit bourgeois sector itself, whereas the other part is obtained through exchange with other sectors.

Here, as earlier, we use the term "nonproductive consumption" to mean the part of the surplus product of a given sector that enters into the income of groups in Soviet society that represent nonproductive consumption: expenditures for the state apparatus, the army, the nonproductive part of expenditures on trade, and so on. The difference between the second and first departments of the petit bourgeois sector is that in department II the nonproductive consumption fund has, from the very outset, the material form of articles of consumption and is not subject to further exchange with other departments, as is inevitable for the nonproductive consumption fund that consists *in natura* of means of production.

As regards the surplus product destined for the fund of socialist accumulation, everything that we have said with respect to department I of the petit bourgeois sector applies without change to department II as well.

The scheme of reproduction in the system of the USSR that we have just presented enables us to define the general conditions of proportionality in an economy of the particular type and in the particular period of its existence that we are investigating. We must define these general conditions before we use the above scheme to analyze numerical data from specific years and before we attempt to replace the algebraic symbols with specific arithmetical figures, such as those of the economic years 1925–26 or 1926–27.

The First Condition of Equilibrium

Let us begin with the conditions of equilibrium between the entire state sector and the two sectors of the private economy taken together, from the standpoint of ensuring expanded reproduction in the state sector. For the time being we abstract from the material composition of the output being exchanged.

Let us assume that the gross annual output of the state sector is equal to 12 billion chervonets rubles (in present prices) and that it can be broken down as follows: $8c + 2v + 2$ surplus product. (In 1925–26 the gross output of the state economy, in producer prices, together with revenue from transport, communications, municipal services, and forestry, plus the gross output of construction, was 14.35 billion rubles, not including some minor items.)

Let us further assume that the exchange fund with private production as a whole totals 3 billion rubles, that is, that the state sector sells means of production, articles of consumption, and transportation services for 3 billion chervonets rubles to the private economy and obtains from the latter an equivalent amount of means of production (chiefly peasant raw materials), articles of consumption, and an export fund.[8] We thus have an even balance of exchange between the two sectors, that is, without any one-sided accumulation of undisposed-of commodity surpluses. Let us now assume that the entire economy of the USSR is integrated into the world economy on the basis of the free operation of the law of value, and that world market prices are forcibly imposed upon our industry, which maintains the same volume of exports and imports—that is, we disregard, for the time being, the possibility of changes in foreign trade flows. The entire equilibrium will then be upset, particularly that between the state sector as a whole and the sector of the private economy. To be more precise, let us assume that the entire output of the state sector is now valued at world market prices, that is, at one-half—or less—the prices it is valued at now. If within the state sector the part of the output of department I that goes to replace part of the constant capital of department II (machinery, fuel for the production of means of consumption) is approximately equal to the part of department II's output that in turn goes into department I (that is, textiles, shoes, sugar, and so on), then the forced lowering of prices will not essentially change the material proportions of exchange within the state sector itself, provided that the relative price increase on the output of heavy and light industry of the state sector does not differ appreciably from the relative price index of heavy and light industry of the world economy (if, say, means of consumption produced in our state industry are twice as expensive as the output of light industry in the world economy, and the prices of machinery are twice as high as the prices of machinery produced abroad). To take a hypothetical example, if one of our machine-building trusts now sells its machines to our textile industry at half the present price, then the textile industry will in turn sell its textiles, which are earmarked for the consumption of the workers and employees of the machine-building industry, at half the present price as well. In short, since the purchasing power of money changes simultaneously for both sides, the material balance of exchange will remain the same as if they valued their output not in terms of 1927 chervonets rubles but in another monetary unit, say, in terms of the purchasing power of the pound sterling on the world market. All this may entail gains or losses for particular branches whose prices are either less than or more than twice world prices. In such an event, when exchange between departments I and II of the state sector does not balance and the remainder is covered by exchange with private production, the principal loss is borne by the department of the state sector that proves to be more dependent on exchange with the private sectors.

In this particular case, however, the most important change occurs in the interrelations between *the state sector as a whole and private production as a whole*. The link between the state sector and the whole of private production is by no means limited by the size of the balance that is not covered internally, that is, through exchange within the state sector. Department I of the state sector must under all circumstances sell to private production a quantity of means of production equal in price to the part of the wages of its workers that is used to purchase consumer goods of peasant origin plus a corresponding part of means of production to compensate for a portion of the nonproductive consumption of department I of the state sector, excluding means of production for war industry. The volume of exchange between department II of the state sector and the private economy is even larger. By means of this exchange, this department replaces a considerable part of both its constant capital and its wages fund. In our example, which is numerically close to the actual figures for exchange between the state sector and the private economy during the economic year 1925–26, purchases by the private sector from the state sector and those by the state sector from the private sector each came to a total of 3 billion rubles.

If the private economy sold this 3 billion of its output at world market prices, then sales by the state sector to the private economy at world market prices—that is, at half-price—would mean that the state sector would make only 1.5 billion rubles on its output instead of 3 billion. That is, the state sector would receive only half of what it would obtain in an economic year in which conditions of nonequivalent exchange prevailed. A mere glance at our numerical example shows quite clearly the kind of disruption this would create in all aspects of reproduction in the state sector. The shortage of 1.5 billion absorbs, first of all, the entire accumulation fund. Secondly, it affects a certain part of nonproductive consumption. Thirdly, it makes it impossible later on to properly amortize fixed capital, as well as to replace the part of circulating capital that consists of peasant raw materials. On the whole, this would mean total breakdown of the process of expanded reproduction and, as long as nonproductive consumption remains substantial, could preclude the possibility of even simple reproduction at the previous year's level.

An even greater disturbance would occur if the establishment of world market prices on raw materials and means of consumption produced in the private economy would mean an effective price rise as compared to the way things stand now.

We thus arrive at a first and most highly significant conclusion: *Given a discrepancy between world industrial prices and domestic industrial prices in the USSR, that is, when domestic prices of Soviet industry are much higher than world prices, an economic equilibrium that will ensure expanded reproduction in the state sector can only be brought about on the basis of nonequivalent* *exchange with the sectors of private production.* This means that, given this sort of price discrepancy, the law of primitive socialist accumulation is the law that maintains the equilibrium of the entire system, above all in its relations with the world economy. This law must of necessity operate until we have overcome the economic and technological backwardness of the economy of the proletarian state as compared to the advanced capitalist countries.*

The Second Condition of Equilibrium

Let us now proceed to the next condition of equilibrium of the system, once again confining our attention for the time being to the interrelations between the state sector as a whole and private production as a whole.

Let us take our numerical scheme for the state sector and assume that a new economic year starts out with the results of the previous year's accumulation. We assume, therefore, that if we have a surplus product of 2 billion in the state sector—of which half goes to nonproductive consumption and half to productive accumulation—and if the exchange fund with private production increases from 3 billion rubles to 3.25 billion,[9] equilibrium in the entire economic system will be ensured. Let us now consider the opposite case, namely, that actual accumulation for some reason—either because of a sharp drop in disposal prices not justified by costs of production or because of a growth of nonproductive consumption—is only 700 million rubles instead of 1 billion. What will be the inevitable consequences of this underaccumulation in the state sector?

It is quite obvious that this will upset the proportionality between the state and private sectors of the Soviet economy. Underaccumulation by 300 million rubles will mean that the reproduction of *c* cannot be expanded within the bounds required

*This thesis, which underlies my theory of the law of primitive socialist accumulation, has evoked numerous laments from my critics, who clamor about "disrupting the peasant-worker alliance, a policy of raising prices, and so on." But despite my invitation to my critics to prove that at the present stage of development of the state economy expanded socialist reproduction is compatible with equivalent exchange, no one has responded. And it is easy to understand why. The formulation I have used merely states what is actually the case. I am simply trying scientifically to understand what is the case. If we already had equivalent exchange, then the very problem of the worker-peasant alliance would not exist at all.

in both departments: there will be a deficit of 240 million rubles in means of production. At the same time, the expansion of v in both departments of the state sector will be 60 million rubles below normal, which, in addition to everything else, will mean a slower increase in the number of workers employed in production and therefore a relative increase in unemployment. Finally, this would result in a 60-million-ruble decrease in the surplus product in the state economy as a whole. With respect to the total output of the state sector, we will have at the end of the year a shortage of production of 360 million rubles as compared to the first example.[10] If, as we have said, the share of the state sector's output absorbed by the private sector is 3.25 billion rubles, that is, almost one-quarter of the total gross output of the state sector, a shortage of 360 million rubles in production can mean a shortage of goods for the private sector of at least 90 million rubles.* But this will give rise to that well-known phenomenon we call the goods famine. If two-thirds of this 90 million rubles represents means of consumption produced in the state sector, the failure to satisfy the effective demand of the private economy, above all, that of the peasant sector, will mean a forced cutback in the peasantry's individual consumption of the products of state light industry and to the substitution of domestic handicraft output for factory products—that is, it will encourage the processing of raw materials (leather, wool, flax, and hemp) by primitive domestic methods and thus tend to delay economic development in this sector. Second, the peasants will refrain from selling their output for export and will consume more of their own foodstuffs themselves. Third, this disproportion will increase the discrepancy between retail and wholesale prices in the trade network, especially in private trade. As regards the remaining one-third, which consists of unmet demand for means of production, the disproportion will have much more harmful consequences: one cannot, after all, smelt metal, produce complicated agricultural machinery, and so on by handicraft methods. Under conditions of expanded reproduction, peasant agriculture will not be able to increase the quantity of machines, stocks, and other means of production it needs. In both departments of the petit bourgeois sector, recurrent goods famines will inevitably—since sales cannot be followed

*We say "at least" because the urban demand for goods of state production is naturally to be satisfied first of all; and in the present case, the *bulk* of the deficit may be transferred to the demand of the private economy.

by purchases—cause the peasantry to refrain from selling a part of its output and will encourage the appearance of the familiar phenomenon of accumulation of unsold stocks in kind in the peasant economy. This disproportion can be alleviated only by monetary accumulation in the peasant economy, which is generally possible only if there is either a stable currency or if the purchasing power of money is rising because of falling prices. However, it is self-evident that such accumulation, insofar as it corresponds to the part of the peasant economy's reserves that ought to have been converted into means of production produced in the state sector, inevitably means an artificial delay in the process of expanded reproduction in the peasant economy as compared to the possibilities for expansion that actually exist within it.

It follows quite clearly from this discussion that (1) the volume of accumulation in state industry at a given price level is not an arbitrary magnitude but is subject to iron laws of proportionality, the revealing of which constitutes one of the most important tasks of a theory of the Soviet economy and of the practice of planned management of economic life, and (2) any perturbation in the necessary minimum of accumulation not only is a blow to the state economy and to the working class but also retards the development of the peasant economy by artificially slowing the pace of expanded reproduction in agriculture.

Let us now look at the same question, but from a different angle: let us look at what some economists, who draw an uncritical analogy between the Soviet system and capitalism and who fall into petit bourgeois philistinism, at one time tended to call "overaccumulation in state industry" and "industry running ahead." To begin with, we have to decide what we mean by the term "overaccumulation." If by overaccumulation we mean a relationship between production and consumption throughout society such that new means of production put into operation in both departments lead in the final analysis to so sharp an increase in the production of means of consumption that these goods cannot be absorbed by the consumer market at existing prices, as a result of which the corresponding accumulation in department I proves to be useless—well, then, such a phenomenon is quite well known in capitalist economy and must inevitably lead to a sales crisis, the ruin of numerous enterprises in both departments, a forced lowering of prices, and a fall in the rate of profit. If, in a theoretically conceivable case, our state economy were on the basis of the previous year's accumulation to turn out means of consumption in excess of the effective demand of both the workers and the entire state economy at given planned prices, then the situation would be much less serious than in a capitalist economy. The reason for this is as follows. Dynamic equilibrium in our system presumes among other things: (1) a growth of workers' wages, (2) a gradual decline in industrial prices, (3) reequipment and expansion of the entire technological base of the state economy. The appearance of a sales crisis may, under such conditions, mean one of three things:

(1) We have miscalculated the time needed to carry out the first two points of the program. In this case, equilibrium can be attained either by raising wages above the levels called for in the program or, more radically, by lowering the general level of prices on articles of consumption produced in the state sector more rapidly than the program calls for. In that case the disproportion may be overcome very quickly and without any special perturbations, and "overaccumulation" will prove to be a crisis in the production plan only in the sense that the plan incorrectly estimated the time needed to fulfill the first two tasks. Moreover, we must not forget that, given our general shortage of reserves in the areas of credit, production and trade, *the disproportion cannot long continue to build up in hidden form*, as is usual under capitalism, and that its elimination must inevitably begin much earlier, before the whole process goes too far. The harmful consequences of this sort of planning error will reveal themselves later, in that there will be a delay in fulfilling the third task mentioned above.

(2) The sales crisis may mean that we have miscalculated the time needed to carry out the third task. That is, we have expanded the production of means of consumption, *at prevailing prices*, too far and too fast: the technological base of the state economy and the degree of rationalization of labor that has been achieved are inadequate to permit a lowering of the cost of production, a lowering of selling prices or, in the worst case, even just an increase in wages. In this situation, "overaccumulation" proves to be the result of an incorrect distribution of the productive forces within the state economy, the result of the fact that the process of technological reequipping of industry has lagged behind the overall development of the economy as a whole. What we have here is an internal disproportion within the state sector,

not overaccumulation in terms of the interrelations between the state economy and private production. Solving this crisis by lowering prices—a lowering of the cost of production for which the economic basis has not been prepared—could temporarily delay the entire process of expanded reproduction, just as it would be delayed if we tried to solve the problem by letting a part of production remain in the form of a nonliquid fund while maintaining the prevailing price level. This lack of correspondence would continue until a redistribution of productive forces restored equilibrium.

(3) The reequipping of fixed capital, which proceeds unevenly, draws so many means of production into the production of means of production that themselves do not begin turning out goods until several years later, that all this retards the growth of the population's consumption fund and, with the occurrence of a goods famine, arrests the process of lowering prices. In that case *we will have not general overaccumulation* (otherwise a goods famine could occur, even if only with respect to means of consumption) in the state sector but a temporal disproportion in the particular tasks of expanded reproduction. We would then be confronted not so much with an error in drafting the plan as with the natural result of the transition from the restoration process to the reconstruction process. We would be confronted with the natural consequences of the situation wherein the country's fixed capital, which had been severely depleted by the failure to make up for the depreciation losses of previous years, was being renewed under conditions of limited ties with the world economy and of a general shortage of internal accumulation in the material form of means of production. *What appears superficially as overaccumulation in heavy industry is merely a special form of underaccumulation throughout the state economy, taken as a whole.* The very nature of the renewal of fixed capital under the conditions we have described is such that this process must necessarily occur unevenly. To expand the annual production of means of consumption in state light industry by, let us say, 100 million rubles, we first have to increase the production of means of production by 400–500 million. This may temporarily slow down the necessary rate of production of means of consumption, bring about a special kind of goods famine, and delay the lowering of prices, especially in the case when a shift in the structure of the peasant budget leads to a heavier demand for means of consumption than before the

war. But in return, it will within a few years enable us rapidly to reduce the cost of production, lower selling prices, and rapidly increase the consumption fund. Instead of a systematic lowering of prices (let us say, 2–3 percent per year), and a systematic increase in the production of means of consumption (let us say, 6–7 percent per year), the same program can be carried out in three to four years, only in more uneven form. If we disregard the political difficulties of this period, the harmful economic consequences of such a development of the state economy will essentially amount to the fact that production of export crops will be slowed down in the peasant economy and the production of industrial crops will prove to be lower than the demands made upon it by the rapid development of state light industry. For the most part, this latter difficulty for our economy still lies before us, whereas the artificial cutback in peasant exports is already at hand. In terms of the overall progress of the state economy, the case we are examining will imply not a crisis of overaccumulation and overproduction in the strict sense but simply the material impossibility of harmoniously coordinating the development of all aspects of expanded reproduction *with respect to time*. In the transition from restoration to reconstruction this will, generally speaking, be unavoidable, because the transition itself, as we will see in more detail below, implies a sharp change in the overall proportions of distribution of the country's productive forces. The fact that new plants do not start turning out goods until three to four years after their construction has begun is more the result of technical than economic necessity. An initial delay and then a forward jump are inevitable. The only possibility of partially evening out this jump is through greater exports and foreign credits. But these latter alternatives are impossible precisely because in the Soviet Union we have not merely expanded production but expanded *socialist* production of industry—a process that world capitalism is not inclined to assist.

Thus, we arrive at the conclusion that the volume of accumulation in the state economy in any given year is not an arbitrary magnitude, but that a certain minimum of accumulation is harshly dictated to us by the overall proportions of the distribution of the productive forces between the state and private sectors, as well as by the extent of our ties with the world economy. Second, we arrive at the conclusion that overaccumulation in the state sector, given the tremendous task of rapid reequipment and expansion of the fixed capital of industry (a task that will take decades to complete), is an absolute impossibility. This reequipping constitutes essentially a domestic market of colossal capacity, not to mention the growth of the domestic market on account of increased demand from the private sectors of our economy. Rather than talk about a crisis of overaccumulation in the state economy, a sector that does not have as its goal the production of surplus value, we can speak of a colossal underaccumulation, which is reflected in the peasant economy as well, in that it slows down its development. We may also speak of insufficient accumulation in the sphere of peasant production of industrial raw materials. We will deal with this sort of disproportion when we analyze the material composition of exchange between state and private production.

It must also be noted at this point that the two general conditions of equilibrium that we have so far examined differ from one another in the following respect. Equilibrium of nonequivalent exchange when there is a gap between domestic prices and world prices—that is, equilibrium of an economy regulated by the law of primitive socialist accumulation in struggle with the law of value—is a distinguishing feature of our economy; it is the law of our existence as a Soviet system throughout the entire period of struggle to overcome our economic backwardness relative to advanced capitalism. Here, equilibrium is attained as a result of the constant struggle waged by still backward collective production, the struggle waged by the only country with a dictatorship of the proletariat, against the capitalist world and against the capitalist and petit bourgeois elements in its own economy. Equilibrium of this type is the unstable equilibrium of a struggle between two systems; it is not attained through the workings of a world-wide law of value but on the basis of constant violation of this law, on the basis of constant violation of the world market, on the basis of the withdrawal—if not complete, then partial—of an enormous economic area from under the regulatory influence of the world market.

Things are considerably different when we talk about the second condition of equilibrium, that is, the proportions of accumulation in the state sector needed to maintain equilibrium in the economic organism after the first condition of equilibrium has already been met for a certain length of time. Maintaining equilibrium within an economic organism that is divided into a system of collective production and a system of private production *brings state planning policy, guided by the law of primitive socialist accumulation, into a different sort of conflict with the law of value.* If we do not in planned fashion hit upon the required proportions of distribution of the productive forces, given the existing correlation between domestic and world price levels, the law of value will burst through with elemental force into the sphere of regulation of economic processes and, forcing the planning principle into a disorderly retreat, will thereby encroach upon those specific proportions of the distribution of labor and means of production that will have been created as a result of the existence of the collective sector of the economy—those specific proportions that guarantee not merely expanded reproduction, but expanded reproduction in a system of the Soviet type.

The Third Condition of Equilibrium

Let us now go on to the third condition of equilibrium, which has to do with the extent of our participation in the world division of labor and the specific conditions under which this participation takes place.

Let us take our previous numerical example relating to reproduction in the state sector. Now, however, the nature of the question we must answer requires us to divide the annual production of the state sector into two departments. Let us assume that the distribution of the productive forces and of the output between the two departments is as follows: department I, 40 percent; department II, 60 percent.* To stick to reality, let us assume further that the organic composition of capital in department I is lower than in department II (in contrast to Marx's scheme; details on this later). The ratio *c*:*v* in department I is 3:2, whereas in department II it is 2:1. Let us further assume that the surplus product equals 100 percent of the wages and that it is broken

*In 1925–26 the output of means of consumption was 58.8 percent, and the output of means of production 41.2 percent, of total industrial output. See *Perspektivy razvertyvaniia narodnogo khoziaistva SSSR na 1926/27–1930/31 gg.* [Prospects for the Development of the National Economy of the USSR for 1926/27–1930/31], Gosplan SSSR, pp. 123–24, and the table on pp. 54–58. The corresponding data for 1913 and 1924–25 presented in the *Kontrol'nye tsifry na 1926/27* [Control Figures for 1926–27], p. 163, seem incorrect to me, but more about that later.

down in both departments into two equal parts: one part goes to accumulation in the same department, and the other goes into the nonproductive consumption fund of Soviet society. The entire scheme will then have the following form:

I. 2,100c + 1,400v + 1,400 surplus product (700 to the accumulation fund; 700 to the nonproductive consumption fund) = 4,900

II. 3,550c + 1,775v + 1,775 surplus product (887.5 to the accumulation fund; 887.5 to the nonproductive consumption fund) = 7,100

Even a cursory glance at this scheme shows a major difference as compared to the corresponding schemes used by Marx to illustrate capitalist production. Not only is IIc of the state sector considerably greater than wages and nonproductive consumption in department I of the state sector, but it is also greater than the wages plus the entire surplus product of department I. All this is quite natural in a peasant country where a very large part of IIc of the state sector is reproduced by exchange with the the petit bourgeois economy, which provides our light industry with such means of production as cotton, flax, hemp, hides, wool, sugar beets, oil seeds for the oil-extraction industry, grain for the mills, and potatoes for the alcohol industry. Let us assume that half of IIc of the state sector, or 1,775c, is reproduced through exchange with private production.[11] That is, we choose in advance a figure that exceeds the actual size of what IIc reproduces through exchange with petit bourgeois economy. The question now arises: How can the other half of IIc be reproduced?

For the reproduction of that half, we have first of all a wages fund of department I that is equal to 1,400. However, not all of this sum can go to replace half of IIc, because part of the wages of department I must be exchanged for peasant means of consumption. Let us assume that the latter exchange required one-third* of

*A study of workers' budgets shows about 40 percent, that is, more than the proportion we have chosen. However, when we take into account the processing of grain into flour and bread in state flour mills, the volume of state and factory woodcutting, and so on, the figure we have chosen will not be very far from the truth.

1,400, or 466.6. A fund of 933.4, which has the material form of means of production, then remains for exchange against II*c*. Furthermore, since 700 of the surplus product goes to accumulation in department I, a nonproductive consumption fund of 700 remains from the surplus product to be exchanged with departments II of the other sectors. If we take the same proportion of exchange of that fund with department II of the state sector on the one hand and with the private economy on the other, as we did with I*v*—that is, if we assume that two-thirds, or 467, goes to department II of the state sector, whereas the remaining 233 goes to private production—then the entire exchange fund of department I of the state sector that goes to replace half of II*c* will be equal to 933.4 + 467 = 1,400.4 or, rounding off, 1,400.[12] However, the amount to be replaced was equal to 1,775. Thus, there is a deficit of means of production in the state sector to the tune of 375 million.

Let us go further. If we assume that this deficit is somehow covered, then all we need do is construct a scheme of expanded reproduction for the following year on the basis of the data of the initial scheme in order to see how the disproportion that we have noted will persist, decreasing somewhat under certain conditions, increasing under others. To be precise, of the 887.5 of surplus product in department II that is subject to accumulation, 295.8 will go to increase *v*, and 591.7 to increase *c*. Thus, II*c* will now equal 4,141.7, whereas the part of it that must be covered by exchange with department I will be equal to 2,070.8. At the same time, as a result of the growth of *v* and of nonproductive consumption, the exchange fund of department I increases proportionately, and the part of it that must go to replace II*c* will now be 1,680 instead of 1,400. This means that in the following year the deficit of means of production will equal 2,070.8 – 1,680 = 390.8 million instead of 375—*with the same rate of growth of nonproductive consumption.*[13] Conversely, maintenance of the same absolute volume of nonproductive consumption must necessarily increase the disproportion because maintenance of the old volume, or a reduction of the rate of growth of nonproductive consumption, will cause a depletion of the exchange fund of department I of the state sector at the same time that II*c* of the state sector is growing in relative terms.[14] The question arises whether the disproportion that we have discovered is the result of the numerical relationships we have chosen as an illustration (although the proportions are close to the actual ones) or whether it represents a real disproportion in our economy.

There can be hardly any doubt that the example we have chosen illustrates precisely the real disproportion that exists in our economy and that is caused by (1) the suspension of foreign capital investment in our industry; (2) the reduction of the nonproductive consumption of the bourgeois class; (3) the failure to make up for depreciation losses on fixed capital in previous years; (4) the withdrawal of a part of the means of production for the construction of new plants that have not yet begun to yield any output; (5) the general necessity of more rapid accumulation in department I during a period when the country is undergoing industrialization.[15]

Thus, we observe a sharp and continuously growing deficit of means of production in our state economy. The question now arises: What role in eliminating this disproportion can be played by foreign trade, which we must now introduce into our analysis? This role is an extremely important one. Let us assume that the deficit of means of production in department II signifies a deficit of machinery for light industry, the electric power industry, the basic chemical industry, and so on, and that the deficit in heavy industry expresses itself in a shortage of equipment in the fuel industry, in engineering plants, high-power turbogenerators, air compressors, and other equipment of ferrous and nonferrous metallurgy. What is the effect of introducing foreign trade?

The introduction of imports achieves the following:

(1) Light industry will not be arrested in its development and will not have to wait for the moment when department I can, on the basis of its own development, provide it with the elements of *c* that are in short supply. Instead, it can cover its deficit immediately from abroad. That is, the problem of time is solved. In contrast, trying to solve the problem by the long, roundabout way of developing our own department I would lead to a growing crisis and to one difficulty piling up on top of another, including those in the area of exchange between the state sector and private production. In this connection we must keep in mind another extremely important circumstance: To increase its output by 100 units, light industry must expend its constant capital correspondingly—in the present case the part of *c* that is reproduced in department I of the state sector. But if in that department there

happens to be a general deficit of means of production required by light industry, then the additional demand of light industry can be satisfied only by constructing new enterprises in heavy industry. This construction, however, necessitates each year the withdrawal—for the entire construction period—of resources from the general accumulation fund of the state economy that far exceed the value of the means of production needed to supply light industry with additional elements of fixed capital. The addition of a new 100*c* to the constant capital of department II may require a simultaneous investment of 400 to 500 in new capital in department I. Yet, if we turn to the world market we can solve this problem, directly and without delay, by importing the necessary amount and type of means of production for department II.

(2) Heavy industry will not have to wait until its own deficit of means of production is covered by its internal development, nor will it have to equip new industries with machinery of its own production, which would mean an extreme delay in putting new enterprises into opeartion and lead to a crisis within department I itself, as well as in its exchange relations with department II. Instead, heavy industry can cut through the contradictions by importing equipment that, if produced domestically, would intensify the crisis by channeling an already inadequate accumulation into enterprises whose construction is hardly of primary importance as long as we have links with the world economy.

(3) Both light and heavy industry solve not only the temporal problem of developing their production, but also, to a certain extent, the problem of accumulation at the expense of the private economy. Let us illustrate this concretely. In our example, the state sector has a shortage of 400 million rubles, calculated in domestic prices, in means of production for replacing fixed capital. To cover this deficit, our state has only to export, let us say, consumer goods from the peasant economy for 200 million rubles or $100 million and buy foreign equipment for that same sum. This foreign equipment, which in world prices costs $100 million or 200 million chervonets rubles, costs 400 million rubles inside our country, if we consider the difference between our domestic industrial prices and foreign prices. Thus, thanks to the import of means of production, we profit by the difference between world prices and domestic prices and automatically accumulate fixed capital in our developing industry.

Thus, the link with the world market, which solves the temporal aspect of the problem of reconstruction and expansion of fixed capital of both departments in the state sector, also solves to a certain degree the material aspect of the problem of accumulation, specifically, by methods of primitive socialist accumulation.

In addition to the case we have just examined, however, there is another disproportion that can also be solved by imports. This involves replacing a certain part of the elements of II*c* in their material form, since our own domestic production of raw materials is insufficient in certain areas. We would probably retard the normal development of our textile industry by a decade if we were to wait for our own cotton production to develop to the point where it could satisfy the entire demand of this industry for raw materials.

In addition to the cases we have just listed, reliance on imports is an absolute necessity in cases where, for natural reasons, we simply do not produce a particular raw material (for example, natural rubber) or certain means of consumption (for example, coffee). But I deliberately avoid going into that aspect of our link with the world economy, because in that case participation in the world division of labor is advantageous and necessary for us *in general, regardless of the structure of the economy and the degree of its development*. Rather, I am speaking of the import of those means of production that we can, in general, produce ourselves and whose domestic production we will in fact expand, but which, at the present stage of the state economy's development, we have to import—first to maintain equilibrium in the system of expanded socialist reproduction, and second to promote the accumulation of fixed capital.

Thus we arrive at the conclusion that the third precondition for equilibrium in our system is the closest possible link with the world economy, built upon the very distinctive nature of our exports and imports. When there is a general deficit of domestic production of means of production, in particular, when heavy industry is underdeveloped relative to the demands of the domestic state and private market and relative to the overall rate of industrialization necessary for the country, *our planned import of means of production must be of such a volume and material composition as to serve, so to speak, as an automatic regulator* *of the entire process of expanded reproduction without ceasing to be a source of accumulation.**

The Fourth Condition of Equilibrium

Let us proceed further. The fourth condition of equilibrium of our economic system is proportionality in the distribution of labor, in particular, proportionality in exchange between the state economy and the entire private economy within the country, both with respect to the value of that exchange at given price levels and with respect to its material composition. Here we assume equilibrium of value exchange to be understood in a conditional sense, that is, in the sense of an equilibrium of nonequivalent exchange, or exchange as the mechanism of socialist accumulation. To give a more graphic picture of this fourth condition of equilibrium, let us take our provisional numerical example for the state sector and add to it an arithmetical scheme of reproduction in the private economy. To simplify matters, we will for the time being not divide the private economy into two sectors, capitalist and petit bourgeois, as should be done in a more detailed analysis. As was done in the state sector, we will divide the surplus product of each department of the private economy into two parts: an actual accumulation fund and a fund of nonproductive consumption.

Let us set the total annual output of the entire private economy at 17 billion.** We shall assume that this gross output is divided

*Of course, the above disproportion could also be resolved, from the standpoint of private production and its interests, by direct imports of means of consumption, but it is quite clear that such a solution of the question would mean a most serious delay in, if not the elimination of, expanded socialist reproduction. Generally speaking, many of the problems of the private economy could be solved by eliminating socialist industry or even by merely eliminating the monopoly of foreign trade. The entire struggle between the state and private sectors of the Soviet economy is reduced precisely to the question of the basis on which equilibrium can be attained within that economy: on the basis of integration into the world economy "on general terms," that is, on the basis of the law of value, or in a new way, unprecedented in economic history, through planned imports subordinated to the task of primitive socialist accumulation.

**In the 1925–26 economic year the total output of the private economy, according to the Control Figures of Gosplan, was 16,397 million rubles in terms of producer prices.

between the two departments of private economy as follows:

I. 2,200*c* + 2,200 consumption fund + 1,100 surplus product = 5,500

II. 3,300*c* + 6,600 consumption fund + 2,100 surplus product = 12,000

Department I includes the production of industrial crops in the peasant economy, as well as all raw materials in general, plus those enterprises in artisan and craft industry that produce means of production—for example, private smithies and repair shops; artisan production of agricultural implements, wheels, and carts; and animal-drawn freight transportation for transferring goods destined for further processing.

All production of means of consumption in the peasant economy takes place in department II, and it will constitute the overwhelming part of that department's total output: field cultivation, animal breeding (the part of it that yields consumer goods such as milk, butter, and meat), truck farming, fishing, and manufacture of homemade clothing. Department II also includes handicraft and private capitalist production of fabrics and clothing, the private leather industry, and the private food industry.

Having divided the peasant economy into two departments in this fashion, we must always keep in mind that this division is a methodological abstraction. The same indivisible peasant farm almost always figures in two departments at the same time, because no matter how many means of consumption it produces, it must also produce a certain quantity of means of production; and conversely, a peasant farm that specializes in industrial crops always produces a certain amount of means of consumption.

Reproduction in department I occurs in such a way that part of the means of production for the peasant economy, which produces both raw materials and means of production for craft and artisan industry, is produced within the same department I of the private sector. This includes production of seeds in the cultivation of flax, cotton, sugar beets, and hemp that are to be used for further cultivation of the same crops. The same sector produces dray animals and animal feed grown on cultivated or natural meadows, and also breeds animals for raw materials (sheep that give wool are the means of production of wool, and the breeding of such sheep is production of the means of production of wool).

However, there remains another part of the means of production that can only be obtained from department I of the state sector. This includes metal and coal for smithies and small repair shops, agricultural machines for peasant production of raw materials, artificial fertilizer, rail and water transport to service the replacement of I*c* of the private sector, etc. The following question arises: Department I of the state sector, which is composed of the engineering and fuel industries, metallurgy, the construction and supply of electrical power, etc., purchases very little from department I of the private economy—in any case, less than this department must buy from heavy industry. Yet, everything that heavy industry sells to replenish its wages fund requires corresponding sales of means of consumption from the other sectors, which department I of the private economy is unable to provide. This is the source of an extremely complex set of relationships that extend throughout the entire system of reproduction and that Marx did not investigate directly in his famous chapters on accumulation in vol. II of *Capital*, because he was assuming purely capitalist reproduction, where the entire equilibrium of exchange is concentrated solely on the relationship between the volume of II*c* and its rate of growth on the one hand and the magnitude of $\mathrm{I}(v + s/x)$ and its rate of growth on the other. The part of I*c* of the private sector that is not covered by its own production of means of production or by internal exchange with I*c* of the state sector may still fall into department I of the private sector via realization of the nonproductive consumption fund of department I of the state sector. This problem may also be partially solved by foreign trade: flax, hemp, raw wool, bristles, etc., are exported, and the required amounts of means of production are obtained in return.[16]

Thus, we see that reproduction of one part of I*c* of the private sector represents a rather complex task, which can be solved by drawing into exchange all the departments of all the sectors, mainly through the channel of nonproductive consumption plus foreign trade. It is not enough that this particular part of I*c* of the private sector, which initially has the material form of industrial raw materials or means of production of private industry, be sold. It is also necessary that the money thus earned can buy a sufficient quantity of precisely those means of production that are needed. The systematic shortage of means of production described above, mainly in the form of fixed capital (a shortage that characterizes the period of reconstruction of the state sector's technological base) must increase still further as a result of that disproportionality in the exchange of I*c* of the state sector for I*c* of the private sector of which we have just spoken.

Before it is exchanged, the consumption fund of department I of the private sector consists of the same elements–that is, all types of industrial raw materials produced in the peasant economy, as well as means of production of craft and artisan origin (the output of smithies, repair shops, and cart shops; the production of all other types of agricultural implements; and the cutting of wood for further processing). Part of these means of production is realized within the private sector itself and goes to reproduce that sector's II*c*, which in our example totaled 3,300*c*.[17] Department II of the private sector offers means of consumption in exchange with department I of its own sector. The other part of the means of production of department I of the private sector that is destined to replace its consumption fund goes to department II of the state sector in the form of raw materials for the textile, leather, sugar, dairy, and alcohol industries and is exchanged for cloth, footwear, and sugar.

The surplus product of department I of the private sector, at least as regards its main and most interesting part—that is, the surplus product in the production of industrial crops in the peasant economy—consists of three basic parts: (1) the portion of the nonproductive consumption fund that falls to that particular department and from which is paid a proportionate share of state taxes, expenditures on the trade apparatus, and so on; (2) a productive accumulation fund within the department itself; and (3) a fund that goes to socialist accumulation in the state sector. In our example, the entire surplus product of department I of the private sector is equal to 1.1 billion, of which 500 million, let us say, goes to the accumulation fund, 400 million to the nonproductive consumption fund, and 200 million to the socialist accumulation fund.

As regards the nonproductive consumption fund, the bulk of it must be exchanged for means of consumption of department II of the state and private sectors, since means of production are not consumed individually. The conduit for such exchange is the reproduction of *c* in the departments II of all three sectors of the economy. As regards the accumulation fund of 500 million, this fund must also be divided into two quite distinct parts: (1) a fund of additional means of consumption for expanded reproduction, that is, the part of this 500 million that must be exchanged for means of consumption and serve as a consumption fund for new workers who will be employed in production; and (2) a fund of additional means of production in the strict sense. If we assume that the division between the consumption fund and the fund of means of production occurs in the same proportions as in the preceding year, then the accumulation fund of means of production will be 250 million. Let us now examine the elements that make up this latter figure. The smaller part of this 250 million will consist of means of production that department I of the private sector must purchase from department I of the state sector, that is, from state heavy industry. The greater part of this 250 million consists of means of production that are produced within the peasant economy itself and are added, to use the term imprecisely, to the capital of production. This includes (1) seeds of industrial crops, which are obtained within the department itself and go to *expand* the sown area; (2) the expanded reproduction of cattle, fodder, and manure; (3) all types of land improvements aimed at extending the area of cultivation of industrial crops and increasing soil fertility; (4) farm buildings constructed of peasant timber by the peasant's own means; (5) additional means of production obtained within the department itself, but through exchange with private and craft industry.

It is quite obvious that expanded reproduction of industrial crops is most intimately connected in its development with the conditions of reproduction and accumulation in state heavy industry, since it requires means of production from the state sector. On the other hand, however, expanded reproduction in department II of the state sector is intimately connected with progress in the expanded reproduction of industrial crops in the peasant economy, from which it obtains its raw materials. Thus, as a result, expanded reproduction of department II of the state sector requires *the prior* expanded reproduction of department I of the private sector—specifically, the part of it that produces industrial crops—whereas expanded reproduction of industrial crops requires *the prior* expanded reproduction of the part of department I of the state sector that provides it with the necessary additional means of production. Thus both state light industry and peasant production of industrial crops have a common interest in seeing that accumulation in heavy industry, which must always *precede* the expanded reproduction of these branches, be as rapid as possible.

Let us present one more particular example that is often encountered in practice in a peasant country and is related to the question we are examining. It is a well-known fact that in our peasant economy the process of accumulation takes place unevenly, in years of good harvest. In one year of good harvest hundreds of thousands of peasant farms manage to "put themselves in the black" and increase their means of production to an extent that they may not be able to achieve again for perhaps another five years. Let us assume that we have an above-average harvest of flax, cotton, oil-bearing seeds, and so on. As a result, the peasant economy can put into the accumulation fund a sum that exceeds the usual average annual increment of accumulation. This also gives rise to an increased demand for, among other things, means of production produced by state industry, as well as for those produced in handicraft production. However, since there is no such thing as a good harvest of machines, metals, and so on in heavy industry, the peasant economy's demand for additional means of production will not be satisfied unless accumulation in heavy industry takes place at a consistently faster pace than in other branches of the economy, specifically, unless it can ensure that the necessary commodity stocks are on hand. If this does not occur, then in the best of cases the accumulation fund earmarked for the purchase of means of production in heavy industry will be temporarily frozen in monetary form, and provided there is a well-developed credit system, it will, on the basis of a redistribution of the country's monetary accumulation, permit credit expansion and thereby also make possible additional production in the corresponding branches of heavy industry. At worst, however, this accumulation fund will be exchanged for means of consumption and will simply be consumed within the peasant economy, having increased the consumer budget of the peasant department producing industrial crops. This is not to mention the fact that the disproportion will be even greater in the case where heavy industry has already exhausted all its reserves of old equipment, and the new additional demand can be satisfied only by new fixed capital investments that far exceed the total commodity deficit for the year in question.

Let us now move on to department II of the private sector. If we exclude private industrial production of means of consumption (craft and artisan production of footwear, clothing, and fabrics;

the private food industry),* we will be left mainly with peasant production of means of consumption. The reproduction of the constant capital—in our example, equal to 3,300*c*—occurs as follows. The bulk of *c* consists of means of production obtained within peasant production of means of consumption itself. This includes seeds of grain crops, cattle fodder, manure, reproduction of cattle, buildings constructed from the peasant's own timber by his own means, land improvements, the clearing of forests to provide new arable land, and cultivation of virgin soil. The second part of the means of production is obtained by the exchange of articles of consumption of the department in question for means of production from department I of the private sector of the economy. Finally, the third part of the means of consumption of department II of the private sector that go to replace its *c* is sold to the workers in heavy industry of the state sector. In return, heavy industry provides means of production in the form of agricultural machines, equipment, nails, roofing iron and other forms of iron, freight transportation and so on.

The overwhelming part of the consumption fund of department II of the private sector is produced and consumed within the department itself, and in fact most of it does not enter at all into the "commodity" part of the output of the peasant economy. In addition, only a minor part of this fund participates in internal exchange with the wages fund of department II of the state sector, that is, with state light industry. In other words, if we take the wages fund of state light industry to be 1,000, and if we take the part of the fund that consists of articles of consumption of peasant and other private production to be 400, then according to the makeup of his expense budget, the worker in light industry will use that amount to buy what he needs (grain, butter, and so on) from the consumption fund of department II of the private sector, whereas the peasants and the craftsmen of department II will buy articles of consumption produced in the state sector.

However, this does not at all mean that we must have the same sort of complete or approximate arithmetical equality as Marx establishes in his analysis of capitalist reproduction, where II*c*

*In 1925–26 total private industrial production—capitalist, handicraft, and artisan—was 2.165 billion chervonets rubles, including the production of both means of production and means of consumption.

is exchanged for $(v + s/x)$. When we analyzed exchange between department I of the private sector and department I of the state sector, we already established that department I of the private sector—because of the material composition of the commodities exchanged—must obtain more from heavy industry than heavy industry can buy from this department. However, this means that department I of the private sector must make up the balance by selling its means of production elsewhere and using the money earned to buy means of production from heavy industry. It is quite obvious that this problem may be solved by means of foreign trade. Part of the flax, hemp, and so on is exported; heavy industry obtains the equipment it needs by import; and the sellers of flax, hemp, and so on purchase, in chervonets rubles, the means of production they need from Soviet heavy industry. In this way, the disproportion in the material composition of exchange between department I of the private sector and department I of the state sector is eliminated by drawing on the foreign market, which makes it possible to regroup the elements of production within department I itself and to free the resources needed for exchange with department I of the private sector. The problem may be solved even more simply in a direct way, that is, by importing machinery and other means of production for department I of the private sector. If the problem cannot be solved in the requisite quantitative proportions—either because of underdevelopment of the domestic machine-building industry or the production of artificial fertilizers, or because of limitations on the import quota allotted the private economy—we have a goods famine in means of production of heavy industry, that is, one of the forms a disturbance in the equilibrium between the state and private economies takes as a result of the underdevelopment of our heavy industry.

In precisely the same way, let us assume that the part of the peasant economy that produces means of consumption must exchange more of its products for means of consumption of industrial production than the wages fund of light industry, which we mentioned above, can provide; then the problem can, generally speaking, also be solved by resorting to foreign trade. Whether or not recourse to the foreign market is practically possible under present conditions is another question. To take a hypothetical example, let us assume that the workers and employees of state light industry purchase 400 million rubles' worth of means of consumption in the private sector, whereas the private sector's department of means of consumption requires 600 million rather than 400 million rubles' worth of goods in exchange for its consumption fund; that is, its effective demand, accompanied by sale, is 600 million, and it manifests a demand in that amount for products of state light industry. Specifically, the peasantry has an extra 200 million rubles' worth of grain, butter, eggs, and so on to sell, and it wants to use this extra 200 million to purchase an additional amount of clothing, footwear, sugar, and other manufactured consumer goods. But let us assume that department II of the state sector, that is, state light industry, provides only 400 million rubles' worth of goods and no more. Foreign trade could offer a solution in this case as well: an additional 200 million rubles' worth of peasant products could be exported, and the money earned could be used to import foreign manufactured consumer goods for the peasantry. In practice, however, given the shortage of resources for export, even for the importation of vital means of production, this method turns out to be impossible for the Soviet state during the first years of the reconstruction process. To draw this 200 million rubles' worth of additional export resources into circulation, we would first have to purchase the products of light industry abroad, for which we would have to dip into the import fund for the year in question, that is, we would have to cut down on imports of means of production, which are already in short supply. Because such a measure is impossible, and because its own state light industry is still insufficiently developed, the Soviet economy will also find itself faced with a protracted goods famine of industrially produced means of consumption. As a result, part of the liquid resources from the fund of means of consumption produced in the peasant sector are not drawn into commodity circulation, and the Soviet village begins the familiar process of increasing internal consumption of eggs, butter, and so on, increasing grain stores beyond the emergency reserves kept in case of bad harvests, and a number of concomitant phenomena. *As a result, agriculture as a whole effectively produces relatively less for the market than would be objectively possible with a more rapid development of Soviet industry, even with the existing very high prices,* not to mention the possibility of a still greater growth of the marketed share that would result from a more rapid reduction of production costs and industrial prices. This is the source of a second disproportion between state industry and the peasant economy, one that under the present circumstances can only be overcome by the more rapid development of state industry.

It is theoretically possible to solve the problem in another way as well. As mentioned above, the additional export fund of means of consumption comes to 200 million rubles. Of this, only 100 million goes to buy consumer goods from abroad, and these goods are sold within the country by taking advantage of the difference between domestic and foreign prices—that is, for a sum that is perhaps equal to that 200 million. At the same time, the other 100 million rubles of the export fund is used to purchase means of production from abroad. As a result, at the same time that the peasantry's consumer demand is being met, the problem of how to accelerate the development of domestic industry also finds a partial solution. But, although such a solution to the problem is fully possible in principle, it is quite obvious that under present circumstances it will, in practical terms, do no more than alleviate the difficulty pointed out earlier, not eliminate it. The point is, even in this case, that it is necessary to *advance* 100 million rubles out of the import fund for the purchase of means of consumption.

Our study of the present question would be incomplete if we did not point out that the disproportion we have indicated has one positive aspect: the hoarding of unsold surpluses of means of consumption in the village makes it possible to hold agricultural prices at a stable, low level. What seems here to be fully the product of the planning principle in economic life, and evidence of the strength of that principle, is in fact to a much greater degree the result of the disproportion we have indicated—that is, a phenomenon that is familiar to every commodity economy. The fact that we hold prices more or less stable results from the planning principle; the fact that we hold these prices stable at *a low level* is to a very great degree the result of the obstruction of the development of agriculture in the sphere of production of means of consumption, an obstruction that stems from the underdeveloped nature of our industry and the inadequate actual accumulation within it.

In analyzing the internal conditions of equilibrium between state industry and the private economy, we have so far disregarded the changes introduced into this whole process by the presence of the nonproductive consumption fund. We will return to this question below, in our concrete study of reproduction in the economy of the USSR in 1925–26, and will only touch upon it in the theoretical part. This question cannot be examined without an investigation of several new questions that are only peripherally related to the topic under consideration.

After all we have said so far, we can now formulate the following very important proposition on the law of proportionality of exchange between the state sector of our economy and the two sectors of the private economy.

If in the Soviet economy II*c* of the state sector plus II*c* of the private sector, minus the means of production obtained by department II of the combined private sector within its own department is equal to *v* plus the nonproductive consumption of department I of the state sector, plus the consumption fund and the nonproductive consumption fund of department I of the combined private sector,* then: (1) when department I of the combined private sector suffers a deficit of means of production of department I of the state sector, the disproportion may be eliminated only through ties with the world economy; (2) the part of the consumption fund of department II of the combined private sector that consists of means of consumption from state light industry must equal the part of the wages fund of department II of the state sector that consists of means of consumption purchased from department II of the private sector with wages—that is, the part that to a very great extent consists of means of consumption of peasant production; (3) if internal exchange of the consumption fund of department II of the combined private sector against a corresponding portion of II*v* of the state sector reveals an excess of demand on the part of the private sector, the disproportion may be solved either with the aid of ties with the foreign market or by redistributing the national income in such a way as to provide resources for additional development of department II of the state sector—a solution that, however, would require an even more rapid development of heavy industry; (4) if the disproportion in the economy cannot be solved in any of these ways, a goods famine arises throughout the private economy, affecting both means of production and means of consumption produced in the state economy.[18]

*Minus means of production of war industry, as is clear from the entire preceding account.

Throughout our analysis we have assumed a division of the peasant economy into two departments, along the same lines as Marx did with respect to the capitalist economy. Is this method correct, if we consider that there is an extreme lack of differentiation in the peasant economy as regards the division of labor among the various branches of agriculture? Is it not true that the same medium-size peasant farm, growing predominantly grain crops, produces raw materials such as wool and hides at the same time that it produces means of consumption such as grain, butter, and meat? Is it not true that cotton- and flax-growing regions simultaneously produce meat, butter, eggs, grain, and so on?

This is all quite true. Nevertheless, Marx's method—which we have applied in dividing peasant production into departments I and II—remains the most appropriate. First of all, we must not forget that both departments in Marx's analysis included capitalist agriculture, which, though more differentiated in the sense of specialization of crops, is nevertheless always characterized by a close intertwining of the production of means of consumption and the production of means of production. For example, a modern large-scale capitalist farm in Germany combines livestock breeding and field cultivation with the production of sugar beets. Second, if we were to begin the analysis from the other direction, if we were to take the peasant economy of the USSR as a whole in its relationship to state industry, we would still find it necessary to use the same method. To be more precise, let us determine, say, the total amount of raw materials the peasant economy can provide for our industry and export; without this a solution to the question of proportionality in the development of agriculture and industry is inconceivable. As we determine the total raw materials potential of the peasant economy, we will necessarily distinguish the part of its output that makes up department I. Similarily, as we determine the marketable surpluses of food production, we will set apart "department II." Just as in Marx's analysis one part of the output of every large-scale capitalist farm figures in department I and another part in department II, in our calculation each individual peasant farm that produces a mixed output figures sometimes in department I and sometimes in department II. Thus, the same plow, horse, and so on figure simultaneously both as means of production of means of production and as means of production of articles of consumption. This may complicate the general analysis of reproduction, but it is not sufficient grounds for rejecting Marx's method of investigation. There is no other method of investigation to replace it. If we want a detailed analysis of reproduction in agriculture, all we need do is make an additional study concerning the relative extent to which these means of production figure in department I and department II.

We have yet to consider the role of nonproductive consumption in the economy of the USSR from the standpoint of its influence on the conditions of equilibrium between the combined state and combined private economies.

To better deal with this question, let us take one of Marx's schemes of expanded capitalist reproduction. Let us take, for example, the following numerical scheme:

I. 4,000*c* + 1,000*v* + 1,000*s* (500 accumulation fund + 500 capitalist consumption fund)

II. 1,500*c* + 500*v* + 500*s* (500/*x* + 500/*y*)

In this case 1,500 II*c* is exchanged for 1,000*v* plus 500 capitalist consumption fund of department I. Assume now that nonproductive consumption is reduced by one-half in department I, but total production remains the same. We will then have in department I

I. 4,000*c* + 1,000*v* + 1,000*s* (750 accumulation fund + 250 consumption fund)

In this case, because of the growth of accumulation at the expense of nonproductive consumption, department I reduces its exchange fund with department II from 1,500 to 1,250, whereas the reproduction of II*c* requires 1,500 worth of means of production from department I (providing no changes have occurred in department II). Even if that reduction of nonproductive consumption is relative rather than absolute—that is, the nonproductive consumption fund of department I either remains unchanged at the level of 500 while the accumulation fund grows, or both these magnitudes grow but the accumulation fund grows more rapidly than the nonproductive consumption fund (in other words, if the change is not so drastic as in our example)—the tendency will nevertheless remain the same. This tendency consists in a growing deficit of means of production for department II. This is because the exchange fund of department I systematically lags behind the demand for maens of production on the part of department II.

If a corresponding cutback in the nonproductive consumption fund also occurs in department II, then all we need do is perform the same operation with department II that we did with the numerical example of department I in order to see where it must lead. In this case the additional accumulation fund obtained by the cutback in nonproductive consumption is distributed between *c* and *v* of department II proportional to the organic composition of capital, and department II will no longer require 1,500 worth of means of production from department I, but considerably more. This means that the disproportion will grow from both directions at the same time: as a result of the relative reduction in the exchange fund of department I and as a result of both the absolute and relative growth of II*c*.[19] How this disproportion in the economy can be eliminated in the future is another question. (Obviously, it can be done by a general reapportioning of the productive forces between departments I and II.) However, when we simply take the transition to a lower level of nonproductive consumption and to a higher level of accumulation, this inevitably alters the proportions of exchange between departments I and II, increasing department II's demand for means of production and decreasing their temporary supply. *In that case, the country's economy becomes more progressive from the standpoint of the development of the productive forces, the surplus product grows throughout society, and the aggregate gross and net output of society, as well as accumulation, grow more rapidly; however, the actual transition onto the new path—the growth of the relative share of department I—must cause a temporary disproportion throughout the economy.* From this general theoretical proposition we are obliged to draw the following important conclusion for the economy of the USSR. If, throughout the economic domain in which the state sector has replaced private prewar capitalist production,* the accumulation fund increases as a result of a decline of the nonproductive consumption of the industrial bourgeoisie, this must necessarily mean a decline in the exchange

*We assume here that the production of surplus product remains at the same level.

fund of department I of the state sector, along with a simultaneous *increase* of accumulation in department II, that is, a relative growth of II*c*, and an increase in II*c*'s demand for means of production. However, since the means of production of department II of the state sector consists not only of machinery, fuel, and other means of production obtained from department I of the state sector but also of a tremendous quantity of peasant raw materials, the actual transition to a system of reduced nonproductive consumption and more rapid accumulation (assuming that production in department II of the state sector and production of raw materials in the peasant economy have reached their prewar levels) must necessarily give rise to a *chronic crisis in the supply of raw materials to state light industry*. Thus, even if we disregard the changes in the structure of the peasant budget associated with the revolution (which will be discussed below), the cutback in nonproductive consumption in industry alone must result in both more rapid accumulation and more rapid growth of the shortage of means of production.

But the state economy of the USSR eliminates only a *part* of the nonproductive consumption that existed in the bourgeois economic system. To take a practical example, let us assume that out of every 100 units of surplus product of prewar capitalist industry 40 went to accumulation, of the remaining 60 the capitalists nonproductively consumed 20, and 40 went to the nonproductive consumption of the entire capitalist system (that is, these units represented industry's share in maintaining the bureaucratic apparatus and the army, paying the interest on foreign loans, covering the nonproductive expenditures of the trade apparatus, and so on). Our state industry can use this 20 percent of the surplus value for additional accumulation, but instead of capitalist nonproductive consumption it has its own Soviet nonproductive consumption: we still have the army, the state apparatus, expenditures on the nonproductive consumption of the trade apparatus, and so on. Moreover, if nonproductive outlays of this type had turned out to be larger in our economy than they were under capitalism, they would have eaten up the entire saving of 20 percent and even reduced the accumulation fund as compared to the prewar level, especially if the fund of surplus product in Soviet industry had turned out to be less in absolute terms than before the war. I will not, in this connection, go into how matters actually stand, that is, as it is expressed in numerical terms. It should be mentioned that some of our nonproductive outlays have grown (the trade apparatus), whereas others have been reduced (the state budget). For the moment, it is important only that we establish two facts. First, if the nonproductively expended part of our surplus product is declining or has declined as compared to the prewar level, this must of necessity alter the proportions in the distribution of the productive forces, giving rise to stronger demand for means of production. Second, to one extent or another nonproductive consumption* unavoidably continues to exist in our economy. However, this in turn implies different proportions in the distribution of the productive forces as compared to the scheme that could be constructed for the Soviet economy if we were to abstract from nonproductive consumption. To be more precise, if we allow for the presence of nonproductive consumption in the Soviet system this means we must set aside a certain part of the general consumption fund of the country for the maintenance of nonproductively employed strata of the population. To produce this nonproductive consumption fund, the means of production for the fund must be produced somewhere. But this means that all departments of all sectors of the economy must be employed to some extent, in supplying nonproductive consumption. However, this does not at all mean that the distribution of the bulk of nonproductive consumption between the individual sectors of the economy and between the individual departments of these sectors must be proportional to the changes that the very existence of nonproductive consumption provokes in the equations for exchange between these departments.

Concretely, the situation with respect to the individual departments is as follows: The nonproductive consumption fund of department I of the state sector has the material form of means of production. One part of this fund, which will go directly into nonproductive consumption in the form of means of production themselves, will provide everything that will be used for war industry: equipment for arms plants, metal for the production of armaments, fuel consumed in production, and so on. The second part of the nonproductive consumption fund of department I must enter into exchange with departments II of both the state and pri-

*The term "nonproductive" is used here in a socioeconomic sense and not at all in a moral sense. There is, after all, *necessary* nonproductive consumption as well.

vate sectors. The situation is approximately the same with respect to the nonproductive consumption fund of department I of the private sector, the only difference being that the role of war industry in absorbing the means of production of the department in question, with the possible exception of horses for the cavalry, is very small. As regards the departments of production of means of consumption, their nonproductive consumption fund, in its material form, enters into the consumer budget of the groups of the population that are not employed in productive labor. It is quite obvious that in value terms the entire fund of personal nonproductive consumption will be less than the share of the total burden of nonproductive consumption that will be borne by the departments II of both sectors, since one part of this nonproductive consumption will be covered by the departments I in the form of supplying the departments II with their own means of production, minus the means of production that go to war industry. But this means that, on the one hand, the existence of nonproductive consumption in Soviet society reduces accumulation and the rate of growth of society's gross and net output, but on the other hand it also reduces—albeit by purely negative means—the disproportion between departments I and II of both sectors which we discussed earlier and which amounts to a shortage of means of production. In particular, as regards the exchange of a part of the consumption fund of department II of the private sector for a certain part of the wages fund of the workers of department II of the state sector, the relative decline in the growth of IIv of the state sector reduces the exchange fund with that department, while the decline in accumulation in department II of the private sector reduces its demand for additional means of consumption coming from department II of the state sector and its demand for means of production from the state sector's department I.

On the other hand, when nonproductive consumption declines, both the gross and net income of society and accumulation increase, yet at the same time there is also a growing goods famine of means of production. However, as we have already shown, the development of the economy as a whole on a broader basis will in the future create within the economy itself the means for overcoming the disproportion, specifically on the basis of exports and imports.

To conclude the question of nonproductive consumption, we still must go into one very important methodological question whose practical significance will become more evident later on.

How do we correctly determine the volume of nonproductive consumption in the USSR and the influence of this consumption on the entire process of production?

There are two possible methods for doing this. The first of these is the method Marx used in his analysis of capitalist reproduction in vol. II of *Capital*, where v represents the part of the advanced capital that is *actually* spent by the working class as income. Hence, Marx classifies all taxes on wages as surplus value. The advantage of this methodological approach is that the entire v then participates fully in exchange, uncomplicated by the part of v that, although *formally* representing wages, essentially goes to pay for a part of the nonproductive consumption of the bourgeoisie. If we want to make a detailed investigation of the economy of a particular country, we have then only to make an additional study of exchange within the nonproductive consumption fund, a study that is necessary, in particular, for determining both the role of war industry in this consumption and that of the nonproductive part of the expenses of the trade apparatus. This will also require additional investigation of the money savings of the working class. As regards the petit bourgeois sector, this method means that we must take into account *only the real consumption fund of independent producers engaged in production*, whereas their entire real accumulation in the economy, plus the part of the nonproductive consumption of the society in question that falls on this sector, must be classified as surplus product. This by no means prevents us from making an analysis of the exchange of the real magnitudes of the means of production of departments I, which, in exchange for means of consumption, go to replace the constant capital of the departments II. Generally speaking, the difficulty here is that it is impossible to define precisely the necessary consumption of the class of petty producers, since the consumption fund of the petty producers, as we have already shown, is not regulated by the law of value, even under concrete capitalism, and in our economy it is also governed to a certain extent by the law of primitive socialist accumulation. Furthermore, we must remember that the meaning of the term "productive labor" changes as compared with its meaning in Marx.*

*In discussing our economy, the concept of productive labor as labor creating surplus value is one of the several concepts of Marxist political

The second method would consist in simultaneously drawing up two balance sheets, one for production and one for consumption. This second method does not exclude the first but must, in our opinion, follow it, since beginning immediately with a double balance would mean beginning not with a simpler general balance but with a complex concrete one, not to mention that without a preliminary general balance this double balance might simply hide an *inability* to draw up a single general one.*

Furthermore, we must emphasize at this point the great practical difficulty in distinguishing the part of the outlays on trade that goes to pay productive labor from the part that goes to pay for the nonproductive consumption of the apparatus. The trade markups involved in the payment of transportation expenses are easily allowed for and included in the production balance of transport as one of the branches of *production.* Similarily, all taxes on trade, with the exception of that which returns to production via the state budget, should be included in the nonproductive consumption fund. On the other hand, it is much more difficult to distinguish the productive labor used in moving a commodity to the site of its individual consumption, storage expenses, and so on from the numerous other outlays that are connected not with this physically specific labor but rather with social expenditures on the given *system* of distribution, including primarily the nonproductive consumption of the agents of private merchant capital, and the useless agents of the state and cooperative network, as well as the educational expenses involved in passing on the science of how to carry on trade in a "civilized" manner.

Another very important methodological question is the general question of the indexes that should be used to calculate social production and consumption. It is quite obvious that we will have to use a dual system of accounting: accounting in prewar prices, which represents a form of *in natura* accounting, and accounting

economy that must be replaced by another definition. Without going into this question in detail, we will simply note that we use the term "productive labor" in the *social* economy of the USSR to mean the social labor of workers and independent petty producers that creates means of production and articles of consumption for all of Soviet society.

*The derivation of a general balance on a methologically correct basis, is, among other things, one of the most important methods of verifying all the data of our industrial and general statistics.

in real wholesale and retail prices in chervonets rubles, which represents a form of value measure.

With this let us wind up for the time being our general investigation of the conditions of equilibrium between the state and private sectors of the economy. For the moment we shall leave aside the question of how the conditions of equilibrium, particularly the rate of expanded reproduction in the state sector, are influenced by quantitative changes in the distribution of the bulk of society's nonproductive consumption between the socialized sector of the economy and the entire private economy.

The Fifth Condition of Equilibrium

The fifth condition of equilibrium of the entire economic system of the USSR is the systematic growth of wages. We are speaking here not of the natural growth of the entire fund of v of the state sector that results from a growth in the number of persons actually working but rather of the growth in this fund that results from an increase in the average wage of the individual worker. The social structure of our state economy is such that, if there is a systematic rise in the level of the productive forces in it, the gap between the price and value of labor power must widen steadily, and thus the very concept of labor power as a commodity must be gradually eliminated. A rise in wages is also inevitable because of the very fact of the industrialization of the country, since a change in the technological base of the entire state economy and increased rationalization of labor inevitably require a rise in the skill level of the workers. The collective ownership of the means of production in the state economy inevitably demands that the cultural level of the proletariat be raised and that the elements of a new socialist culture be created. If the growth of socialist culture lags behind the development of the productive forces of the collective sector of the economy, this lag itself can become an obstacle to the further development of the productive forces. As every system of social production develops, it works out a system of a labor discipline and incentives that is most suited to it and develops an average worker that is most appropriate. Socialist industry, too, must mold its own type of worker and develop its own work incentives. This type of worker can emerge only if the working class has a sufficiently high general material standard of living, a standard considerably higher than the one capitalism can provide for workers under the same technology.*

The enormous nonproductive expenditures of the state and cooperative trade and industrial apparatus, which has yet to develop even the rudiments of the methods of work suitable to the collective mode of production, are due not only to the general low level of development of the productive forces in the state sector but also *to the rudimentary level of socialist culture of the working class itself.* The culture of all bodies of society always tends to be drawn to the same level as that of the ruling class. Raising the cultural level of Soviet society means above all raising the culutral level of the working class. A steady rise in the proletariat's material standard of living is necessary not only for social reasons but for economic ones as well.

Furthermore, we must not forget the fact that we established earlier: if the country cannot import large amounts of industrially produced means of consumption for the peasantry, which produces means of consumption, then the increase in internal exchange of means of consumption between state light industry and department II of the petit bourgeois economy will be limited for the latter by the proportion of IIv of the state sector that goes to purchase peasant means of consumption and, indeed, privately produced means of consumption in general.

Even if we grant that this exchange may increase as a result of occasional additional imports of means of consumption, it is still the part of IIv of the state sector we have mentioned that constitutes the basic exchange fund. This means that at a given price level an increase in the wages fund of the workers of light industry (and this increase may result from an increase in the

*It must be clearly understood that the peasant protest against the growth of wages and improvement of labor protection and of the workers' entire mode of life is profoundly reactionary not only from the social and class standpoint but also from the narrowly economic one. Socialism knows only one way of equalizing the material conditions of the town and the village, and that is (if we disregard the temporary improvement in the situation of the petty producers) the elimination of the very foundations of individual petty production. A highly developed collective economy in agriculture is capable of providing its workers with a level of material welfare no lower than that in urban socialist industry. We cannot overcome the contradiction between the town and countryside, which constitutes one of the historical tasks of socialism, by turning the urban worker into something like a village blacksmith, who plays a subsidiary role in the petty economy.

number of workers, as well as from an increase in the average wage level) *must precede* an increase in the effective peasant demand for articles of consumption produced in state light industry. State industry's leading role becomes evident in this sphere of the economy as well. Along with a general reduction of prices, the growth of wages appears here as a factor that helps decrease the disproportion of exchange between agriculture and industry, doing so not in a negative form but in a socially and economically positive form.

The Sixth Condition of Equilibrium

The sixth condition of dynamic equilibrium in the economy of the USSR is a systematic reduction of prices on the output of the state economy. An equilibrium of this type is simultaneously economic and social.

Let us begin by discussing the economic aspect of this equilibrium.

We have already shown earlier that one of the bottlenecks in the development of state light industry is now to a certain extent, and will be in the future to an even greater extent, the lag in peasant production of industrial crops behind state industry's demand for raw materials. However, an increase in the production of industrial crops requires, above all, an increase in accumulation in that branch of the economy. And, to increase accumulation given the same level of individual consumption in that department, there must be (1) a cutback in nonproductive consumption in general, and hence also in the part of it that involves the department in question; (2) an increase in prices of industrial crops; (3) a reduction in prices of articles of consumption; (4) a reduction in prices of the means of production that department I of the peasant economy obtains from department I of the state sector; (5) a cutback in individual consumption in department I of the peasant economy itself; and (6) an increase in labor, using the existing means of production. Some of these possibilities are purely theoretical. A decrease in individual consumption in this particular department is impossible, or almost impossible, since it is already quite low. A reduction of prices of means of consumption of peasant production is, on the whole, also impossible, because relative to prices of industrial articles these prices are much lower than prewar prices, which were also quite low. The only thing that can be done is to bring the selling prices of grain in regions producing industrial crops closer to the procurement prices of grain-producing regions—that is, essentially, to reduce the nonproductive consumption of the trade network, to lower transport costs, and to improve the means of transportation, above all highways and rural roads. A systematic increase of the prices of industrial crops is also impossible—except for the correction of occasional, clearly incorrect calculations made by the purchasing bodies—because such an increase of prices would tend also to raise the prices of the output of state light industry. The remaining alternatives, then, are to raise the intensity* and productivity of labor and of soil fertility in peasant production of industrial crops, reduce nonproductive consumption throughout the political and economic system of the USSR, cheapen the means of production produced in department I of the state sector, and cheapen the means of consumption produced in state light industry. In this last case, it is by no means a question of artificially reducing accumulation in these branches, but rather of reducing real production costs through reequipment of the technological base and rationalization of production. On this point, the interests of state industry coincide with those of the peasant production of raw materials: a reduction of industrial prices is an incentive to expanded reproduction in department I of the peasant economy. In addition, on the basis of increased accumulation in that department of the peasant economy it will be easier to achieve decisive successes in improving land cultivation, enhancing livestock breeding, and increasing the productivity of labor in general, which will increase the aggregate annual production of industrial crops.**

As regards the peasant production of means of consumption, the situation differs somewhat in the following way. The domestic market of the USSR does not absorb all the articles of con-

*It must be emphasized at this point that, even with the existing means of production, peasant agriculture in the USSR could considerably increase its gross output by a greater expenditure of physical labor, in particular by putting into effect a number of simple agronomic improvements. The struggle against rural fear of work and traditional laziness is one of the most important problems in the industrialization of the country.

**This is why the Soviet government's policy of selling agricultural machinery at artificially low prices is absolutely correct. In the future this must become a systematic pattern: means of production must always be sold at lower prices and means of consumption at higher prices, given identical costs of production.

sumption of the peasant economy, and their export is quite necessary to maintain a general equilibrium throughout the system. But, under the conditions of reproduction in state industry that we discussed above, the state's import fund obtained from these exports cannot be devoted to any considerable extent to imports of peasant means of consumption and can be used only in part for imports of agricultural means of production. This contradiction, along with unfavorable exchange ratios of peasant output for the output of state industry, plus the purely material shortage of the latter, acts as a brake on the entire process of expanded production of peasant means of consumption and reduces both the economic effectiveness of accumulation and the purchasing power of the part of the consumption fund that is exchanged for the part of v of light industry mentioned above. All this inhibits the development of the marketable share of peasant production of means of consumption, increases the nonproductive consumption of the peasant masses themselves, and inhibits the growth of the export fund. However, even when agricultural production has reached the prewar level and the volume of exchange of agricultural output of means of consumption has approached that of prewar Russia, the decline in the nonproductive consumption of the bourgeoisie, the elimination of the nobility's ownership over the land, and the elimination of foreign debts will create the preconditions for very significant growth of the surplus product of agriculture, capable of contributing to the fund of expanded reproduction. Here, too, the way out of the partial impasse and disproportion is to more rapidly reequip industry, reduce costs of production, systematically lower prices, and, finally, raise the productivity of labor in the peasant economy itself. For every 100 units of its output that the peasant department of means of consumption exchanges for a part of Iv of the state sector and that replaces its means of production, this department will obtain more of those means of production in their material form. On the other hand, every 100 units of the consumption fund will permit the acquisition of more means of consumption in exchange for part of IIv of the state sector.

However, a systematic reduction of industrial prices is important not only from the standpoint of maintaining the economic equilibrium but also from that of maintaining the *social equilibrium of the entire Soviet system*. The sharp divergence between domestic industrial prices and world market prices—that is, a system of far-reaching nonequivalent exchange—is an exceptional system and one that by its very nature is temporary. It corresponds to the period of infancy in the development of the state economy in a backward peasant country. It is historically destined to provide state industry with the necessary economic resources to replace its technological base, to enable it to accumulate on the basis of modern, improved technology rather than old, obsolete technology. It is not until this process has been completed that the state economy will be in a position, as we have repeatedly stated, to develop all the advantages that collective production provides over capitalist production. In that period, however, the peasant economy also must develop. The peasant economy is unconcerned with the stage of development through which socialist reproduction is passing: what it needs is cheaper industrial goods in the necessary amounts and of the appropriate quality. This economic contradiction turns into a social contradiction, into the growth of peasant dissatisfaction with the foreign trade monopoly and into efforts to eliminate the peasant market's compulsory bonds to Soviet industry—efforts to break through to the value relationships obtaining on the world market and to avoid paying the multibillion-ruble tax into the fund of primitive socialist accumulation. This social contradiction represents a whip that drives the state economy to bring domestic industrial prices of the state economy closer to world market prices. Rapid success along this path, accompanied by the expansion of state credit to organize the economy of the middle and especially the poor peasants and provide then with additional means of production, will weaken this social contradiction. A delay along this path will heighten the contradiction and expose the socialist sector to the risk of a revolt by, above all, the capitalistically most developed elements of the peasant economy and the corresponding groups of the peasant population, which are most impeded in their development along the bourgeois path by the process of expanded socialist reproduction.*

*Here we have arrived at the most fundamental question of the relationship between socialist development of the city and capitalist development of the countryside. In the present, difficult period, the Soviet system can exist only on the basis of a proportionality between their respective rates of growth. A more rapid rate of socialist development will permit a larger dose of capitalist development as well, without any great danger for the system as a whole.

The Seventh Condition of Equilibrium

Finally, the seventh condition of equilibrium of the Soviet system is the gradual absorption of the country's excess population by the developing state economy and by intensified agriculture, an absorption that includes both the overt and the hidden unemployment inherited by the Soviet system, primarily from the agrarian relationships of the old regime. It is in this respect that the situation is most difficult and most contradictory. Improving the technology of the state economy and rationalization of labor—which are the natural preconditions for lowering production costs and disposal prices—essentially means reducing the expenditures of labor power per unit of output. Even in the best-equipped Soviet enterprises these expenditures are considerably higher than in advanced European industry, not to mention America. The only way to keep the whole process of rationalization of labor from leading to stagnation in increasing the number of key personnel employed in state industry is to ensure that it is accompanied by a sufficiently rapid expansion (in absolute terms) of the industrial base of the country. But such rapid expansion presupposes a considerably more rapid accumulation in industry than we now have (1927). Since the Soviet economy is presently developing in breadth, not at the level of advanced capitalist technology but only while it is in the process of catching up to that level, there must necessarily be a relative slowdown of the rate of growth of the labor force and a relative slackening of the pace of absorption of the army of the unemployed. In the history of the Soviet economy a similar process was to a certain extent observed in the transition to NEP, when a more rational use of the labor force and means of production in 1921–22, together with a sharp rise in the overall level of output as compared to 1920, led to a reduction in the labor force in state enterprises relative to the last year of War Communism. Gosplan's five-year plan for the economic development of the USSR provides for a 70.4 percent increase in the total output of state industry by 1930–31 (that is, at the end of the five-year period), whereas the employed labor force will increase during that time by only 27.9 percent or 2,053,000 persons.* As regards unemployment associated with the migration from the village to the town and the in-

*See *Perspektivy* . . . , op. cit., appendix, pp. 2 and 21.

crease in the work force within the town itself, its possible extent is defined by the five-year plan in 1926–27 as 1,189,000 persons, with a gradual, slow, almost imperceptible reduction to 1,146,000 at the end of the five-year period. However, in the first half of 1927, unemployment already exceeded the projected Gosplan figure by several hundred thousand. This shows that Gosplan's calculations, which are in themselves highly pessimistic, are actually turning out to be too optimistic. And from the standpoint of the ratio of the work force employed in the socialized sector as compared to the capitalist and petit bourgeois sectors, we can expect only very modest success: the proportion in the socialized sector has risen from 11.2 percent to 12.6 percent—that is, a total of 1.4 percent. The situation with agrarian overpopulation, which Gospan sets at 6.8 million* turns out to be even more serious. At best, this figure, according to Gosplan calculations, will not decline. Most indications show that it will rise, and thus that the figure for urban unemployment will rise considerably as well.

On the other hand, the intensification of agriculture, *whose possibilities are directly proportional to the backwardness of our farming as compared to foreign peasant economy*, will mean the absorption of new labor power by agriculture on the one hand and increased productivity of labor in agriculture—that is, a relative decline in expenditure of labor power per unit of output—on the other. However, intensification in agriculture requires increased accumulation in agriculture. At the same time, if this accumulation were to occur at the expense of the part of the fund of surplus product that the village provides to the town for socialist reconstruction, this would lead to a slowdown in the rate of expanded reproduction in state industry, that is, in precisely the sector that is decisive in the sense of overcoming in the future all the basic contradictions of the transition period.

* * *

We have had only to present the very broadest outlines of the foundations of dynamic equilibrium in the economic system of the USSR in order to show the totality of economic and social contradictions that are inevitably revealed by our development toward socialism under conditions of our isolation:

---

*The data are those of Narkomzem [People's Commissariat of Agriculture].

(1) Accumulation based on nonequivalent exchange versus the necessity of eliminating this nonequivalence—together with the lack of correspondence of these processes in time.

(2) Accumulation at the expense of the surplus product of the workers versus the inevitability of a systematic growth of wages.

(3) The necessity, in the interests of reducing the "birthpangs of industrialization," of the fastest possible integration into the world division of labor and an increase in foreign credit versus the growing hostility toward the USSR shown by the entire capitalist world.

(4) Accumulation at the expense of peasants who produce industrial raw materials and of the peasantry in general versus the necessity of stimulating expanded reproduction of these raw materials as much as possible.

(5) Accumulation at the expense of peasant exports of articles of consumption versus the necessity of stimulating these exports under conditions of an extremely slow reduction of industrial prices.

(6) The economic necessity of having the peasant economy produce more for the market versus the social necessity of materially maintaining the part of the peasantry that produces least for the market–namely the poor peasants and the weak groups of the countryside.

(7) The necessity of lowering prices on the basis of the rationalization of production versus struggle with growing unemployment.

The sum of these contradictions shows how closely our development toward socialism is connected with the necessity–for not only political but also economic reasons–to make a breach in our socialist isolation and to rely in the future on the material resources of other socialist countries.

* * *

We conclude our general survey of the equilibrium conditions in the economy of the USSR. This outline is far from complete, even in its purely theoretical part. It undoubtedly suffers from a number of shortcomings, as does every first attempt of this nature. But even on the basis of what has been presented here we can proceed to a study of the concrete figures of our economy for particular years. From here on, our task will consist in filling in the algebraic scheme of reproduction in the USSR that we have outlined here with concrete data provided by Soviet statistics and, above all, by the Control Figures of Gosplan. We will focus the primary attention of this concrete study on the economic years 1925–26 and 1926–27, as the most typical years for the end of the restoration period and the beginning of the reconstruction process. Our concrete study will also compel us to touch upon certain theoretical questions that, in the interests of shortening the purely methodological section of the study, we prefer to illustrate with figures from the present-day living Soviet economy.

EDITOR'S NOTES

[1] Soon after the October Revolution in 1917 a system of illegal trade grew up that rivaled the "official" trading network right up to the institution of NEP. "Bag trading" (*meshochnichestvo*) came to be so called after the practice of private traders who scoured the countryside, buying up whatever food or other items they could acquire, and smuggled them into the cities in sacks, where they resold them at extremely high markups. Despite repeated attempts at repression and control over this type of black-market trade, the Soviet authorities never succeeded in doing away with it—the drastic shortages of the War Communism period made this a virtual impossibility. Eventually, in the last years before NEP, it became a more or less accepted fact of life. For a fuller discussion of the phenomenon, see E. H. Carr, *The Bolshevik Revolution*, vol. II (London: Macmillan, 1969), pp. 118-19, 240-44.

[2] *Capital*, English edition, vol. II (Moscow: Progress Publishers, 1967), p. 397.

[3] It is difficult to precisely render into English the difference between the Russian terms *razmen* and *obmen*. *Obmen*, as is perhaps clear from its usage in the passage at hand, refers to the system of market exchange, that is, to a system of exchange that presupposes the need to establish a basis of equivalence between the items being exchanged. In short, it implies an *exchange of values*, and in Russian the terms for "exchange economy" (*obmennoe khoziaistvo*) and "commodity economy" (*tovarnoe khoziaistvo*) are synonymous. The term *razmen* refers to the concrete act of exchanging, or changing, for instance, to change money.

[4] The consumption fund of the capitalist sector here refers to the sum of the variable capital plus the fund of individual capitalist consumption.

[5] That is, the fund of nonproductive consumption within the state sector, which the peasantry must help cover.

[6] Preobrazhensky discusses this point in greater detail on pp. 201-02 and 212. Essentially, the prices the state pays for peasant grain are below those prevailing on the world market. Its costs of producing its own means of production are generally higher, given the relative backwardness and inefficiency of Soviet industry. If the state exports peasant grain and sells it at world market prices, it receives a "commercial profit" equal to the difference between the domestic and world prices. At the same time it obtains hard currency from capitalist countries, which can then be used to purchase capitalist-produced means of

production; this gives the state a second source of "profit," since it is able to acquire more means of production (in terms of use values) than it could produce for the same aggregate price at home.

[7] There is a misprint in the Russian text, which reads *razmer* ("scale" or "size") instead of *razmen* ("exchange").

[8] The export fund is the commodities purchased by the state at its own procurement prices that it will export for foreign currency.

[9] Accumulation in the state sector would give, at the end of the year's production, 8.8c + 2.2v + 2.2 surplus product = 13.2 billion. This is an increase of 10 percent over the previous year. Technically speaking, therefore, the exchange fund with private production should increase by the same figure, to 3.3 instead of 3.25 billion.

[10] The total drop in productive capital in the state sector would be 240 million in constant capital and 60 million in variable capital. Assuming that the rate of exploitation is 1:1, a cut in variable capital by 60 million will produce an equal drop in the level of surplus product, giving a total cut in state production of 360 million.

[11] There is an error in the Russian text (either a misprint or a calculating mistake by Preobrazhensky), which gives half of IIc as 1,755. This error is carried through all the subsequent calculations and produces a result directly contradicting Preobrazhensky's argument to the effect that the deficit in means of production is growing from year to year.

[12] Here there is a further miscalculation, which gives the sum of 933.4 + 467 as 1,300.4, rather than 1,400.4. This sum was then subtracted from the already incorrect figure for half of IIc, thus giving a deficit of 1,755 - 1,300 = 455. The correct figures are given in the English text here. As is clear from the subsequent calculations for a further year's production (which give a deficit of means of production in the state sector equal to 390.8 million), this would have contradicted Preobrazhensky's argument that the shortage of means of production is becoming increasingly severe. For this reason it is unlikely that the errors here are Preobrazhensky's but are either misprints or "creative editing" by the editors of *VKA*.

[13] Department I accumulates 700 of its surplus product. Of this 60 percent, or 420, goes to increase Ic and 40 percent, or 280, to augment Iv. This will give an increase in the surplus product also of 280, of which half, or 140, is devoted to nonproductive consumption. Thus, the total rise in I's exchange fund is 420, of which two-thirds, or 280, is exchanged against IIc of the state sector. The original arithmetical errors are carried over here. The Russian text lists the original level of I's exchange with IIc as 1,300 and gives the old deficit as 455.

[14] This is true only in the short term. A reduction in the level of nonproductive consumption will create new conditions of proportionality between the two departments to the initial disadvantage of department I, but it will also raise the rate of accumulation out of s. If this rise in the rate of accumulation is uniform in the two departments, the increase in their rates of growth will be the same. If the drop in the share of nonproductive consumption is greater in department I this will, in fact, tend to decrease the shortage of means of production over time. Preobrazhensky provides more detailed treatment of the consequences of reducing the level of the state sector's nonproductive consumption in the next section of the article, and we have added a fuller explanatory note there (see below, note 19).

15 It is again important to recognize why the disproportion Preobrazhensky has identified here is taking place. The organic composition of capital is actually lower in department I than in department II, and so we would have expected the shortage of means of production to decrease over time. It is increasing only because the total size of the productive capital in department II is so great that the accumulated part of its surplus value is able to provide for a greater increase in II*c* than the amount by which department I's accumulation fund is able to raise I($v + s/x$). This, however, hides the tendency for the rate of increase of this deficit of means of production to slow down. After three years the deficit would start to contract, although under the conditions prevailing here it would take quite a substantial time before the lower organic composition of capital in department I would allow it to overcome its insufficient production.

This is only one side of the matter. The other is that this situation, whereby department II has a more advanced technical structure than department I, is a legacy of the backwardness of the Soviet Union's economy and of the devastation that war and civil war wreaked upon its industrial base. It is not a state of affairs that could persist for very long. As soon as department I begins to restore its fixed capital and embark upon positive accumulation, it will replace old, technically outmoded plant and equipment with that embodying modern technical improvements. Thus, the organic composition of capital in department I will start to rise rapidly. At a certain point, once department I has begun to fill the gaps in its fixed capital stock left by the preceding decade, its organic composition of capital will exceed that in department II, and there will appear that very tendency toward underproduction of means of production that Preobrazhensky outlined in the first article of this series, in *VKA*, no. 17. In addition, it is likely that this "switch point" would occur before the already existing deficit of means of production, which is the product of the economic structure inherited from the Civil War, had been overcome. The tendency for underproduction in department I would, therefore, appear on top of this basic famine of means of production (primarily of fixed capital), and the problem would be compounded. Short of a thoroughgoing rearrangement of productive capital in the state sector, which would shift resources into department I and thereby give it greater weight in the economy, the only other way out of this impasse would, of course, be material assistance from other countries.

16 We can illustrate this by slightly modifying the scheme for simple reproduction under concrete capitalism that Preobrazhensky presented in *VKA* 17 (see above, p. 80) where he broke the scheme down to show which part of each department's product went in exchange with the peasant and capitalist sectors. For the sake of simplicity we will keep his designation of K (and *k*) and P (and *p*) for the different sectors. The only other modification is that we have altered the scheme to reflect expanded rather than simple reproduction, so that only half the surplus value, or surplus product, goes toward capitalist (or nonproductive) consumption. The other changes in the figures in brackets reflect the different situation that Preobrazhensky has here described.

KI. $4{,}000(3{,}900k + 100p)c + 1{,}000(500k + 500p)v + 500(250k + 250p)s/x$
KII. $1{,}500(600k + 900p)c + 375v + 187.5s/x$

PI. $750(500p + 250k)c + 1{,}500(750p + 750k)$ consumption fund
PII. $1{,}500(750p + 750k)c + 4{,}000$ consumption fund

Here the balanced exchange between the two departments I no longer pertains. Department I of the capitalist sector (which we can take as the same as the state sector in Preobrazhensky's example) requires 100 in means of production from the peasant sector. Department I of the peasant sector, however, needs 250 in means of production from the capitalist sector. They can exchange 100 of these directly. But how is PI to acquire the other 150 in industrially produced means of production? It can do so only because compensating imbalances exist in the exchange between department II of the capitalist sector and that sector's department I. Here is how exchange would proceed under these conditions:

KII will buy from KI 600 in means of production. This allows KI to realize the entire part of KIv that comes from KII, as well as 100 of KI$s/x(k)$. KI, however, must both purchase 750 in means of consumption from KII and sell that many means of production. KII can sell another 150 means of consumption to KI by dipping into the 900 it had set aside for exchange with PI, from which KII must acquire 900 in raw materials and other peasant-produced means of production. In this way KI receives all of the means of consumption it needs from KII, but to do this it has had to advance 150 in money (since KII still only purchased from KI 600 means of production), whereas it has 150 in means of production left unsold.

Now we must account for the exchange between KII and PI. Here KII had set aside 900 in means of consumption to allow it to purchase a like quantity of means of production from the peasant sector's department I. Now, however, it only has 750 with which to effect this exchange, since it sold 150 of this 900 to KI. It can still *purchase* this many means of production from PI, since in addition to the 750 in means of consumption KII also has on hand 150 in money that it received from KI when it sold means of consumption to KI without making a corresponding purchase. PI, on the other hand, needs only 750 in means of consumption from KII in any case and had allowed only 750 in means of production to carry out this exchange. As things stand the exchange can still proceed. PI, after all, has 150 left over from its very first exchange *with KI*, to which it could only sell 100 in means of production out of a constant capital replacement fund of 250. If PI takes this 150 in means of production and adds them to the 750 it had already designated for exchange with KII, it can sell KII the full compliment of 900 means of production that the latter requires. In return, PI will receive 750 in means of consumption (which is what it demands) plus 150 in money (the same money that KI had advanced in its own exchange with KII).

Thus KII will now have acquired all the means of production it needs from both departments I. PI will have disposed of all its available means of production, and will have 150 in money. Clearly it can take this money and use it to purchase the 150 in means of production from KI that it could not do in the beginning. KI, on the other hand, can sell 150 in means of production to PI since it had this many left unsold after its exchange with KII.

Therefore, PI is only able to realize all of its constant capital by means of the capitalist (or nonproductive) consumption fund of KI. To do this necessitated an extremely complex circuit of exchanges involving three of the four departments (PII had a balanced exchange with both PI and KI). At any point in this series, exchange might have broken down because the products offered for exchange by one department might have been in the wrong material form or available in the wrong quantity for the needs of another department. Had this happened, or had there been a general shortage of means of production in KI, as was actually the case in the Soviet Union, PI could not have obtained the industrial means of production it required. The only other recourse would have been for PI to sell its surplus 150 abroad and purchase foreign-made means of production.

[17] There is a misprint in the Russian text, which gives II*c* as 3,500.

[18] The condition Preobrazhensky is describing here can be put more simply in terms of the scheme we used in note 16. Designating the state sector as S (instead of K), if SII*c* plus PII*c* (less the means of production PII produces on its own) equals SI($v + s/x$) plus PI's consumption fund, then (1) if PI*c*(s) is greater than SI*c*(p), the disproportion can only be solved by exporting PI's excess and importing the means of production it needs. This is not entirely true, as we have shown. A complex circuit between the various departments could allow PI to obtain these means of production, *provided that they are available through prior production in SI.* (2) The part of SII*v* not covered by SII itself but purchased from PII must equal the part of PII's consumption fund not covered within PII and purchased from SII. If these conditions are not satisfied, as they were not in the Soviet Union during this period, Preobrazhensky's third and fourth conclusions prove valid.

[19] The example Preobrazhensky has chosen here is somewhat misleading, for the same reasons as was his discussion of the effects of a rise in the organic composition of capital in *VKA* 17. The scheme he presents here has a built-in disproportion, in that the organic composition of capital in department II is lower than that in department I. If their organic compositions of capital were the same, and if they each reduced their nonproductive consumption by exactly identical shares, then their exchange funds would continue to grow at the same rate, all other conditions being equal. There would still be an initial disproportion, however, which would necessitate a rearrangement of the social capital and a shift of resources into department I. If we modify Preobrazhensky's scheme here, so that the organic composition of capital is 4:1 in both departments, we will, if we also change the ratio of accumulated to nonproductively consumed surplus product to 3:1, have the following:

I. $4{,}000c + 1{,}000v + 250s/x + 750$ for accumulation
II. $1{,}500c + 375v + 93.75s/x + 281.25$ for accumulation

Here I($v + s/x$) has fallen to 1,250, whereas II*c* has remained at 1,500. If we were to carry out accumulation and production in the following year we would have

I. $4{,}600c + 1{,}150v + 287.5s/x + 862.5$ for accumulation
II. $1{,}725c + 431.25v + 107.8s/x + 323.4$ for accumulation

There is a rather massive deficit of means of production, equal to $1{,}725 - 1{,}437.5 = 287.5$. What would be necessary would be a rearrangement of the productive forces in the state sector as a whole, so that proportionality was reestablished between I($v + s/x$) and II*c*. Then, given the conditions we have assumed, that is, equal organic compositions of capital and equal, though larger, rates of accumulation, proportionality would be maintained with each successive period of expanded reproduction.

This does not change the essence of Preobrazhensky's argument. As long as the state sector was able to reduce its levels of nonproductive consumption, there would need to be more or less constant rearrangements of the newly available productive resources in order to meet society's increased demand for means of production.

A Select Bibliography of Preobrazhensky's Works

The bibliography we have compiled lists the books and articles written by Preobrazhensky from 1920 to 1931 that we know to exist in Western libraries. It does not claim to be complete, in that we have culled this list primarily from the catalogs of libraries that we knew to have major Soviet holdings: the Hoover Institution of War, Revolution, and Peace, Stanford, Calif.; the Library of Congress, Washington, D.C.; the New York City Public Library; the British Library (British Museum); and the British Library, London School of Economics. Although we also scoured the catalogs of the major Continental libraries, none of them listed works by Preobrazhensky not already held by the above-mentioned institutions. The bibliography also makes no pretense to listing every one of Preobrazhensky's articles, as not all journals were examined comprehensively over the entire period. Finally, we have listed none of Preobrazhensky's lectures and speeches other than those we knew to have been subsequently published in booklet or pamphlet form. Nevertheless, to our knowledge no exhaustive list of Preobrazhensky's writings exists in any of the sources dealing with this period, so that this is the first bibliography of his major works to be compiled. We hope it will prove useful to others doing research on the Soviet twenties and early thirties.

The ABC of Communism (with N. Bukharin). (London: Penguin, 1969).

Anarkhizm i kommunizm [Anarchism and Communism] (Moscow: Gosizdat, 1921).

Bumazhnye den'gi v epokhu proletarskoi diktatury [Paper Money in the Epoch of the Proletarian Dictatorship] (Tiflis: Gosizdat, 1921).

*"Ekonomicheskaia politika proletariata v krest'ianskoi strane" [The Economic Policy of the Proletariat in a Peasant Country], *Kommunisticheskii Internatsional* 25 (November 1922).
"Ekonomicheskaia priroda sovetskikh deneg i perspektiva chervontsa" [The Economic Nature of Soviet Money and the Outlook for the Chervonets], *Pod znamenem marksizma* 3 (1930).
Ekonomicheskie krizisy pri NEP'e [Economic Crises under NEP] (Moscow: Izdatel'stvo Sotsialisticheskoi Akademii, 1924).
*"Ekonomicheskie zametki I—O tovarnom golode" [Economic Notes I—On the Goods Famine], *Pravda*, December 15, 1925.
*"Ekonomicheskie zametki II" [Economic Notes II], *Bol'shevik* 6 (March 31, 1926).
*"Ekonomicheskie zametki III—O pol'ze teoreticheskogo izucheniia sovetskogo khoziaistva" [Economic Notes III—On the Advantage of a Theoretical Study of the Soviet Economy], *Bol'shevik* 15–16 (August 31, 1926).
"Ekonomicheskie zametki IV—Novoe v khoziaistvennoi situatsii [Economic Notes IV—New Developments in the Economic Situation], *Bol'shevik* 6 (March 15, 1927).
Ekonomika i finansy sovremennoi Frantsii [The Economy and Finance of Modern-day France] (Moscow: Izdatel'stvo Kommunisticheskoi Akademii, 1926).
Finansy i Novaia Ekonomicheskaia Politika [Finances and the New Economic Policy] (Moscow: Gosizdat, 1921).
Finansy v epokhu diktatury proletariata [Finances in the epoch of the dictatorship of the proletariat] (Moscow: Narodnyi Komissariat Finansov, 1921).
From NEP to Socialism, trans. Brian Pearce. (London: New Park Publications, 1973).
Itogi Genuezskoi konferentsii i khoziaistvennye perspektivy Evropy [The Results of the Genoa Conference and the Economic Outlook for Europe] (Moscow: Gosizdat, 1922).
"Izmeneniia v stoimosti zolota i tovarnye tseny" [Changes in the Value of Gold and Commodity Prices], *Problemy ekonomiki* 1–2 (1930).
*"Khoziaistvennoe ravnovesie pri konkretnom kapitalizme i v sisteme SSSR" [Economic Equilibrium under Concrete Capitalism and in the System of the USSR], *VKA* 18 (1926).
*"Khoziaistvennoe ravnovesie v sisteme SSSR" [Economic Equilibrium in the System of the USSR], *VKA* 22 (1927).
Krest'ianskaia Rossiia i sotsializm (k peresmotru nashei agrarnoi programmy) [Peasant Russia and Socialism (Toward a Reconsideration of our Agrarian Program)] (Petrograd: Priboi, 1918).

*Essay appears in this collection.

The New Economics, trans. Brian Pearce. (London: Oxford University Press, 1965).

Novaia ekonomika: Opyt teoreticheskogo analiza sovetskogo khoziaistva [The New Economics: An Attempt at a Theoretical Analysis of the Soviet Economy], 2nd ed. (Moscow: Izdatel'stvo Kommunisticheskoi Akademii, 1926).

Nuzhna li khlebnaia monopoliia? [Is the Grain Monopoly Really Necessary?] (Moscow: Vserossiiskii Tsentral'nyi Ispolnitel'nyi Komitet, 1918).

"O dvukh spornykh voprosakh marksovoi teorii deneg" [On two contentious Questions in Marx's Theory of Money], *Arkhiv K. Marska i F. Engel'sa* 1930.

O krest'ianskikh kommunakh (razgovor kommunista-bol'shevika s krest'ianinom [On the Peasant Communes (Conversation of a Communist-Bolshevik with a Peasant)] (Kiev: Narodnyi Komissariat po Voennym Delam Ukrainy: 1919).

O material'noi baze kul'tury v sotsialisticheskom obshchestve [On the material Basis of Culture in Socialist Society] (Moscow: Vserossiiskii Proletkul't, 1923).

"O metodologii sostavleniia Genplana i vtoroi piatiletki" [On the Methodology of Drawing up the General Plan and the Second Five-year Plan]. (Submitted to *Problemy ekonomiki* in 1931 but never published.)

O morali i klassovykh normakh [On Morality and Class Norms] (Moscow: Gosizdat, 1923).

Ot NEP'a k sotsializmu: Vzgliad v budushchee Rossii i Evropy [From NEP to Socialism: A Glimpse into the Future of Russia and Europe] (Moscow: Moskovskii Rabochii, 1922).

*"Perspektivy Novoi Ekonomicheskoi Politiki" [The Outlook for the New Economic Policy], *Krasnaia nov'* 3 (September–October 1921).

Prichiny padeniia kursa nashego rublia [The Reasons for the Fall in the Exchange Rate of our Ruble] (Moscow: Narodnyi Komissariat Finansov, 1922).

*"Problema khoziaistvennogo ravnovesiia pri konkretnom kapitalizme i v sovetskoi sisteme" [The Problem of Economic Equilibrium under Concrete Capitalism and in the Soviet System], *VKA* 17 (1926).

[Reply by Preobrazhensky to critics during the debate in the Communist Academy over his theory of primitive socialist accumulation], *VKA* 15 (1926).

Russkie finansy i evropeiskaia birzha v 1904–1906 [Russian Finances and the European Stock Exchange in 1904–1906], comp. B. A. Romanov, ed. E. Preobrazhensky (Moscow: Moskovskii Rabochii, 1926).

Social Revolution and Finances [a collection of articles for the Third Congress of the Communist International, ed. People's Commissariat of

*Essay appears in this collection.

Finances] (Moscow: First Moscow Factory for the Manufacture of Government [Currency] Notes, 1921). (Preobrazhensky was one of the contributors to this volume. Also published in Russian as *Sotsial'naia revoliutsiia i finansy*.)
"Sotsialisticheskie i kommunisticheskie predstavleniia sotsializma" [Socialist and Communist Conceptions of Socialism], *VKA* 12-13 (1925).
[Speech given at the graveside of V. I. Lenin], *VKA* 11 (1925).
Teoriia padaiushchei valiuty [A Theory of Depreciating Currency] (Moscow: Gosizdat, 1930).
Trekhletie Oktiabr'skoi revoliutsii [The Third Anniversary of the October Revolution] (Moscow: Gosizdat, 1920).
Voprosy finansovoi politiki [Questions of Financial Policy] (Moscow: Gosizdat, 1921).
Zakat kapitalizma [The Decline of Capitalism] (Moscow: Gosudarstvennoe Sotsial'no-ekonomicheskoe Izdatel'stvo, 1931).

About the Editor

Donald A. Filtzer was educated at Wesleyan University and the University of Glasgow. He is presently an Honorary Research Fellow at the Centre for Russian and East European Studies, University of Birmingham. In addition to scholarly articles on Preobrazhensky's thought, Dr. Filtzer has published a translation of Isaac Ilyich Rubin's *History of Economic Thought* (1978). He is currently engaged in a comparative study of labor unrest and labor policy in Nazi Germany and the USSR during the 1930s.